PIPER ALPHA

A Survivor's Story

Ed Punchard with Syd Higgins

S T A R

published by
the Paperback Division of
W.H. Allen & Co. Plc

A Star Book
Published in 1989
by the Paperback Division of
W.H. Allen & Co. Plc
Sekforde House
175/9 St. John Street
London EC1V 4LL

Copyright © Ed Punchard and Syd Higgins, 1989

Printed and bound in Great Britain by
Cox & Wyman Ltd, Reading

ISBN 0 352 32527 5

WE REMEMBER

ROBERT M. C. ADAMS
GEORGE ANDERSON
IAN GEDDES ANDERSON
JOHN ANDERSON
MARK DAVID ASHTON
WILSON CRAWFORD BAIN
BARRY C. BARBER
CRAIG A. BARCLAY
ALAN BARR
BRIAN BATCHELOR
AMABILE (JIM) BORG
HUGH W. BRACKENRIDGE
ALEXANDER R. C. BREMNER
HUGH BRISTON
HENRY BROWN
STEPHEN BROWN
GORDON C. BRUCE
JAMES BRUCE
CARL W. BUSSE
DAVID CAMPBELL
DAVID ALLAN CAMPBELL
ALEXANDER W. CARGILL
ROBERT CARROLL
ALAN CARTER
ROBERT CLELAND
STEPHEN COLIN COLE
HUGH CONNOR
JOHN COOKE
JOHN THOMAS COOPER
WILLIAM NUNN COUTTS
WILLIAM JOHN COWIE
MICHAEL JOHN COX
ALAN I. CRADDOCK
EDWARD J. CROWDEN
BERNARD CURTIS
JOSE HIPOLITO DASILVA
JOHN STEPHEN DAWSON
ERIC DEVERELL
ALEXANDER DUNCAN
CHARLES EDWARD DUNCAN
ERIC DUNCAN
JOHN DUNCAN

THOMAS IRVINE DUNCAN
WILLIAM D. DUNCAN
DAVID ALAN ELLIS
DOUGLAS FINDLAY
HAROLD E.G. FLOOK
GEORGE FOWLER
ALEXANDER P. FREW
SAMUEL QUEEN GALLACHER
MIGUEL ESTEVEZ GALVEZ
ERNEST GIBSON
ALBERT S. GILL
IAN GILLANDERS
KEVIN BARRY GILLIGAN
SHAUN GLENDINNING
JOHN EDWARD T. GOLDTHORP
STEPHEN ROBERT GOODWIN
JAMES E. GORDON
DAVID LEE GORMAN
KENNETH GRAHAM
PETER J. GRANT
CYRIL J. GRAY
HAROLD E. GREEN
MICHAEL J. GROVES
JOHN HACKETT
IAN HAY
THOMAS A. HAYES
JAMES HEGGIE
DAVID W. HENDERSON
PHILIP ROBERT HOUSTON
DUNCAN D. JENNINGS
JEFFREY G. JONES
CHRISTOPHER KAVANAGH
WILLIAM HOWAT KELLY
IAN KILLINGTON
JOHN B. KIRBY
STUART KNOX
ALEXANDER LAING
TERENCE MICHAEL LARGUE
GRAHAM LAWRIE
FINDLAY WALLACE LEGGAT
BRIAN LITHGOW
ROBERT RODGER LITTLEJOHN

MARTIN GEORGE LONGSTAFFE

SIDNEY I. McBOYLE

ROBERT B. McCALL

JAMES McCULLOCH

ALISTAIR J. McDONALD

ALEXANDER McELWEE

THOMAS O. McEWAN

WILLIAM G. McGREGOR

FREDERICK THOMAS S. McGURK

WILLIAM HUGH McINTOSH

GORDON McKAY

CHARLES McLAUGHLIN

NEIL McLEOD

FRANCIS McPAKE

DAVID McWHINNIE

DUGALD McLEAN McWILLIAMS

WILLIAM RAYMOND MAHONEY

JOHN MORRISON MARTIN

CARL MEARNS

DEREK K. M. MILLAR

ALAN D. MILLER

FRANK MILLER

JOHN MOLLOY

LES J. MORRIS

BRUCE ALEXANDER F. MUNRO

GEORGE FAGAN MURRAY

JAMES COWIE NIVEN

GRAHAM S. NOBLE

MICHAEL O'SHEA

ROBERT RENNIE PEARSTON

IAN PIPER

WASYL POCHRYBNIAK

RAYMOND L. PRICE

NEIL PYMAN

TERENCE STEPHEN QUINN

WILLIAM W. RAEBURN

DONALD REID

ROBERT WELSH REID

GORDON M. RENNIE

ROBERT M. RICHARD

ALAN RIDDOCH

ADRIAN P. ROBERTS

ALEXANDER J. ROBERTSON

DONALD N. ROBERTSON

GARY ROSS

MICHAEL HECTOR RYAN

STANLEY SANGSTER

JAMES J. D. SAVAGE

MICHAEL H.B. SCORGIE

WILLIAM ALEXANDER SCORGIE

JOHN FRANCIS SCOTT

COLIN D. SEATON

ROBERT SELBIE

MICHAEL JEFFREY SERINK

MICHAEL M. B. SHORT

RICHARD SKINNER

WILLIAM H. SMITH

JAMES SPEIRS

KENNETH STEPHENSON

THOMAS STIRLING

MALCOLM STOREY

JAMES C. STOTT

JURGEN TILO STWERKA

STUART DOUGLAS SUTHERLAND

TERENCE JOHN SUTTON

ALEXANDER R. TAYLOR

ALASTAIR A. THOMPSON

ROBERT A. VERNON

MICHAEL A. WALKER

JOHN E. WAKEFIELD

BRYAN THOMAS WARD

GARETH H. W. WATKIN

FRANCIS JOHN WATSON

ALEXANDER WHIBLEY

KEVAN D. WHITE

ROBERT WHITELEY

GRAHAM GILL WHYTE

JAMES GILBERT WHYTE

ALAN WICKS

PAUL C. F. WILLIAMSON

DAVID WISER

JOHN RICHARD WOODCOCK

ERIC BRIANCHON

ACKNOWLEDGEMENTS

I wish to thank the many people who have helped and supported me both in the writing of this book and during my time in the offshore industry.

There are too many to mention in total but they include:

The staff and facilities of Prodive Ltd in Falmouth whose training helped me to stay alive; Mike Chew for his encouragement and assistance in my early diving days; Comex Houlder Diving Ltd for their consistency and for always doing the right thing by me in the end; Len Porter for offering me a leap in my career. Also, the divers offshore as a whole. I am privileged to have many as my friends. They are often misunderstood or put down; certainly they have been generally unappreciated. As far as I am concerned they are the ablest people I know and I am happy to say it.

I must mention all those involved in the rescue work of July the 6th last year, whether on the *Silver Pit*, the *Tharos* or the other craft or in helicopters. Nobody should have been put through what they had to endure and they all did whatever they could.

Above everyone I acknowledge those from the small boats, the Z-boats and others whose actions were indescribably brave. Also Gareth Parry-Davies, my wife Vicky and especially my daughter Susannah who, in various ways, enabled me to hang on.

I must also mention Chip Scott and Jean Lornie for their love and attention that terrible morning, and the nurses and doctors whose consistent care, especially in Ward 39, continued for months; the flight staff and ground assistance crews of British

Airways and Brymon Airways (Aberdeen, Heathrow and Newquay) who treated us with such simple consideration on our journey home that I will never forget their kindness; my friends who called Vicky and me on my arrival home and the many whom I know wrote to me, but due to a clerical error were provided with the wrong address. I never saw any of those letters as they were destroyed by the post office, so if you are out there and you wrote to me – thanks, whoever you are.

In the period after Piper I received the support of a large number of individuals whether family, friends or professionals. I owe them a great deal, in particular they are: Patrick Handscombe, my consistent friend, and his parents; Anne Bone, David Tumelty and the Piper Outreach Group whose work has been superlative; Dr Angela Rouncefield, who keeps me sane. Dr D. A. Alexander; Dr Phillip James; Chris Wright; Chris Dobson, the journalist, for his invaluable advice and repeated generosity; Michael Shaw and Andrew Best of Curtis Brown; Graham Bagley and Allan Miller of the Professional Divers Association (at various times); Mr Frank Lefevre; the EEPTU and their representatives who I have been dealing with at our many Department of Energy meetings, including David Short and Steve Blunt; the MPs David Mudd, Frank Doran, Alex Salmond, Alick Buchanan-Smith for their diligence and help; Lord Cullen, Alf Vannet and many others at the public inquiry for their various kindnesses; the many members of the media who have shown me their willingness for accuracy and for fulfilling an essential function; my wife and her family for their support.

My dear mother, my brothers and their families, for their love through a difficult time.

Finally, to my friend the biographer Sydney Higgins and his wife Anna, my thanks. Their constant care and happy disciplining was essential. Without them this book would never have been completed. Cheers, Syd!

CONTENTS

PREFACE

I have no interest in blame or retribution. To me, they serve no purpose and have no value. Consequently, though it may seem strange to some, I have no bitterness towards Occidental or to any of its employees. What happened, whilst no surprise, could have happened on many other rigs.

It has been said that there are no mistakes in life, only lessons. This is a maxim that I've followed and have found especially useful in maintaining a perspective in the aftermath of Piper. Any other philosophy seems too low on hope for the human condition. However, we must never forget that lessons are repeated until they are learned.

Finally, just in case anyone should doubt my motivation in writing this book, let me share with you my recurring nightmare. It is of a young boy on his paper round in Aberdeen, delivering morning newspapers which showed the charred remains of Piper Alpha. On his return home, he says, 'Mummy, Dad's on Claymore, isn't he?'

But he wasn't. He'd been on Piper Alpha.

And it's no dream. The story's true.

ED PUNCHARD

PROLOGUE

ELEVEN MINUTES OF HELL

It was my last shift on Piper Alpha before I went on leave.

I'd spent some time clearing up the paperwork in the office of the diving module I shared with Stan MacLeod, the diving superintendent.

At about a quarter to ten that evening, both of us were called into the office next door by Barry Barber, Occidental's diving representative.

When we arrived, he and his clerk, Dick Common, were sitting behind their desks. Stan leant with his back against a filing cabinet and I stood just inside the doorway, my arm resting on the other filing cabinet.

We were talking, when suddenly, for a split second, all hell broke loose. The lights went out, shelves falling off the walls spewed files across the room, and one of the ceiling's metal panels crashed on to my head.

There had obviously been an almighty explosion, but enclosed as we were within the bomb-proof office module we had no way of knowing its extent or where it had taken place. We hadn't seen a flash. But what had happened was much more than a bang. It was completely overwhelming. My entire body shook – every organ I possessed vibrated violently and my brain went numb.

'Jesus Christ!' I heard Barry exclaim.

Somewhere in the gloom, Dick Common was scrabbling around

on the floor where he'd been flung by the blast.

I could see hardly anything. Until the explosion, there'd been bright fluorescent lighting in the offices. Now, only the glimmer of the emergency light in the corridor showed that the building was filled with what seemed to be clouds of smoke. But from the smell I knew it wasn't smoke. It was the dust thrown up by the falling debris and the insulating material that had been packed above the ceilings.

Having been smashed on the head, my first thought was to find my hard hat. I stumbled along the corridor to my office. I had a quick grub around, but there wasn't any sign of my hard hat. I came across one on the workbench but, when I tried it on, I realised it wasn't mine. Thinking it might be needed, I put it back on the bench.

Stan arrived in the office and began searching around in the gloom. 'Where's the fuckin' breathing apparatus?' he said. 'It's fallen off the bloody wall.'

I got down on my knees and hunted around until I came across it among the debris on the floor. Then I began helping him into it, because it was heavy and unwieldy.

As he was putting on the full-face mask, he said to me, 'Fuck off to your lifeboat.'

Unthinkingly, I followed him out into the corridor where we bumped into Andy Carroll, one of the divers.

'What the hell's going on?' he asked.

'Don't ask me,' Stan replied. 'What's going on down there? Are all the divers OK?'

'Yes. But the door on one of the decompression chambers has been blown in and Gareth's still in the water.'

'Well, let's get him out.'

They both went one way, I went the other. Being the diving superintendent, Stan was responsible for the divers' welfare. In an emergency, I'd no specific duties. So I set off for the diving team's lifeboat – two levels, or thirty-nine feet, above me.

I left the dive module and walked out into the evening light of the cellar deck – the lowest deck on Piper. There was a peculiar silence. On a rig, there's normally a lot of working machinery – but much of it was no longer running. Although I could smell it in the air, there was hardly any smoke around and everything seemed almost normal. I felt quite calm and in no danger. It was better, more orderly, being outside than in the eerie chaos and gloom of the offices.

As I went round the corner, people were rushing around, intense and preoccupied. It was as though all of us were seeking a purpose, a sense of direction. As I strode past them, I noticed that Davey Elliott, the divers' rigging foreman, had sooty marks all over his face and what appeared to be a smear of blood. With him was Brian Jackson, one of his riggers, hopping along on one leg, a drawn grimace on his lined face.

Glancing over the side towards the diving-support vessel *Lowland Cavalier*, I was amazed to see on the back deck several men who appeared to be cutting adrift the remotely operated vehicle that was being used on the sea-bed. Then suddenly, the *Lowland Cavalier* set off like a bat from hell. 'Stupid bastards!' I thought to myself. 'Haven't they any idea how much that ROV costs? They've just dumped eleven million quid over the side. It's insane! What the hell do they think they're doing?'

I walked around the cellar deck to the north-west corner where a stairwell led up to the 85-foot level. On the deck above that – the 107-foot level – was my lifeboat.

As I reached the stairs and was about to climb up, I had to stop. Three or four blokes in Occidental overalls were carrying down an injured man, who I think worked in the control room.

'Forget it,' one of the men said to me. 'Don't bother trying to get up there. There's no way up. It's all blocked with smoke and fire.'

Still the seriousness of what was happening hadn't sunk in. What the man had said really didn't register. If it did, I just dismissed it as an over-exaggeration.

I walked briskly back towards the diving module, assuming that I'd be able to use the stairs beyond. But when I reached the corner of it, I saw that the way up was completely blocked by smoke. Looking on eastwards towards the centre of the platform, I saw flames flicking around machinery that I took to be condensate pumps. It was only a small oil fire – nothing serious. It was clearly not fierce enough to be a gas leak. But I was slightly shocked.

Then glancing back to the diving offices, I saw that there was thick, black smoke billowing around by the southern end, a fractured electrical cable was sparking and dancing on the deck, and showers of burning debris were cascading on the divers' changing-room.

I rushed back to the office. Several divers were already assembled there.

'Which way are we supposed to get up to the lifeboats?' I asked

Barry. As the diving representative, he should have received information about the safe route direct from the control room. That was the drill in the case of a fire.

'I've phoned the control room,' he replied. 'But the lines are dead. And so's the radio. Everything's broken down. So I don't know a thing.'

'Well, we can't go south. A fire's blazing there, just where all the oxygen's stored. If that lot goes up, it could bring down a whole block of flats on its own.'

'OK. Go north.'

'I've tried it once and was told the north-west stairwell's blocked. But I'll try again.'

'OK. If you're not back soon, I'll know it's OK. When the rest of the lads are up, we'll be hot on your heels.'

It seemed a good joke at the time. We smiled and I left with Andy Carroll, one of the divers. Within an hour, Barry Barber would be dead.

Andy and I hurried back towards the north-west corner. By this time, I was very conscious of the wind direction. I'd realised that there was an immense amount of smoke coming from somewhere because it completely obscured the centre of the platform. But I knew that, as the wind was blowing from the south-west, the north-west corner was being swept clear of smoke. And it was important to be up-wind of the smoke and fumes. On oil rigs, it's possible to have all kinds of gases, including H_2S, which is quite deadly.

When Andy and I arrived, there was a group of men by the north-west stairwell. Several were attending to the injured man I'd seen being brought down the stairs earlier. Everybody seemed very calm. There was no panic. A few men appeared shocked, but most were moving around, apparently looking for something to do.

'It can't be all that serious,' one of the men said. 'They still haven't set off the fire alarms.'

'Perhaps they can't.'

'Don't be bloody daft.'

Close to the stairwell was a very large air-compressor, that I was told was used both by the painters and as a back-up for the diving systems. It was racing away. A few weeks earlier, I'd spotted sparks coming out of its exhaust. Although I assumed it had been repaired, I was concerned it might still be dangerous, especially if a gas leak did develop. I decided to deal with it. At first I couldn't find the off button.

Davey Elliott suddenly appeared at my side.

'Are you all right?' I asked, glancing at the sooty marks on his face.

'O.K.'

'What happened?'

'I was on the landing stage away by the gritting-shack. Then a bleedin' great fireball flashed over us heads. Before I knew it, I was smack flat on the groun'.'

'But you're OK?' I asked, glancing at his blood-smeared face.

'Dinne worry aboot me. Thar's the bloody button yew're lookin' for,' he said, jabbing forward his index finger. 'Switch the bugger off.'

I pushed the button and the compressor shuddered to a halt.

Strangely, I still had no sense of imminent danger. I'd heard people talking about an explosion in 1984 on Piper Alpha when everyone was evacuated safely. I just assumed we'd all be back on shore in a little while, having a couple of pints in the pub.

'If we're going to get out of here,' Andy said, 'we've got to get up those bloody stairs.'

'Come on, then,' I said. 'Let's go.'

'It's blocked up there, mate,' one of the blokes called. 'Yew might get trapped if yew go up.'

'We'll bloody-well be trapped if we stay here,' Andy said. 'The fucking lifeboats and the helideck are all up there.'

We ran up the stairs. At the top, on the 85-foot level, a strong wind blew thick, black smoke into our faces, making our eyes run. I walked along the west face for a short distance towards the stairway leading up to the control room. Although I could feel the heat, I still couldn't see the fire. Then I realised that the smoke ahead of me was billowing out so heavily it was masking the flames shooting out around the crane-pedestal area.

Above me, on the 107-foot level, I could see my lifeboat, but it was obviously going to be impossible to reach it.

I hurried back to the north-west corner, where there was a small area still smoke-free. About fifteen men were crowded there and others were still arriving. There really wasn't enough room for us all – some repair work had been taking place to the grating and an area of it had been roped off with plastic tape. I stepped over it and jumped up and down on the deck to make sure it was secure. Then I ripped the tape away.

That gave us more room, but the space was rapidly filled. Men stood around as though waiting for a bus on a Sunday evening.

One of the chaps there was Derek Ellington, a fitter who worked for Wood Group. 'Did yer hear that noise before the explosion?' he asked.

'No, I didn't hear anything,' I said.

'Well we were in the workshop and there was a long high-pitched scream like a man being gripped by his balls.'

'What the hell we doing standing here?' somebody asked.

'Waiting for some bugger to tell us what to do.'

'And who's ganna do that?' asked another.

'The control room. Who d'ya think?'

'Yew'll be lucky,' a man said, hunched on his haunches.

'What yer mean?'

'Yew should see the fuckin' state of the place. There's wires hanging down everywhere. Even the bloody bulkheads've buckled in.'

'How d'yer know?'

'I was in it, wasn't I? The explosion blew me straight across the fuckin' room on me chair.'

While they were talking, I looked around for a possible way of escape. I tried to see if I could squeeze through the three-barred guardrail, just to check how quickly I could manage it if things really got bad. It'd be a long way to jump. We were eighty-five feet above sea-level.

The wind changed slightly and the smoke -free area became much smaller. I began to see fine glowing embers drifting by and so I realised there was quite a fire burning somewhere. Suddenly, there was an extremely loud, constantly-pitched scream. Once or twice it stopped, briefly, but then it started again – as loud and as shrill as before. It was impossible to say where it was coming from, but we all knew instinctively it was the sound of escaping gas. At last, I realised the situation was dangerous.

About six precious minutes had passed since the first explosion. As the conditions were worsening, it was pointless staying where we were. So all of us in that small north-west corner of the 85-foot level began hurrying down the stairs to the deck below. As we were descending, the rest of the dive team arrived at the foot of the stairs.

'What's going on up there, Ed?' Barry Barber asked.

'God only knows,' I replied. 'But there's no way up. It's blazing up there.'

Somebody said, 'There's a box of life-jackets here, chaps. Get 'em on.'

The box was at the bottom on the stairs. The people around it began putting on the life-jackets. The *mêlée* prevented everybody else getting to the life-jackets and brought to a halt our group's scramble down the stairs.

'There's a lot of guys behind me, fellers,' I shouted down. 'Pass the life-jackets up here.'

I handed back three or four and then went to reach for another one – but there weren't any more. With a wry smile, I turned back briefly and watched the last of the life-jackets being passed up the stairwell.

Stan MacLeod arrived with a group of people including Barry and Gareth Parry-Davies, the diver who'd been in the water. 'Where's all the life-jackets?' Stan asked.

'Sorry, mate. They've all gone,' I told him.

When they realised there was a shortage of life-jackets, most of the divers who were wearing them took them off and handed them to the older men.

But they were bloody stupid life-jackets. I'm sure they'd keep you afloat, but they were those great thick kapok jobs that are completely unwieldy. Later, many of the men had to remove them so they could climb down a rope to be rescued.

Keith Cunningham, one of the divers, threw the nearby inflatable, modular life-raft into the sea and pulled the painter which was supposed to inflate it. But nothing happened and we watched it float uselessly away. So that was a lost cause.

Tied to the handrail was a knotted rope, which we were supposed to use to climb down into the life-raft. This had also been thrown over and left dangling down into the sea.

Although I was well aware that the situation was dangerous, I still wasn't worried. I hadn't seen anyone being injured, nobody around me was panicking and nothing really frightening had happened. I'd spent every minute since the explosion being very busy. It hadn't yet dawned on me that we were running short of options – although, in truth, we'd just about run out of them all.

The smoke around us was getting thicker. I felt I had to do something positive. I knew a small vertical metal ladder went from the corner on which we were all standing, down by the north-west leg of the rig to a small beacon platform suspended about ten feet below. Somebody else had clambered down and back up again, but I decided to have a look for myself.

'That's a dead end, Ed,' a chap shouted as I climbed over. 'It don't go nowhere.'

'I don't care. I want to see for myself.'

By climbing down that ten feet, I saw for the first time what was going on. Because I was under the deck, I could see that a large area, including the entire dive skid in front of the diving module, was ablaze. Where a few minutes earlier the dive crew had been working, massive flames were billowing down. Now I knew there was a major fire on Piper Alpha.

'What can you see, Ed?' somebody called.

'I can see things are pretty bad over there, fellers,' I said, all too aware of the understatement. 'I think it's time to go.'

The knotted rope that had been thrown over the side was actually brushing against the platform just beside me. I grabbed hold of the rope and pulled it in. Then I started to tie it to the handrail – being a diver, I never trusted anybody else's knot-work. But several people called out, 'It's all right, Ed. The rope's secure up here.'

I undid the rope and shouted, 'Are you sure the rope's fast?'

They assured me it was and I clamped my hands and legs on to the rope. As it took my weight, it suddenly dropped. I was sure I was just going straight down. And it mightn't have been into the sea. Almost below the beacon platform was the heavy steel boat-buffer. But after a drop of ten feet or so, the rope pulled taut and I managed to hold on.

I scurried down the rope and swung on to the boat-buffer, which was at the extreme north-west corner of the platform. Then I held the rope for the next man, to make sure he was also able to swing on to the boat-buffer.

When he was down safely, I gave him the rope and said, 'Hold on to it for the next guy and make sure he does the same thing.' And so he did, but after a couple more people had come down, somebody had the more sensible idea of tying the rope to the boat-buffer.

Meanwhile, I hopped around on to the spider deck – a series of metal companionways and handrails extending round the lower part of the platform. By being that much further down, I could see the intensity and extent of the blaze above me. There were flaming objects the size of cars dropping into the sea. I'd no idea what they were.

Only when I began to wonder what the hell they could be did I realise that up to then, from the time of the first explosion, I'd been virtually without thought. Everything had been done in automatic gear, on auto-pilot, by reflex action. Now I was thinking, the dangerous time had begun.

PART ONE

TRIUMPHS AND DISASTERS

CHAPTER ONE

A CHANGE OF MIND

My elder brother, Bernie, became a professional diver while I was at university. I kept in fairly regular contact with him and one day I called up his office in Aberdeen.

'Bernie Punchard, please,' I said, when the phone was answered.

'Who's speaking?'

'His brother, Ed.'

'Well, don't worry, Ed. It looks as though he's going to be OK.'

'What are you talking about?'

There was a brief pause. Then the chap said, 'Don't you know? I thought that's why you were phoning.'

'Know what?'

'There was a bit of trouble while he was diving. But don't worry. He's in hospital and it looks as though he'll be all right.'

I was then told what had happened.

Bernie had been part of a dive team working from a small drilling rig off Aberdeen on a massive sewage outfall pipe. Several divers had complained about the taste of the air before Bernie went off to do his dive. He'd not been down there long when he started to feel dizzy. He informed the diving supervisor, but the last thing he remembered was crying because he knew he couldn't make it back to the diving basket which would take him up to the surface. Then he passed out.

It turned out that a petrol-driven welding generator had been accidentally sited right next to the air intake for the diving compressor. When it was started, the exhaust fumes were sent through his air system directly to the diver. During his dive, Bernie had been breathing carbon monoxide mixed with his air. On the surface that can be deadly, but under water the increased pressure compounds the effect. Even at a depth of thirty feet, carbon monoxide has twice the effect it does on the surface.

It was something like ten minutes before Bernie was pulled out of the water. Another diver had been sent down to get Bernie into the diving basket so he could be hauled up to the surface. When they pulled his helmet off, he was still unconscious, had been vomiting and his lips were cherry red – all classic symptoms of carbon-monoxide poisoning. Fortunately, he came round and was put on a boat to be taken ashore.

When he arrived at Aberdeen Royal Infirmary, a doctor said to him, 'I'm going to take a blood sample, I'm afraid it'll be very painful.'

'Why?' Bernie asked. 'I've had blood samples taken before and it's no big deal.'

'Yes, but with this condition, we cannot take the blood from your arm. We have to take it from a particular part of your body.'

'What part of my body?'

'Your groin.'

'By "groin", do you mean what I think you mean?'

'I'm afraid so!'

It was, Bernie told me, excruciatingly painful.

An hour later, the doctor came back and said, 'Congratulations! You've withstood what's generally recognised to be a lethal percentage of carbon monoxide in the bloodstream.'

Bernie recovered and his next job was working as the diving supervisor for a civil engineering project in the Thames. They were lifting off the river-bed huge lumps of concrete from a demolished oil-tanker mooring platform.

I called to see Bernie on a freezing cold winter's evening. The diving team was working from a dirty old barge with a load of diving equipment and some containers strapped on top of it.

Just as I arrived, a couple of divers went off to get changed. They went into a cold, damp container. Hanging inside was a row of 'woolly-bears' – thermal diving undersuits that are just like babies' romper-suits. They were all dripping wet. The poor bastards had to get all their clothes off and climb into these things and then pull on a rubber suit. It looked horrific to me. Then they put on an enormous, bloody-great hard helmet, called a Swindell, that looked like an upturned bucket with a window in it. The air supply to those things is on a constant-flow basis. So there was a continuous swishing noise.

They then went on deck, leapt over the side into a thick pea soup and vanished, leaving behind nothing more than what seemed like a length of rope sticking out of the water.

I joined my brother, who was inside another, equally freezing container, listening to the two divers wandering around the bottom of the Thames. As they could see nothing, they had to work entirely by touch. When they managed to stumble into a lump of concrete, they secured it with cables so it could be lifted to the surface.

It was difficult to believe that divers were expected to work in such awful conditions. I decided there and then that I would never have anything at all to do with commercial diving.

Later that year, in the summer of 1979, I finished at Swansea University. My degree was in political theory. I'd really enjoyed the courses, but I'd no idea what I was going to do next. The only thing I'd decided was that I could never be a faceless company man imprisoned behind a desk. To delay having to make any decision about my future, I spent the best part of eighteen months taking odd jobs and travelling through Europe and across North America.

I was at home again in early summer of 1981. One day, Dave, another of my three brothers, drove me to a little beach close to Brixham in Devon. He was a very keen sports diver and had a load of diving equipment in the car.

'I'll take you diving,' he said.

It was a warm, sunny afternoon and we carried all the equipment down to the beach. I was given very brief instructions as to what to do. These mainly seemed to consist of hanging on to David at all costs. Then we put on diving suits and rapidly warmed up in the sunshine. Even though sports-diving equipment is far less complex than that used by commercial divers, I was shocked by how hot and heavy it all was.

But as soon as I walked into the sea, it was a complete release. Suddenly I became more or less weightless. That day, the visibility in the sea was extremely good. It was absolutely amazing. Since then, I've often taken people sports diving for the first time and their eyes seem to grow to the size of saucers. I know mine did.

All around me, I could see all kinds of incredible things.

That year, there was a mass of spider-crabs around the south coast. There were literally hundreds of them lying around. In places I could see piles of twenty spider-crabs. Some of them were eighteen inches long with huge claws and pear-shaped, rock-like bodies, covered in spines.

I swam around in very shallow water, not really knowing what I was doing, but mesmerized by all the wonderful sights. It was the most fabulous experience.

It was a totally contrasting experience of diving from the one I'd had when I watched Bernie at work in the Thames.

A few weeks later, Bernie took me sports diving just off Plymouth. It was equally enjoyable. But, when we got out of the water, he said, 'I'm glad you enjoyed it, but that's enough. Unless you do some training, neither Dave nor I will ever be taking you diving again. Even sports diving is a very dangerous activity. You should never dive unless you've been trained.'

'All right,' I thought, 'I'll do something about it.'

I then set off for a quick jaunt to the south of France in an old VW camper I'd bought.

When my cash ran out, I returned to stay with my mother in Dartmouth. After a few days I was bored. The only money I had to my name was the hundred pounds left on the credit limit of my newly acquired Access card. 'OK,' I thought, 'I'll go and spend it.'

I went to Fort Bovisand Underwater Centre in Plymouth and booked in for a one-week snorkelling course. It isn't diving as such – it's the stage before you do any scuba diving with an aqualung, but it is the essential preliminary to any sports diving training.

Much of the week was spent attending lectures on what you must and mustn't do when you're under water. We were taught the rudiments of diving physiology – what happens to your body and lungs when you're diving. We also went snorkelling. The first thing we had to do was called the A-test. At the time, it seemed to be an horrific experience. We had to swim back and forth wearing weight-belts so we had no buoyancy. Then we had to tread water with our hands above our heads – which to me then was no mean feat. We also had to do exercises and practise rescuing people under water.

I really enjoyed it all and found it very straightforward. But it stopped short of the good bits. So I sold my sports car and borrowed from my family to get together another couple of hundred quid. This enabled me to stay on for two more weeks so I could obtain the basic qualification in the British sub-aqua club scheme, which was then called the Third Class Diver.

During the fortnight's course, we were taken out on small boats and dived on shipwrecks. The weather was perfect. It was all great fun and I loved every moment I was diving. I'd never been the kind of person who jogged or did exercises for pleasure, but I suddenly found that I enjoyed a physical activity that had some kind of structure to it.

On occasions, I saw the commercial divers doing their training at the centre. I couldn't believe it. They just looked insane. In the blazing heat, wearing black rubber suits, they were running up a hill carrying empty beer kegs on their backs. That further persuaded me that I'd never be interested in diving for a living.

But I'd definitely got the bug. One day, Alan Bax, the director of the centre, told me they were planning a new course to enable sports divers who'd reached a certain level of proficiency to convert to the first level of professional diving. Called the HSE Part Four qualification, it meant you could dive professionally with scuba equipment. Not that it was much use. There were few companies that would use a diver who could use only scuba gear.

But Alan said, 'As you're so keen, why don't you come on the first course? It's in September and we're treating it as a kind of pilot and so we'll knock a few bob off the fee.'

I said I would. But by then financial realities had hit and I realised I had to earn some money. So I went off to London and did some temping.

A couple of weeks later, I duly returned and completed the new course which gave me the first part of the professional diving qualification.

I found that I enjoyed diving more and more. There seemed to be some purpose to the whole thing. I found particular satisfaction in working in a difficult environment. What I was doing might on the surface have been very mundane, but under water it seemed somehow special.

By the end of the course, I was absolutely stony-broke. All the time I'd been at Plymouth, I'd been living in my VW camper to save the costs of accommodation. It'd worked out very well. I used to bum meal vouchers from guys on the course. They always had a couple spare. I collected so many, I've still got some left. If things really get bad in the future, I suppose I can always get a couple of free lunches at Fort Bovisand!

In October, I returned to London and parked my camper on the South Bank, near the site of Shakespeare's old Globe Theatre, immediately opposite St Paul's. As I was right against the embankment wall, I could wind down my window and spit into the Thames.

I got a job as receptionist and hall-porter at the Royal Society of Arts – a splendid old building in the Adelphi, just behind the Strand. As part of my duties, I took the coats of a whole battalion of well-known people. Every morning, I'd get up, put on my blue pin-striped suit, slide open the door of my camper, and join the commuters walking towards Blackfriars Bridge.

In the evenings, I went along to the Royal Commonwealth Society, which I'd joined as a student member. It was tremendous. There was a café there, a bar, and a beautiful old reading-room with tapestries and leather Chesterfields where old gents were slumped snoring. For fifty pence I could have the biggest bath I'd ever seen – complete with a towel and soap. So, despite sleeping in a camper, I lived in an extremely civilised fashion.

Just after Christmas, I woke up to find five inches of snow on top of my camper. On the way back from work that day, I bought a small camping stove. At nights, during that freezing cold spell, I used to wear a diving undersuit, climb inside my sleeping-bag and direct the reflective bowl of the stove on to my face. I'm sure it was incredibly dangerous, but I kept extremely warm!

Despite my frugal life, I was not saving as much money as I would have liked. So in February, I managed to get a second job as a night security-man at Barclays Bank in Kensington High Street. It was being completely rebuilt. There wasn't a roof and at the back of the building was a mountain of scaffolding draped in canvas. So they required somebody just to hang around there. It was great. I'd arrive, find an old armchair, sleep for an hour, wander around for ten minutes, sleep for two hours, and then wander around for another ten minutes. But getting from one job to the other was a bit of a race. I'd only half an hour at either side of each job to dash half-way across London.

Although I was saving a lot of money, I was getting fed up with working twenty-three hours a day. One afternoon, I began to think about the earnings of professional divers. They earned in a day what I was managing to save in a week.

'This is ridiculous,' I thought. So I walked into a call-box and rang up my bank in Dartmouth. I told the bank manager what was what and said, 'I need two thousand pounds to take a professional diving course.'

Much to my surprise, he said, 'Sure. That's fine. Good to hear it. Glad you're doing something sensible.'

I quit both my jobs, went back to my camper, dusted it down, started it and set off for the Prodive Commercial Diving Centre in Falmouth. I'd chosen to go there because, for some reason, its course at the time was much cheaper than the one at Fort Bovisand.

I arrived in Falmouth one Sunday evening, the day before I was due to start the course. I had a quick look round, parked the camper, went to sleep and got up in time to be at the centre by nine o'clock on Monday morning.

I'd never met such hostility in my life. I was absolutely staggered. The staff there were really horrible to me. I was expecting at least a hello and a quick introduction to the course. Instead, all they said was, 'Get on the boat, Mr Punchard!'

I was wearing fairly decent gear and so I said, 'Any chance of a pair of overalls?'

The two instructors ignored my request and bellowed at me to get on the boat.

There were eleven guys apart from me on the course and all of them appeared to be in a state of shock. They were dashing around like blue-arsed flies, intense fear written all over their faces. It didn't take me long to work out why. It was because of the way in which we were all being treated. Nobody was called by their first names. All the students were addressed as Mr. We had to refer to the instructors as Mr Norman and Mr Lewis. All the instructions were shouted and if you didn't do everything at the double you were shouted at even more. I was quite disgruntled by the whole business. It was the type of military environment I'd always hated. But I decided it would be best to button up and keep my head down.

That was the start of the course. And it didn't get any better. All the students felt they were treated like dirt. But none of us complained.

The course was very exhausting. The rest of the students were staying in digs. I was trying to economise by sleeping in my camper, but after a fortnight I was an absolute wreck. So I moved into a flat with one of the other guys.

Every morning, we had to be at the centre by eight o'clock. The first half hour was spent running around Falmouth docks or doing exercises. Even worse were the dock swims, when we had to swim up and down No. 1 Dock in huge diving suits. I've never been much of a swimmer and everybody seemed to be able to do it better than I could. And the one who was last always had to do the swim again. That really pissed me off.

The course was very structured. We used the full range of diving equipment, we dived at different depths, and then we were taught how to use all the tools we could expect to encounter working offshore in the North Sea. There were also a large number of practical tests.

One day, Colwyn Darlow, who was another student on the course, and I were sent down to lay some explosives on an old wreck. Anybody who's worked with explosives will tell you it's great! There's nothing quite like setting off great bangs underwater. Unfortunately, it also kills a lot of fish, most of which float to the surface.

After we'd set off our explosives, we went out in a Zodiac – a fast inflatable boat – and began scooping up all the fish. Then some distance away, we saw in the sea what appeared to be the classic cartoon Loch Ness monster. It looked like half an inner tube sticking up out of the water. We glanced at each other and then sped across.

The monster was a sodding great conger eel, about six feet long. It was floating, stunned, arched half out of the water. But every time we touched it, it woke up and started snapping its football-sized jaws. I got hold of the anchor and Colwyn grabbed the oar.

Apparently, what happened next looked hilarious from the diving boat. The chaps on there could only see the two of us trying for brief spells to beat hell out of something in the sea, before jumping sharply back into the boat.

Eventually, Colwyn managed to grab hold of the conger eel and haul it into the boat. As soon as it was landed, it started snapping around. Lying next to it in the bottom of the boat was a bass. The conger eel took one look at it and with a quick movement snapped the fish in two. At this stage, we were almost jumping out of the boat – the conger eel seemed determined to have a snap at us as well.

Fortunately, at this point, the diving boat arrived. The instructor told us to stop arsing around and passed us a lump-hammer to dispatch the still-very-active conger eel. After it'd been pulled into the diving boat, one of the chaps gutted it, but it was still snapping away. Half an hour later it was still trying to bite people, even though it had been filleted and nothing was left of its insides.

Despite such occasional lighter moments, the course continued to be both extremely strenuous and thorough. The instructors never let up or showed any sign of friendliness towards any of the students.

When I'd successfully completed the course, I felt absolutely terrific. It gave me an immense amount of personal satisfaction. I was also fitter than I'd ever been – I felt just like a well-trained race-horse.

I'd still no idea why the instructors had behaved as they'd done. But at the end-of-course party their attitude changed completely. Suddenly, they were calling everybody by their first names. I couldn't understand what was happening and so I said to them, 'What on earth's been going on all this time? Why have you been such bastards?'

'It's quite simple,' one of them said. 'Some day, you may find yourself in the most horrific of situations. Then you'll have to be able to perform, when an immense amount of pressure is suddenly put on you. It's difficult for us to produce the conditions that may exist in an emergency. So the only thing we can do on the course is to apply continuous pressure. If you can't handle that, we think it's a fair bet you won't be able to handle a situation where your life and those of others around you are on the line. So that's why we're so strict. It may seem old-fashioned and boring, but we think it works.'

One day, I was to find out just how right they were.

CHAPTER TWO

IN TRAINING

After finishing the eight-week basic air-diving course at Falmouth, I decided to stay on for another fortnight to take a course on underwater inspection. Several people who worked in the North Sea had told me it was a qualification that would give me a far better chance of finding work offshore. The construction phase of installing platforms was all but over and the existing ones were getting older. As defects in them became more apparent, there was a growing awareness of the need for regular inspection.

So once again, I had to ring the bank and ask for a loan. Without a murmur, the gallant bank manager coughed up another six hundred quid.

Much of the work on the course was concerned with inspecting welds on underwater installations. Defects in welds can be caused by corrosion or fatigue. We were taught to find them visually and by more advanced techniques such as magnetic particle inspection. During this, the weld is magnetized and sprayed with a magnetic, fluorescent dye. Ultraviolet light is then used to reveal any existing cracks.

We were also taught about the effects of seawater on oil rigs – about the causes of corrosion and the methods used to prevent it. For example, to protect a steel structure, a metal more likely to corrode – such as zinc or aluminium – is placed in electrical contact with the steel below water level. The added, more-active metal – called 'a sacrificial anode' – will then corrode in preference to the steel, which is thus protected. Corrosion can also be discouraged by impressed current. In this system, a DC current is passed from the surface through non-corroding anodes plated with platinum and niobium. As the current passes through the sea water, it inhibits the normal corrosive process in the submerged steel members.

Although I found some of the theory a little tedious, I thoroughly enjoyed the diving work. The atmosphere was far more relaxed than on the basic course. The instructors were pleasant and I got on well with all the other guys.

One of them was Dougie Wright, a nice bloke who was a bit older than the rest of us. I knew he was living at the time with a woman called Vicky. Their relationship, by all accounts, was somewhat tempestuous.

One night , a few of us were sitting in the digs when she walked in with him. We all chatted away for a while about the inspection course. I can't remember what I said, but I know it didn't impress Vicky. A few months later, she told me she'd concluded that night she'd never met such a pompous arsehole in her life!

We met again, because Doug invited me a couple of times to their place for supper. Vicky always had something different to say about whatever was being discussed. She was an extremely intelligent woman with a most unusual outlook on life. As she was also a keen sports diver, we had a lot in common and I spent a long time chatting to her.

At the end of August 1982, on the last day of the course, I was finishing off some magnetic particle inspection at the bottom of No. 1 Dock in Falmouth harbour, when Dave Ryeland, who runs the dive school, spoke to me over the intercom. 'Ed,' he said. 'There's some chap on the phone here who says he wants to speak to you urgently. I think it's your brother.'

I'd all kinds of thoughts about his having had another accident. I came straight up, took off my helmet, and in my dripping suit went into the reception at Prodive.

It was my brother, Bernie.

'What's the matter?' I asked.

'Nothing. Do you want a job?'

'Yes. Where?'

'Aberdeen, be here at two o'clock tomorrow afternoon.'

'Great!'

Back on the site where he'd had his near-fatal accident three years before, he was the diving superintendent on a job that had started a few days earlier. They needed an instant replacement for a diver who'd suffered a bad case of the bends (decompression sickness). This can happen when the changes of pressure a diver experiences while being brought to the surface cause bubbles of inert gas to form in the body. There are two types of decompression sickness – the more serious can be fatal.

Delighted to be given my first diving job, I quickly changed and went into town. By the time the other guys arrived back at the flat, I'd collected my British Airways ticket and it was lying on the table.

'You bastard!' they said in unison. I was the first one on the course to find a diving job. It wasn't offshore on a rig where most of the divers wanted to work. It was a civil engineering job, but the rate of pay was £65 a day. That was an absolute bloody fortune!

That evening, I called briefly in the pub to say goodbye to the chaps on the course before I caught the night train to London. While I was there, Vicky came in and told us all that she'd slung Doug out that day. As I was leaving, Vicky gave me a big hug and a kiss. 'If you want to come back to Falmouth any time,' she said, 'you're welcome to sleep on my floor.'

With that, I left the pub and caught the train. The next morning, I flew from London to Aberdeen.

An inflatable took me two miles offshore to a Dutch coaster, called the *Tugro*. I was put in a tiny cabin in the stern where there were four bunks. They exactly followed the contours of the ship and so they could only comfortably be slept in by somebody with a pronounced curvature of the spine.

The food was cooked by the wife of the Dutch mate and so we had such things as plates-full of cheese for breakfast. We got very fed up with that and, after the crew had turned in, I used to be dispatched to the kitchen to make piles of bacon sandwiches.

'You divers are all animals,' the mate said to me once.

'Why's that?'

'All you want to eat is pig!'

The bearded skipper was the spitting image of Captain Ahab in *Moby Dick*. When he was shouting down from the bridge in his thick Dutch accent, I had a constant vision of him going over the side tied to the great white whale.

The hold of the coaster was filled with five-ton bags of stone chippings. The divers' job was to use these to stabilise the sea-bed around the diffusers of the sewage outlets to prevent scouring by the tides.

At first, we started off by using the ship's derrick to lower one bag at a time to the sea bed. We'd find the diffuser and then guide the bag of stones into place. We'd cut them open and then send the empty bag back to the surface. But once we'd found the location of all the diffusers, we cut the bags at the surface and let the stones sprinkle into place. That speeded the job up.

I really enjoyed working for the first time with my elder brother. But, although I didn't realise it at the time, he was absolutely paranoid. Because I was his kid brother, he was shitting himself every time I went into the water.

The other divers were a mixed bag, but I got on with them fine. A couple had been working for only a few months, while others had been with the same civil engineering company for years. One of the chaps, Steve Oliver, was very proud of the tattoo round his belly-button. It read 'Made in Sheffield'. Another, a huge ex-Marine, took great delight in throwing people overboard. There was absolutely naff-all you could do against this bloke – he was a giant.

We only went ashore a couple of times. The whole team of twelve of us piled into one Zodiac and sped to Aberdeen, where we were dispatched to have a few drinks. I didn't know Aberdeen at all and we ended up hanging around the harbour bars. They were a bit grim, full of strippers and drunks looking for a fight. But a good time was had by all.

The job lasted just over six weeks. Almost to the penny, I'd saved enough to pay back all the money I'd borrowed to take my diving courses. I'd never earned so much money in my life.

The contractor was Shiers Diving, one of the largest civil engineering diving companies. My brother had worked for them for years. The owner, Don Shiers, said to me, 'Do you want to carry on working for us? We've got another job coming up.'

But I said, 'No, thanks. I want to work offshore.'

All the diving team said, 'No way you'll get a job offshore, Ed. You're just a baby diver. No chance!'

Bernie and the rest of the team went down south to do a job in a reservoir near Manchester and I stayed on in Aberdeen.

Justin Mayhew, the guy on the diving course who'd driven

my camper up to Aberdeen, had already managed to find work offshore. I was determined to do the same.

The oil companies who operate the rigs and platforms do not employ most of the offshore workers, including divers. Most of the work is put out to tender and then organised by contractors.

There are two ways in which diving work can be put out to tender. When I entered the profession, the most common way was for approved companies to be asked to bid on a day-rate basis. The personnel and equipment that would be used had to be specified. The oil-production company would look at the bids, consider the companies' track records and accept what was considered to be the best value. More recently, because of the pressure to reduce costs, it has become increasingly common for diving companies to make a fixed-price bid for a specific job. The lowest bid is then often accepted. It doesn't matter what the record of the company is – providing the price is the cheapest.

At the time, there were about six major diving contractors who recruited divers to work on specific contracts. I set off on a tour of them all, making detailed notes of everybody I'd seen and what their reaction was. I even parked my camper within sight of their offices so they knew I wouldn't go away until I'd been given a job.

Very slowly, I started to learn the fundamentals of the offshore business. For example, before anybody could be accepted on a job, his C.V. had to be approved by the oil-production company. It was a legal way of controlling not only their own employees but also the people working for contractors.

The more I learned about the industry, the more people's attitudes towards me softened. It also helped that my brother, Bernie, was a respected professional diver. So I got to know many of the people working in the offshore oil industry.

In some places it was impossible to get past the battleaxe of a secretary; at others, I'd encounter someone like an operations manager who was so staggeringly aggressive he made me feel like dirt.

But the people at Comex – one of the most important diving companies – were absolutely superb. Even though they didn't have a job for me, they gave me a new diving medical and sent me on courses in offshore survival and underwater cutting. I rapidly realised that Comex was far better than most companies – it was more of a club than an employer. One of the great tragedies in the decline of the industry is that Comex have been forced to make brutal economies. The medical department has closed down, divers are no longer given free courses and the squash courts and divers' accommodation have been turned into offices.

As I was spending all my time in Aberdeen, I got to know the place quite well. It's a dominant city of grey granite, with a centre focused around one long, wide street – Union Street. Apparently, in the late seventies it was a riotous place, but it was never quite like that while I was there.

But there were lots of pubs and bars. One of the favourites was the bottom bar in the Imperial Hotel, which was known as the Snake Pit. It was always full of divers chatting up women and getting drunk on pints of heavy with Scotch chasers. There was also a bar called Gabriel's in a converted church that was very popular at the time. It was then the haunt of some South African and Zambian divers who used to pile in there flashing their tans and Rolex watches. I discovered then that a hell of a lot of divers are terrible poseurs.

After four weeks of hassling, I was offered a job by the Operations Manager at Comex.

'Where?' I asked.

'The Byford Dolphin.'

'Great. When?'

'Tomorrow afternoon. So go and pick up all your kit.'

I then discovered that getting a job with Comex was like joining the army. I arrived in the stores, stuck my arms out, walked down a long counter, and was given a pile of goodies. There were overalls, rig-boots, Parkas, foul-weather gear, a hard hat. It was like Christmas.

I was told to be at the airport at two the following afternoon for a flight to Stavanger in Norway. Then I'd be taken by helicopter to the Byford Dolphin. I'd spend a couple of weeks there and then be transferred to the main Frigg complex in the Norwegian sector to work on TPC2 – a concrete-leg rig, where we'd be diving inside the legs.

When I arrived at Stavanger, I checked in at the heliport. I was really very excited. I'd never travelled in a helicopter. Before we set off, we had to put on a survival suit and watch a safety instruction film which told us how to fasten our life-jackets. Then we were led to the helicopter. It was a Puma – quite modern, but a bit cramped. Before we started, the woman pilot told us how long the trip would be and the rigs we'd be stopping at.

Then they put on some music. It was bugger-all use. When we

took off, it was so noisy and there was so much vibration that we had to wear ear-plugs. It felt very unsound – it just didn't seem as though the thing should be flying at all.

Having left behind the fiords of Stavanger, we flew over occasional supply boats sailing backwards and forwards to the rigs. Then eventually we reached the Frigg complex. It was a staggering sight. Operated by Elf, there were three massive rigs connected to each other by bridges. Close by, there was another huge concrete rig. Sticking out of the sea beside it was the bare steel jacket of a rig that was erected wrongly and left there unused and useless.

As we landed, the complex looked just like something you'd expect to see springing out of the desert in a Mad Max movie. Everything about it was completely alien. It was noisy and dirty, with bizarre bits sticking out and flames shooting up into the air – like a blazing, second-hand Pompidou Centre on stilts.

From Frigg, we flew to the Byford Dolphin. Though much smaller, it looked equally alien. To stop the helicopter slipping on the helideck, it was covered with a rope net. The first thing I did was trip over it. That caused the snarling, deep-sea diver behind me to start tut-tutting.

There was a lot of activity on the helideck. The controller, with his headset on, was talking to the pilot. Luggage was being unloaded from the hold. The co-pilot had hopped out and was being passed a pile of packages. At one corner, a chap in an asbestos suit stood next to a massive foam-gun in case of fire.

For the first time, I was on an oil rig. Far below me and as far as I could see in all directions was the turbulent expanse of the grey North Sea. It suddenly dawned on me that my training was over. Now I had actually to do the work!

Carrying my bag, I walked from the helideck, down one flight of steps and along a companionway to the check-in area – an office with a glass door. I was told the number of my cabin and where I could find it.

I left the noisy, smelly environment and walked into the pristine, air-conditioned acccommodation area. Having put on my rig boots, I then wandered out to the dive control on the large expanse of deck.

The Norwegian superintendent told me what shift I'd be on. I was then sent to get my instructions from the life-support technician. He showed me around.

My job was to assist – not to dive. But I rapidly discovered that

I didn't know what the hell I was supposed to be doing. I'd trained as an air-diver and all the diving there was with a saturation system that was far more complex than anything I'd encountered.

There was a massive gas-control system to ensure the divers breathed the correctly adjusted mixture of helium and oxygen. This was fed both to the diving bell from which they worked and to the saturation chamber complex on deck in which the off-duty divers could live for several weeks at a stretch.

After looking around the dive platform, I was taken to meet Chris Dobson, the supervisor, in the Dive Control. It was a small building, full of big brass taps, several television screens, digital read-outs and huge dials twice the size of dinner plates.

'Where've you been working?' Chris Dobson asked me.

'Nowhere. It's my first time offshore. I've just finished my ticket.'

'What rate are you on?'

At the time, Comex paid divers on the D-scale. The highest air-diving rate was D10. That was about £80 a day. As soon as you qualified as a saturation diver, you went on to D11 and supervisors were on at least D15.

'D5,' I replied.

He looked at me for a moment in astonishment. Then he guffawed, turned round, switched on the intercom and spoke to the divers in the saturation chamber. 'Here, fellows,' he said. 'We've got a new guy on board. Guess what rate he's on.'

Because the divers were breathing helium, they all sounded like Donald Duck. 'Oh, fucking hell,' one of them squeaked. 'D14, I expect. Bet the bastard's getting more than us.'

'No. He's just started. He's on D5.'

'What! I didn't know it bloody-well existed!'

The hysterical laughter coming from the chamber sounded like a Walt Disney chorus. I felt really put in my place.

'Don't worry about it,' Chris Dobson said. 'We've all got to start somewhere. There's not much you can do now. It's too rough for diving. So find something useful to do. Go and make everybody a cup of tea.'

A little while later, a cheerful red-faced fellow called Eddie Coward took me to get some 'scran' – the offshore term for food.

We clambered up the metal stairwells and changed out of our overalls and rig-boots. Then in our trainers, we squeaked along a maze of corridors to a large round recreation room, inside one of the legs of the rig. A group of dour Norwegians was staring transfixed at a television screen. I took a quick glance and saw the programme was in Norwegian. I wasn't going to be watching much television there!

Next to the rec. room was the galley. On one side was a table with salad and ice-cream machines. As we walked towards the hot-food counter, Eddie said, 'Now you can have the chance of sampling some of the infamous offshore scran.'

The first thing I saw was a huge pile of T-bone steaks.

'Just help yourself,' Eddie said.

So I did. I'd never had a T-bone steak before in my life! 'This is great,' I said.

'Christ,' he said. 'This is rubbish. Wait till you work on a Norwegian production platform. The food there's brilliant.'

We chatted about the work on an oil rig and Eddie told me a lot about the saturation-diving system. 'It's a bit old hat,' he said, 'but it's still pretty efficient. On the diving deck, there's two saturation chambers that can be connected to the diving bell. That's why there were so many dials in diving control. Each of the three units had its own controls.'

After we'd eaten, he took me back down to the dive control.

For the next two days, the weather remained too bad for diving and so I had time to familiarise myself with the diving system. One of my jobs was to collect food for the divers in the compression chamber. This was then passed through the medical lock – a steel tube that penetrates the wall of the chamber with an air-locked door on either end.

On the third day, when I came on shift, they'd already started diving and the divers were nearly at the end of the first bell-run. So the bell was about to be hoisted back through a hole in the deck known as the 'moon-pool'. While the bell was being held above it, the moon-pool would then be closed with a door. In this door were three sockets which held the legs of the bell. When they were in place, the bell and the door would be slid across pneumatically so the bell could be connected to the compression chamber. It's just like docking a spaceship. Then the divers would transfer under pressure from the bell to the chamber.

I went outside with Roy Lucas, a tall friendly chap from Caernarfon. The bell came up showering streams of water and we coiled up the umbilical cables through which the gas mixture was fed to the divers. When the moon-pool door was shut and the bell had been slid across to the chamber, Roy said, 'Come on, Ed. Now we've got to put the clamp on.'

There wasn't much space between the trunking of the chamber and that on the wet, dripping bell. At the chamber end were two halves of a heavy, circular clamp. We lowered them into position. On the far side, there was a bolt in the clamp that had to be pulled up into place to make it secure.

'If it won't quite go,' Roy said, 'you'll have to tap it in gently with a hammer.'

The bolt slipped into place. Then Roy picked up a long steel tube with a socket welded to one end and a handle to the other.

'You hold the socket on the nut,' Roy said, 'and I'll tighten it up. But, for Christ's sake, Ed, make sure we get this right. 'Cause a lot of people have been killed this way.'

After we'd tightened the nut, the divers opened the doors in the bell and the chamber and so were able to pass through the trunking from one to the other. When the new pair of divers were in the bell and the divers who'd completed their bell-run were back in the chamber, the two doors were closed again, the clamp was undone and the bell was wheeled back into place ready for the next bell-run.

It was a routine job that was tackled several times a day in a saturation-diving system. Yet it was obvious that the way the clamp was opened and closed was potentially very dangerous. There was no safety device to stop the clamp being removed when the interior of the trunking was under pressure. Yet for a hundred quid or so, a gauge and lock could have been fitted to prevent this ever happening.

Fourteen months later, there was a major accident on Byford Dolphin. The diving bell had come up through the moon-pool and had been connected to the compression chamber. There was then obviously a breakdown in communications between dive control and the deck crew. One of the chaps thought the trunking between the bell and the chamber was ready to be disconnected. He undid the nut, but couldn't open the clamp. He picked up a lump-hammer and gave it a clout.

The divers had transferred into the chamber from the bell. The doors in both the bell and the chamber were still open. As the chap hit the clamp, it shattered. There was a huge gas explosion as the bell and the chamber decompressed. The massive bell, with nothing holding it, was flung across the deck.

Five men were killed. The man who'd opened the clamp was hit in the chest by the hammer and killed. One of the divers who'd just transferred, on hearing the clamp being opened, tried to close the chamber door, but was spat out in dozens of butchered pieces, past the partially closed door. The massive drop in pressure instantly killed the other divers, two of whom were lying quietly on their bunks in the adjacent chamber. One was Eddie Coward. The other was Roy Lucas.

CHAPTER THREE

MAKING OUT

Like everybody working offshore for the first time, I was very
green. But I managed to survive without upsetting too many
people.

One day, I went to the galley to collect the food for the divers.
I was wearing my overalls and heavy rig-boots. Then I noticed
that everybody was staring at me. Nobody said anything, but
I felt most uncomfortable and scampered out as soon as I could.

Later, the Norwegian diving superintendent came up to me
and said, 'No rig-boots. No rig-boots in the galley. You do it
again, you won't stay here. So you better not do it again.'

'Nobody told me,' I protested.

'You should know these things,' he replied sharply and strode
off. It was pretty stupid.

After I'd been on the Byford Dolphin for about a fortnight,
I was told that I was wanted for the diving job on TCP2 – one
of the rigs in the Frigg complex.

I flew across on the regular shuttle – an in-field helicopter that
was permanently based on the rigs. It was small – only a six-
seater – and flying in it was great fun.

The pilot was an American guy, chewing gum and wearing
a baseball cap. As I had my camera with me, I leaned over his
shoulder and said, 'This is my first time on the rigs. Do you
mind if I take a few photographs?'

'Why sure!' he said, and did some flash passes round all the rigs in the area.

We landed on QP – the accommodation module, which on Frigg was separate from the working rigs.

When I went down into the reception area, I met the rest of the dive team. There were several guys I knew, including Justin Mayhew, my friend from the training course who'd taken my camper up to Aberdeen. We all had a noisy reunion.

While we were eating a meal, the diving superintendent said to me, 'Sorry, Ed. You and three other guys have got to stay on CDP1. They're short of accommodation on QP.'

I was really put out. I'd already seen that QP had splendid facilities such as a full-size cinema. The food was out of this world. Everything was brand-new and immaculately clean. It was just like a palace in the middle of the North Sea.

A couple of hours later, I flew in another shuttle to CDP1, where I was given a cabin with Justin. We'd just arrived, when I saw a chap walking over to a telephone.

'Is that an outside line?' I asked.

'Yes. Just queue up any time between now and nine o'clock. You're allowed a ten-minute call, or longer if nobody is waiting.'

I was really impressed. After I'd stored my stuff in the cabin, I went to the telephone and called home. Then, as nobody was waiting, I called my eldest brother, Bill, in America. I got straight through. I don't know which of us was more amazed. Then Justin phoned his folks in South Africa. It was an extraordinary perk we'd discovered!

Everything about the place was astonishing. Looking across at night from CDP1 to the three rigs that made up the rest of the Frigg complex was an amazing sight. They stood there, in the middle of nowhere, just like huge Christmas trees covered in thousands of fairy-lights.

In the morning, after breakfast, like commuters queueing for the bus, we waited for the eight o'clock shuttle with a collection of bored riggers and roughnecks. After a half-mile trip, we landed on QP and walked across the connecting covered bridges to TCP1 and then on to TCP2 – the processing platforms in the complex. Then, inside one of the three massive concrete legs, we descended by several vertical ladders to just above sea-level.

It could be dangerous working inside the concrete legs. On some oil platforms, they are virtually dry. You can walk down almost to the sea-bed. But nasty gases build up and there can be sudden fires. People have been killed inside them. I was told by divers after a fatal accident on one of the Brent platforms that they were paid extra money to tolerate the horrible conditions they experienced inside the legs, completely in the dry.

I don't know how they managed to get it down there, but at the bottom of the ladders in the leg where we were going to work there was a dive-spread with a decompression-chamber, compressors and a diving-basket with an air-winch – the whole issue.

The job was to shut forty or so underwater butterfly valves that went roughly a metre straight through the concrete wall. In summer, they were open to allow the sea in to cool down all the internal pipe-work. In winter, when the sea became rougher, divers closed the valves with a socket spanner.

It was my first dive offshore and so the adrenalin was really pumping through my body. I watched a couple of other chaps dive. Then the supervisor said, 'Your turn to go in, Ed. Here's some photographs of what you're looking for. We'll stop you at 60 feet. All the valves are numbered. Start at number 18, and see how many you can get done in your time.'

I put on a Unisuit. It's a dry (that is watertight) suit made from 8mm-thick foamed-neoprene that's sealed around the face and wrists. A zip runs from the middle of the chest, underneath the crutch, and half-way up the back. You have to put your legs in first, wiggle your hands inside the suit and then bend right over. There's a moment of total vulnerability when you're struggling bent-double inside this suit of elasticated rubber. Then you have to try and get your head inside and stand up. Somebody else has to zip you in. On your back, you put the emergency air-supply to what is called a bale-out bottle. It's exactly the same size cylinder as a sports diver uses for the main supply!

The air-supply is then connected to the helmet. We were using a Kirby Superlite 17. Made of yellow fibreglass, it's regarded by many as the best of the helmets. There are two parts. First, a neck dam with an attached yoke is put on. A clamp in it is then snapped onto the helmet. You breathe through what is called an oral nasal assembly. Fitting over the nose and mouth, it gives air on demand. Next are connected all the umbilicals containing the air and communication feeds sent from the surface to the diver. Finally, you put the rubber fins on your feet.

By this time, you're immensely heavy and you waddle

inelegantly backwards into the diving-cage – the open metal lift in which you're lowered into the water. Your only communication is then with the supervisor.

The diving tender checked that all my equipment was properly connected and working efficiently. Then he put a safety-chain across the basket and said, 'Diver's in the cage. Ready to leave surface.'

The supervisor responded, 'OK, Ed. We'll put you down now.'

When the basket started to descend, I reported, 'On the way down.' When I hit the water, the message was, 'Diver left surface.' This was repeated by the supervisor. So all the time, there was a continual dialogue going on over the communication system.

Everything's clear, unhurried and disciplined – a formal procedure that should be followed every time. Sadly, offshore it isn't always. When it doesn't take place, you know you're working with a bunch of cowboys.

Entering the water gave me the same buzz it had done when I first went sports diving. There was the same feeling of weightlessness. Everything began to work as it should – the air and the communications. All the clumsiness I'd felt on the surface in my diving-gear had gone. I was in the environment for which I was dressed.

On the way down, like all divers, I had to equalize the pressure in my ears and sinuses. On the front of the helmet, just below the glass, is a small knob. When it's pushed in, a piece of rubber blocks the nose. So the diver can then blow into his nose with exactly the same effect as when holding the nose on the surface or in an aeroplane.

When I reached a depth of sixty feet, the cage stopped. I leaned forward, took off the safety-chain and looked around. Above me was an enormous chandelier with arc-lamps shining brightly through the crystal-clear water. A gentle surge was flowing through the open valves, which were made to seem much larger by the magnifying effect of water on light. In that underwater world, encased in a concrete round, there was an incredible, surreal atmosphere.

It was the easiest possible work I could have been given for my first job offshore. I closed several of the valves and after what seemed to be no more than thirty seconds, the supervisor came over the intercom to say I had two minutes left before I needed to be back in the cage.

The ascent was at a slow, fixed rate, controlled by the supervisor. This is to prevent not only decompression sickness, but also a gas embolism, or burst lung.

Because such ascents are so slow, it's become increasingly common for air-divers in the North Sea to be brought up quickly and then recompressed in a chamber on the surface to breathe pure oxygen. It's a very controversial technique that's banned in some parts of the world. There's a lot of concern that it may have long-term effects, such as memory-loss and irreparable spinal damage. A friend of mine had a bad case of the bends shortly after leaving the decompression chamber. But it's a very convenient and economic system. The diver can stay down longer and be far more quickly replaced by another one.

The job lasted for a while and then it was back to Aberdeen and my camper. I was keen to get work on one of the long standing air-diving jobs where the work went on all the year round. They tended to be the older platforms like Ninian Northern, Piper and Claymore. They were in such need of additional work that masses of clamps had constantly to be fitted to the corroding underwater steel members.

I'd spent a lot of time phoning all the diving companies and I was just about to give up, when from a phone-box in Aberdeen I rang a company called BIX Offshore in Great Yarmouth. The chap I spoke to was obviously desperate to get a team together that day.

'Did I phone you earlier?' he asked.

'No. But I'm looking for a job.'

'Can you get to Morecambe Bay?'

'When?'

'Two o'clock tomorrow afternoon.'

'Sure I can.'

'I need two more guys. So, if you can get down to Barrow-in-Furness in time to catch the boat at two, you've got yourself a job. There might be anything from a week to a fortnight's work. Oh, what kind of experience have you had?'

'Very little.'

'Never mind. I'll see how you are. Just get yourself there in time.'

So I said goodbye to Aberdeen and headed south. When I arrived at Barrow-in-Furness, I drove straight through the town and out the other side. I had to turn round and drive back again. I couldn't work out where the town was – there appeared to be only one street. Yet there was major industry there, including the Vickers shipyard.

Eventually, I found the quay where I had to report and once again abandoned my camper. The chap I'd spoken to on the phone was waiting for me with a group of other divers. The boat that awaited us was a tatty old tug.

As we chugged along, he told me about the job. A gas-platform was going to be installed and large hoses with a flange on the end had to be attached to the pipe-line. The divers' job was to fit and seal the hose and the pipe-line. All the rust and rubbish would then be scraped from the inside of the pipe-line by a mechanical device driven through at pressure and called a 'pig' because of the squealing sound it makes while on the move.

A team of divers had been out there for a fortnight and had achieved nothing. The American engineering company was becoming really pissed off and had demanded that another team of divers should be recruited. We were a very motley crew. One of the chaps hadn't dived for several years.

After a couple of hours, we saw in the distance a supply-boat and a barge with a lot of equipment on board, including a mobile crane and a dive-spread. We pulled alongside the supply-boat, which was called *Sea Level 7*. A month earlier, it had arrived fresh from Louisiana, complete with its Louisiana crew.

'Who the goddam hell are you?' one of them shouted over the side.

'We're the new team of divers.'

'Well nobody told me you were goddam coming. Where the hell you going to sleep?'

'On the *Sea-Level 7*.'

'Well you'll be sleeping on a mattress in the corridor!'

And that's where we did sleep. And the crew wasn't very happy about that. Nor were the original team of divers pleased to see us.

As soon as we arrived, the weather blew up. Things didn't look good!

To make matters even worse for me, several of the divers started to rag me as a baby diver who didn't know what the hell he was doing. I decided that it would be a good idea if I kept my mouth shut. And I did. Despite this, I was instantly labelled 'College Boy' and was soon more or less ignored.

It was just as well. Around me, all kinds of fracas kept on breaking out.

Once, a Newcastle guy in the team went to get a Coke from the fridge. By this time the skipper was really pissed off with us – not surprisingly, because our unexpected arrival had given him eighteen extra mouths to feed. So he shouted out, 'And where the hell d'you think you're goin'?'

In his broad Geordie accent, the diver said, taking out a bottle. 'Fer this fuck'n' Coke.'

The skipper, just fresh from Louisiana, grabbed him by the scruff of the neck and said, 'What d'you mean, "Suck m' cock!" '

Then all hell broke out.

I could see it was the crassest break-down in communications. 'Stop!' I shouted.

Everybody stopped. Even the skipper and the Geordie paused mid-blow. After all, I was the college boy who never spoke.

'Look, skipper,' I said. 'This guy's got a broad accent and, with the greatest of respect, so have you. Neither of you understand what the other's saying. Believe me, he didn't say what you thought he said and so you're both about to hit each other for the most stupid of reasons.'

As everybody stood around open-mouthed, the two let go of each other and that particular fracas fizzled out.

A couple of days later, the weather calmed down and all the divers tootled off on the tug across to the barge. We could work only at certain times because of the tides, but in the next thirty-six hours, almost everybody was put into the water and nobody achieved anything.

The helmets being used were Kirby 10s. The front is very similar to the Kirby 17, but instead of being a complete hard helmet, the back is made of neoprene and is clipped to the front. A large rubber 'spider' clips over the top and keeps the whole thing sealed. I love them – they're wonderfully comfortable. But all the old divers dismiss them as 'Scooby-do' equipment. The only disadvantage with them is that the coms – the headphones and microphone – can get wet and if they're not properly maintained the clarity of speech is lost.

While one of the divers was in the water, there was a communications problem. He came unexpectedly to the surface and so nobody knew the speed of his ascent. As technically it was a case of what's known as omitted decompression, he had to be put straight into the chamber.

All his gear was dragged off him and he was thrown into the decompression chamber. The superintendent then said, 'Somebody's got to go in with him.'

Everybody seemed reluctant to volunteer and so I said, 'I'll go.' A few of the older blokes moaned that I didn't have the experience, but none of them stepped forward. There wasn't time for a ten-minute chat while everybody had a cup of coffee. And somebody had to be inside with him in case he flaked out and needed an injection.

At regular intervals, I checked his pulse and kept on talking to him. Fortunately, there was nothing wrong with him and after a couple of hours we were let out. As it was then the end of the tide, there was no more diving that day.

The next time we were ready to dive, it was my turn. I fiddled around with the coms, trying to get them to work, but didn't have any success.

The company rep came up to me and said, 'I don't know what to say, Ed. It's getting really serious. There'll be at least a bottle of Scotch in it if you get the job done.'

I went into the water, at first climbing down a ladder and then down the two hoses for about eighty feet. The visibility was very poor. With the light on my helmet, I could just about see as far as the end of my arm.

The hoses had to be attached to the end of the pipe-line. The crane hauled them up from the sea-bed – about five feet away.

'Come up on the crane,' I said and saw the hoses rising in front of me. I waited until they were above the end of the pipe-line and then told the crane-driver to stop. Attached to the two hoses was a square flange with a pin in it. The whole thing had to be lowered so the pin fitted into a guide-hole in a similar square metal flange at the end of the pipe-line.

So the flange could be drawn down, two thick metal wires were shackled to it. These went up to the surface where they were connected to two air-winches, called 'tuggers', on either side of the deck.

To get the thing into place, I had to direct the crane and the two tuggers so the pin on the flange slipped into the guide-hole. It wasn't easy. However, in the first diving job I'd had with Shiers, I'd spent a lot of time controlling a crane, getting the bags of stones into the right position. So I had a good idea of what to do.

Every so often the supervisor would ask, 'How are you getting on, Ed?'

'It's progressing,' I'd reply.

Eventually, I managed to get the pin into the hole – although the flange was twisted slightly. But it was more or less in position. Then I was told I was out of time and had to come up.

When I'd taken my gear off, the supervisor said, 'Well, how is it?'

'It's there.'

'What do you mean it's there?'

'Well, it's not exactly on. Somebody will have to go back down and twist it round, but the pin's in the guide.'

'What do you mean the pin's in the guide?'

'The fucking pin's in the guide! Stop hassling me! It's there.'

He was gob-struck. It was something they'd been trying to do for a fortnight. I don't know how I'd managed it, but I had done it. The supervisor was delighted.

I told the crane-driver that he'd have to keep the tension on the tuggers and balance the crane with the rise and fall of the tide. Otherwise it'd be lost.

The crane-driver was a wonderful chap who came from the Black Country. He stayed on the barge for the next six hours to keep everything adjusted. On the next dive, the flange was fixed.

The following day, all the divers were taken into Heysham and booked into a promenade guest-house. It was at the very end of the season and so it was full of old-age pensioners on cut-price winter holidays.

The divers were determined to get legless and made straight for the bar, where the proprietor was playing an organ and his wife was thumping away at a set of drums. As we walked in, we were all offered song-sheets and invited to join in some community singing. It's not quite what divers have in mind for their first night ashore!

At the end of the bar were some patio-doors leading out on to the prom. Suddenly, one of the guys spotted some girls walking by. With a whoop, three divers raced out and dragged in three screaming ladies of the night.

I could see how the evening was going to develop and soon turned in. Apparently that night, several of the bedrooms were wrecked, three blokes pissed their beds and the three girls were seen running naked in and out of rooms.

The next day, we were all thrown out en masse. But before we left, a telex arrived announcing that one team was demobilized and another team was kept on stand-by with full pay. At the top of the list of those who were retained was the name Ed Punchard! Then before you knew it, the guys who were being stood down were trying to thump hell out of the diving supervisor!

We divers who'd been kept on were moved into a posh hotel where we awaited instructions. I then discovered that most of the other guys were hardened soaks. One of them drank triple gins all day long. No wonder he rattled his cup and saucer when he picked them up at breakfast-time! I was much more couth in those days. When most of them were half-way through their first bottle of the day, I was ordering a second coffee.

While we were there, I came across what I'm told is an old tradition among divers. When some idiot has had too much to drink, he suddenly announces with great solemnity to his group, 'I'm going to do the Dance of the Flaming Arsehole.'

Usually, everybody knows the form. All the glasses are cleared off the tables, which are then all pushed together in a continuous circuit. If the bar can be involved, so much the better. The chap takes off all his clothes. He bends down like a chicken and a rolled-up newspaper is inserted firmly into his backside. The newspaper is then lit and the chap has to run round the circuit before he gets singed. Everybody is supposed to stand there with glasses full of beer, in case the flames need to be extinguished. But, as it did that night, it usually ends with a badly burned bum.

After a week, the order came for us to be demobilized. Just before I left, I was walking along the promenade when I bumped into the crane-driver from the barge.

'You know,' he said, 'I've watched you from the moment you got on board that ship. I couldn't figure it out at first. But I'll tell you – I'm a 55-year-old bloke and you're a young lad, but I learned something from you. Everybody was on your back, calling you names. When you went into the water, I thought, "Christ, I hope he does it." Then when you came out and you had done it and all the wankers were standing there who thought they knew everything and had done fuck all, I thought it was brilliant. I was buggered if I was going to let that flange slip out. So I stayed up all night just to make sure it didn't.'

I was deeply moved.

With the job over, I set off from Morecambe to stay with my mother in Dartmouth. But I didn't really know anybody there.

After a couple of days, I took a drive down to Falmouth to look up old friends. Taking up Vicky's invitation, I ended up sleeping on her floor, passing the time away. She was rebuilding her house and I gave her a hand. I got to know her better and better. In time, one thing led to another, and soon I wasn't spending too much time sleeping on the floor.

CHAPTER FOUR

LEARNING FROM EXPERIENCE

In February 1982, I was phoned by Bill Bain, the Project Operations Manager of Comex. He said there was an air-diving job on the diving-support vessel *Seabex One*.

'Who's it for?'

'Mobil in Beryl Alpha.'

'What's the rate of pay?'

'Oh, we'll talk about that when you get up here.'

As a novice, I was keen for the work and I didn't argue. So off I went to Aberdeen. In those days, companies used to give divers travel expenses. They wouldn't pay for flights, but they did refund the cost of a second-class rail fare plus a sleeper – which was a damned-sight more than the cost of an air ticket. So I used to make a hundred and fifty quid a time by flying to Aberdeen from Falmouth. It was great!

I was put up at the Imperial Hotel and the next morning made my way to the heliport for a chopper flight directly to *Seabex One*, a purpose-built diving vessel with its own helideck. At the time, it was owned by a group of German dentists and was a top-notch vessel.

There were about a hundred people on the ship. A Philippino catering crew prepared superb food. A group of Chinese did all the laundry and ironing. The ship's crew and officers were German. The riggers were French. And all the divers were British.

So there was a wonderful blend of nationalities aboard. Between the Frogs and the Krauts, there was the usual amused animosity, which the Brits were always doing their best to fan.

The Germans ran a very tight ship and were archetypically disciplined – always marching around and never smiling. When they were having their breakfast in the galley, they didn't want the television on in the room next door. At that time, the divers, who'd just worked their balls off for twelve hours during the night, wanted to watch a video and wind down. So there were daily, albeit good-tempered, battles.

The work being carried out by the diving teams was part of the 1983 annual inspection programme agreed with the Certifying Authority.

Every permanent offshore installation has to obtain a Certificate of Fitness. It's issued for a five-year period by one of a small number of Certifying Authorities approved by the government, including Lloyd's Register of Shipping, Det norske Veritas and the American Bureau of Shipping. To obtain the certificate, the owner of the installation has to draw up an annual inspection programme to ensure that the structure remains in a sound condition.

The Department of Energy also carries out routine, brief inspections of the offshore installations. There appear to be very limited resources in the department. The diving inspectorate, which is a specific unit, undertakes spot checks of diving systems, but somehow there is always advance notice. So there's ample opportunity to get the system into trim before an inspector arrives. It's very rare for any of them to see the true picture.

Not only is a variety of bodies involved in safety checks, but the operators are free to choose whatever method they like to organise the routine inspection of their installations. This means that, as far as underwater inspection is concerned, there is an incredible diversity of systems in operation.

Even the criteria used are totally different. For example, a diver inspecting a weld for BP would be invariably required to report every possible defect, including where a welder during construction has spattered hot metal above the weld. It's of no consequence to the safety of the structure unless associated with more serious defects and yet the diving team will spend an immense amount of time recording and reporting such trivial things. Chevron, on the other hand, doesn't wish to know about such fabrication defects that have already been reported in the yard. They look for new in-service defects. The data sheet that is returned on a BP weld may have 150 notes on it. An identical weld on a Chevron platform may have a sheet of paper with the one entry: 'No serious defects.'

Such varieties of practice put the professional diver in a difficult situation. First, he has to obtain unnecessarily advanced qualifications devised by quangos with no experience of offshore work. Then, he becomes a nomad, working on a contract-basis, wandering from one operator to another, unable to maintain any consistent working practice. On every job, his ear is constantly pounded by company engineers who believe that their system is the only one that's correct.

The inspection work the diving teams were required to carry out at Beryl Alpha was on three of the independent installations. These included the flare-stack – a separate tower, rising from the sea-bed to hold the gas flare in place on the platform. Then there were two of the single-point moorings (called SPMs) – long, thin structures, looking vaguely like the Post Office Tower, that were attached to a universal joint on the sea-bed. Their function was to enable oil to be transferred from the storage tanks on the platform to a super-tanker moored against them.

We had to use all manner of standard, visual and photographic inspection techniques, including measuring the levels and coverage of marine growth and corrosion. We also had to monitor three well-known defective welds in the lattice-work structure of one of the SPMs. They occurred at a depth of twenty-two metres, where the steel girders entered a large flotation tank.

Working conditions were pleasant. We were diving with hot-water suits, made of loose-fitting foamed neoprene with a double-sided nylon lining. Threaded throughout is tubing to bathe the diver's body in a constant flow of hot water piped down through the umbilical from the diving vessel. When you first enter the sea, there may be a rush of cold water around the chest that almost takes the breath away. But once the system has been properly adjusted, it's like being in a continuous hot shower. When everything's working properly – and unfortunately that isn't always the case – it's absolutely blissful.

At first, we were diving from a wet-bell, which is a cage with a dome that traps in a pocket of air that could, if required, be used by a diver in an emergency and also has onboard air supplies. One day, it was decided that the wet-bell would be removed from the system, because if an ordinary basket or cage was used the divers would be able to have more in-water time. Wet-bells require addititional turn-around checks.

There was a bit of a debate about this, because all the divers were in favour of keeping the wet-bell. We were used to it and it did provide extra safety back-ups. But the decision was made to remove the wet-bell and use the basket so we could dive from the surface.

The vessel was being held in position by its dynamic positioning system (DP), by which sensors send messages to a computer which can fix the location of the ship within a few metres, allowing for wind speed, swell and tide. This is accomplished by several thrusters – giant electric-powered propellers, jutting down beneath the ship, that can swivel through three hundred and sixty degrees and operate independently with variable thrust. The degree of control is phenomenal.

The DP system can be overridden from the bridge and safety alarms sound if the ship has moved out of position. Such precautions are essential. The thrusters are very powerful. While air-diving, there is always the possibility that the umbilical may be cut when one of the thrusters suddenly starts. In the past, divers have even been sucked through a thruster and chopped into pieces.

It happened that, after the wet-bell had been removed and the basket attached, it was my turn to dive next. I was still a most inexperienced diver and quietly cursed my luck. But I didn't worry about it too much. I still had a blind faith in the people who were in charge.

Down I went into the water, stopping at twenty metres where we were diving. I'd been told to establish a working-line from the surface. I found my bearings, but the visibility was poor. I couldn't see at all where the job was.

'Shall I take my umbilical through the basket?' I asked the surface, knowing that if I did so I'd always be able to find my way back.

'No, no. Don't bother. Just take a down-line across.'

So I headed off towards where I thought the job was. In my inexperience, I didn't ask for a shackle to attach the down-line to the basket.

After I'd struck out for a few seconds, I saw the job. There was a slight tide running. Above me were twenty-two metres of umbilical with a tide pushing against it. Try as I might, I could only get within two or three metres of the job. It was like being part of a nightmarish *It's A Knock Out*, trying to run up a slippery slope with a rubber-rope holding me back. I tried like crazy, but every time I was dragged back again.

I turned round and went back to the basket and paused while I got my breath back again.

'How you doing?' dive control asked.

'There's a bit of a tide running.'

'Well, try again.'

I tried again and exactly the same thing happened. I returned once more to the basket and caught my breath again.

'Try again,' they told me.

At this point, I should have said, 'No. Forget it. This is crazy.' But, knowing no better, I said, 'OK.'

I swam out again into nothing. This time I couldn't find the job. I then turned round and I couldn't see the basket either. So I started spinning round. All the time, although I couldn't see them, I could hear the noise of the thrusters constantly switching on and off above me.

'Can't see the job. Can't see the basket,' I told dive control. 'I'm in mid-water.'

I could sense a note of anxiety in the voice of the supervisor as he said, 'Get back to the basket, Ed.'

'I will, if I can find it!'

For a short period of time, I was swimming around looking for the basket. I could have been anywhere, but all the time I knew there was a possibility of my being chopped up by one of the thrusters. I started to swim in what I took to be the right direction. Then suddenly, I could just see the light-stick attached to the basket. Striking out like crazy, I reached the basket.

I was just about out of time and the basket was pulled up. I had a short period of surface decompression to go through. When I came out, they'd already removed the basket from the system and were putting back the dive bell.

'Jesus Christ,' the supervisor said. 'I've never crapped myself so much in my life. You could have been chopped up down there!'

A few days later, Stuart Porter had a nasty bend on the job. He did his surface decompression, got out, and ten minutes later he collapsed. Afterwards, he told me that he suspected it was because, while he was in the chamber, he'd spent a short time chatting to the other diver and so perhaps hadn't breathed in sufficient oxygen from his face mask.

A couple of weeks into the job, when the saturation diving bell was being brought up, it jammed with the divers still inside. It was impossible to either free the bell or release the divers for a number of hours. Eventually it was recovered and the ship sailed to Stavanger for repairs. Inside the fiord, the bell was fixed and all of us were given twenty-four hours to get drunk. We then returned to Beryl Alpha.

At the end of the job, after a couple of months, the ship sailed to Aberdeen where we were all demobilised. I was immediately told by Comex that in a fortnight there was a job for me on the Murchison platform. I went back to Falmouth to see Vicky again and have a break.

On an early spring day, the two of us went out sports diving with a friend in his fast dory with a 140-hp Yamaha on the back. It was one of those flat, calm days when the sea was as smooth as glass.

We put on our dry suits and launched the boat at the dingy quay, close to the Customs House Quay in Falmouth Harbour. We motored out through the moored boats into the Carrick Roads. As soon as we were clear of the harbour entrance, he opened the thing up and it shot forward like a rocket. We had to hang on for dear life. It spent more time going through the air than it did through the sea.

As we came out the main channel and approached Falmouth Bay, we passed St Maw's Buoy, Black Rock, and St Antony's Head. We turned past Port Scathow towards Gull Rock, where there was the wreck of an old steel sailing ship. When we arrived there, Vicky and I went over the side for a dive.

The visibility was excellent. The wreck was on its side and we landed more or less on its bow. Where the hull had broken apart, it had made a tunnel about fifteen metres long and about a metre high. We gently swam through it together, having a good look round for any old brass we could salvage.

Suddenly we saw a giant angler fish. It was almost a metre long. On top of its head was a thin tentacle, like a fishing-rod, that it flicked back and forwards. Hanging on the end was a little tit-bit to attract small fish. The angler was very wide and had a really big head. When its mouth opened, it displayed huge semi-circular jaws and a cavernous mouth. It was an incredibly ugly fish.

They make fabulous eating and so Vicky grabbed her knife and stabbed it. Although it put up a bit of a struggle, she eventually stowed it away into her goodie-bag. Then, as we were more or less out of time, we came up.

We pulled up the anchor and headed back the four miles to Falmouth. It was still flat and calm and we sped past the occasional fishing boat. Right in front of us, the sun was going down. It was stunningly beautiful and we'd had such a glorious day. Sharing it all with the girl I loved was absolute paradise.

A few days later, it was back again to Aberdeen. On the night before I left for Murchison, I bumped into a diver called Colin Woodwood, very humorous, with a strong cockney accent, who I'd met when I was at Fort Bovisand.

'What you doing here?' I asked. 'Where you off to?'

'I've been with Comex for a couple of years. I've just been on Murchison, but I 'ad a bit of bovver there.'

'Why? What went wrong?'

'I was moving the high-pressure grit blaster underwater when it blew 'alf me fuckin' 'and off.' He then showed me his bandaged hand.

'So what happened?'

'I was cleaning a weld and reached behind me to move the 'ose. One of the joints 'ad gi'en way in the 'ose. So it blasted sand into me 'and. They flew me to 'ospital and now I'm off work for a couple of weeks.'

I commiserated with him and we bought each other a couple of rounds.

The next morning, a helicopter took me out to Murchison. Built in 1978, it was one of the largest North Sea installations and was in the deepest water.

As I'd never worked before for Conoco, the operator, I had to have a photograph taken for the identity card. I queued up with a few others. The guy in front of me had his taken with a red background. When I went in, the photographer said, 'Who are you working for?'

'Comex,' I replied.

'Hang on a sec,' he said and changed the red background to a green one.

'What you doing that for? I like red.'

'No, no. You can't have a red background. It's not allowed.'

'Why not?'

'Conoco personnel have the red background. You have green.'

'Why?'

'So it can be seen immediately that you're working for a contractor.'

It was the first inkling I had that there was a form of class-distinction on the rigs. Until then, I hadn't twigged what was going on.

Although not a patch on the Norwegian platforms, the facilities on Murchison were good. I was very enthusiastic about working there – it was a long-standing Comex job and so it looked as though for the first time it would provide me with long-term employment.

On Murchison, there were four-man cabins, unlike those on the Norwegian rigs, which are never for more than two. Mine didn't seem too bad, although it was rather cramped. There was a toilet, shower and two washbasins in a small bathroom attached to the narrow, windowless cabin.

After I'd had a cup of coffee, the diving superintendent arrived. Called John Boyle, he was a tall Scot with a wonderful, dry sense of humour.

'Have you got your cabin organised?' he asked. 'We're all at one end of the corridor. Our cabins are much better than a lot of the contractors on here. We don't want to lose them. So make sure you keep all the green shirts sweet.'

'Green shirts? Who're they?'

'All the Conoco guys. Look around. All the guys wearing green shirts work for Conoco. They live in a separate accommodation module.'

'Is it any better than ours?'

'I should say. Not that any of us are allowed inside. So for all I know they've got gold-plated taps and a jacuzzi.'

All the new arrivals were assembled to be given a lecture by the safety officer and shown a video which detailed the alarm systems, the location of the lifeboats and the muster-point in case of an emergency evacuation. Much thought seemed to have been given to aspects of safety. The floors were marked with yellow lanes and there were numerous status lights. These were a system of traffic lights that always told you if there was a problem or potential emergency. It was very efficiently done. Everything was explained clearly and professionally.

Afterwards, I set off for the diving platform. To leave the accommodation module, you had to push open an air-locked door, which made a whistling noise as the air escaped. The intention was that the positive pressure from the air-conditioning inside the modules would keep out any gas should there be a leak on the platform.

I climbed down four flights of stairs in a panelled stairwell. Two further, long flights led to the bottom, cellar deck. The equipment there was incredibly noisy, with a constant whine so that you had to raise your voice to be heard. A lot of the guys wandering around were wearing ear-muffs.

In the diving control, I met John Booth, the supervisor. He showed me the hot-water machines, the compressors and how they were started, the fuel store, the changing-room, the two decompression chambers, the stores, the workshop, and where we could make tea. There was a great wealth of equipment – loads of spares, tools and electrical gear. I immediately felt that everything was being done properly – there'd been no stinting.

'You know about the Murchison bends,' John Booth said.

'I've heard vaguely about some sort of problem,' I replied.

'Out here last year, we had the record number of bends for a North Sea rig. It caused a lot of bloody concern, I can tell you. But we think we've got it sussed now. The ruling from Comex is that nobody goes anywhere after a dive for an hour. You're not to involve yourself in any physical task. Under no circumstances do you go up those stairs until an hour is past. So, no showers for an hour after you've dived. Most of the bends we had here occurred after the guys had reached their accommodation. Those two bloody-long flights of stairs must have had a lot to do with it. Anyway, I'm happy to say that since we've been sticking to the rule there hasn't been a single case of the bends.'

After the supervisor had pushed off, I had a bit of a banter with the other blokes and mucked in rearranging the equipment for the next location. There were five moon-pools on the cellar-deck. As Murchison was so large, it was impossible to cover the whole structure from one central point.

The move around took a couple of days and then we were ready to start diving. It was very pleasant and the visibility was good. Although there were a few construction tasks, most of the work was concerned with making detailed inspection of welds. (Comex called them DVIs – Detailed Visual Inspections; Conoco called them CVIs – Close Visual Inspections – which means something different to Comex, another example of the absurd lack of standardisation in the industry.)

A couple of years previously, a severe problem with corrosion had been identified on Murchison – which was why there was so much diving work available. I was told that part of the impressed current system, which was intended to stop the platform rusting, had not been switched on for nearly twelve months. My informant didn't know whether this was because of an electrical fault or human error. Whatever the cause, there had been a certain amount of corrosion, including a particular sort of defect in the toe of welds, which Conoco referred to as 'crevice corrosion'. These regularly showed up in our inspections.

As we worked, it began to dawn upon me that, although an oil rig might appear to be almost new above the surface, underwater, it could be slowly but surely rusting away.

CHAPTER FIVE

A UNION MAN

One day in the galley on Murchison, I met an ebullient chap, called Paddy Handscombe. He was one of the diving representatives, whose job it was to monitor, on behalf of the oil company, the work of the divers.

He told me he was working for a specialist inspection company, called Orca, which was trying to improve the standards of inspection in the North Sea. He said that, when he'd first started diving, he'd worked for Shiers.

'Really!' I exclaimed. 'Do you know my brother, Bernie Punchard? He was with Shiers for years.'

'Bernie! Of course I know Bernie! He was my first supervisor. I was with him on some bloody-horrible job in the Thames.'

'I remember it well. I went along there and vowed I'd never have anything to do with commercial diving!'

Paddy and I got on well together. Over the next few days, I learned five times more about underwater inspection from him than I'd previously known.

Paddy had been working for Chevron on Ninian Northern, which needed a great deal of remedial work because of its high number of weld defects found. Knowing that most inspection work was carried out in a haphazard and inconsistent fashion, he'd been involved in reassessing and redeveloping the process. Assessing the mass of data coming in clearly required a more sensible system than the one that had been operating.

The whole process had been surprisingly archaic. In all kinds of other industries, computers were commonplace. Yet offshore, you hardly ever found anybody involved with the data-collection of inspections using a computer. It was absurd, especially considering the high-tech reputation of the oil-industry.

An inspection should not just amass information, it should identify anything that is unusual. Paddy explained that, as a computer was being used for Murchison, data was being arranged more effectively and anomalies were being highlighted far more quickly.

Already, it'd been shown that there was a serious long-term and worsening corrosion problem on the Murchison platform. Something had to be done about it immediately. Either the cathodic protection had to be increased (through more impressed current or sacrificial anodes) or some of the underwater steelwork had to be removed.

At the time, Murchison still had the pile-guides on its legs. Looking like enormous knuckle-dusters, they'd been attached to enable the piles to be driven into the sea-bed so the oil rig could be secured. The easiest way of preventing the corrosion-protection system being overloaded was to cut off the pile-guides.

'Have you seen the *Arctic Seal* alongside?' Paddy asked. 'That's what they're doing – cutting off the pile-guides.'

The *Arctic Seal* was a support vessel being used for saturation diving, where the divers breathe a mixture of helium and oxygen. As helium is an extremely expensive gas, the vessel was equipped with a gas-reclaim system, which gathered the helium and recycled it on the surface for reuse.

The mix of gas is fed from the surface via the bell panel directly into the diver's helmet. Should anything go wrong with the gas return, there can effectively be an open tube between the surface and the diver, allowing a massive difference in pressure. So a malfunction is potentially fatal for the diver. The gas could be immediately sucked out from around the head, as though it was being vacuum packed. The surrounding water would then try to squeeze his entire body into his helmet.

We heard that there were problems with the gas-reclaim system on the *Arctic Seal*, so that several divers had refused to use it. Apparently, a malfunction did later take place. Fortunately it didn't kill the diver, but it did give him a nasty squeeze, bursting all the blood vessels in his eyes and making him very ill for a while.

While I was on Murchison, incidents like this made me far more aware of the potential dangers of working underwater. So I was very interested when, in common with all the other divers, I received a letter from the Professional Divers' Association. I'd seen some of the literature before, but at that time there was an increasing feeling among many divers that it was an excellent thing to have a professional association interested only in the welfare of divers. So the majority of us on Murchison joined the association.

A letter then arrived requesting that we should select a representative of the Professional Divers' Association on the rig. It was decided that I'd be a good person for the job. I could see no reason why I shouldn't agree. It seemed a sensible thing to do. So I became the representative, along with another chap representing the other shift. He was Dave Nichols, who had a PhD in marine biology.

Shortly afterwards, I finished my second four-week spell on Murchison and went off again on a fortnight's leave. While I was at home, a Chinook helicopter went into the sea by Murchison, fortunately without loss of life. When I returned to Aberdeen, I was shown wonderful photographs of the helicopter body being craned out of the water by *Seabex One*. Everybody was highly amused that, as soon as the Chinook had been put on the back of a supply boat, a couple of technicians arrived and painted out the British Airways markings!

Everybody who's worked offshore knows that helicopters can be extremely dodgy. They're inclined to just drop out of the sky. So when I took off on my return flight to Murchison, I was a touch apprehensive. Ten minutes out, the Puma started vibrating.

The pilot came on the intercom and said, 'We appear to have a problem. We're returning to Aberdeen.'

I was not reassured! There had been a number of problems with the Pumas – one of them had recently crash-landed at Aberdeen airport.

I looked around and everybody else seemed to be casually reading their newspapers. 'God,' I thought. 'There must be something wrong with me. Nobody else seems even slightly put out.' So it was an extremely uncomfortable ten minutes.

As we got off, a rep who was working with Paddy said to me, 'Will you be going to the dry cleaners as well!' I hadn't been the only one in a panic!

We did manage to land on Murchison at the second attempt.

A few days later, we received a communication from the Professional Divers' Association. It asked if we'd support a two-day stoppage offshore in support of a claim for a uniform pay-scale and conditions of employment across the industry.

It all seemed very reasonable to me. At the time, for doing a hazardous job, I was being paid £55 a day, which was sometimes less than the guys cooking the meals and making the beds.

All the divers had a chat and agreed to have a two-day stoppage on Murchison if asked to do so by the Association. None of us had any complaint against Conoco. So, as we didn't want to cause any unexpected disruption to the company, I decided that the correct thing to do would be to explain our intentions and why we wished to take action.

By coincidence, the Chairman and Managing Director of Conoco world-wide was due to visit the platform the following week. So I decided it was best to write him a letter, setting out our case. The letter also pointed out that if Conoco didn't want us on the platform during the stoppage, we'd willingly leave. The draft was thrashed out and finally agreed. The letter was then signed by the entire dive team on both shifts, including both diving supervisors and the diving superintendent.

Just before the Chairman was due to arrive, I went up to reception and said to the chap on duty, 'Would you be so kind as to pass this to the Chairman when he comes on board?'

'You can't do that!' he said.

'Why not? It's a letter. It's got his name on it. Just give it to him.'

'You can't just give a letter to the Chairman of Conoco!'

'Why not? I can write to the Queen if I want to. It's easy. It's a free country.'

Eventually, he agreed.

Later that afternoon, I went along with one of the other divers to meet the Offshore Installation Manager, to whom we'd sent a copy of our letter. We chatted away for half an hour and he was extremely friendly, congratulating us on the proper way we'd gone about everything. There was no problem at all.

A few days later, we received a letter from the Professional Divers' Association saying that as there appeared to be insufficient support for the action, it was called off. We were rather disappointed. We'd made all the preparations. But it was no big deal. We informed Conoco and, in my naïvety, I assumed that was the end of the matter.

I then went off on a fortnight's leave at the same time as Dave

Nichols. After ten days, neither of us had received the expected telephone call telling us when we should return to Murchison. So I called up Comex and was fobbed off with a lame story about there being no more work.

'But I was told it'd go on for at least another six weeks,' I said.

'Not any more,' was the reply.

So I phoned up the platform and spoke to the diving superintendent. 'I'm awfully sorry, Ed,' he said. 'But I can't get you on the crew-change list.'

It was quite obvious then that some skulduggery was going on. I phoned up Comex again and didn't get any sense from them. So I then phoned the Professional Divers' Association. After a lot of pushing and manoeuvering on their part, Dave Nichols and I were called up to Mike Chew's office at Comex. He was the man who'd originally been so kind to me and had since been made the General Manager.

He was really pissed off. As I understand it, a chauffeur-driven car had been sent round to Comex so that a spokesman for the company could report to Conoco and explain why divers were being treated so badly. It was all most unfortunate. I'd always found Comex to be one of the best diving companies and it hadn't been my intention to embarrass them in any way. So we both apologised. But our wrists were slapped and we weren't sent back to work on Murchison.

I returned home and waited.

Four weeks later, the team I'd been working with on Murchison was sent to Stavanger to carry out an inspection on the Alexander Kielland – the semi-submersible accommodation platform that in 1983 had turned upside down in the Norwegian sector with the loss of 126 people. It was, by all accounts, an horrific job.

But I was still without work.

One morning at breakfast, Vicky was talking to me about her family. She mentioned her cousin, Jill, and said, 'Now what was the name of the chap she was married to? John somebody-or-other. He used to fly his plane down to our farm occasionally. John Houlder – that's it.'

I just dropped my sausage. 'You know who I've been working for?' I said.

'Comex.'

'Yes – Comex Houlder Diving Ltd! Your cousin's ex-husband owns the company!'

Vicky just rattled her pearls.

By this time, I was becoming rather agitated. It seemed as though my career had been brought to an early end for a reason that I didn't understand. I couldn't fathom the paranoia that seemed to affect everybody's behaviour or what was wrong with having a divers' association. I was also short of money. I'd missed at least four weeks' work – which is not insignificant when divers work such a limited season.

At eight o'clock one morning in November, Vicky and I were awakened by the clock radio. I heard the presenter say, 'We have in the studio, Tom Hollobone, Chairman of the Association of Offshore Diving Contractors, to explain how much safer diving conditions now are in the North Sea.'

There then followed an interview which dwelt at length on the improvements that had been made since the bad old days. While I was happy to accept that things had improved a lot, there was still obviously so much wrong with the system. So I was irate at what was being said.

I leapt out of bed and started storming around in a real bad temper. 'Fucking arsehole!' I shouted.

'Calm down. Calm down,' Vicky said. 'It's only some dude on the radio.'

'I don't care. When was the last time he had a helmet on his head? What does he know about diving?'

The unjustifiable smugness of the interview had ruined my day.

That afternoon, we drove over to Exeter to see Dale Evans, a friend of ours. I wandered into her sitting-room and glanced at the television which was showing the Ceefax news. To my horror, I saw that there'd been a major accident in the North Sea. It was the tragedy on the Byford Dolphin that had killed five divers, including Roy Lucas and Eddie Coward.

But at that time, the names of the divers were not given. I was terrified that my brother Bernie might be one of them, because I knew he'd been working on the Byford Dolphin.

I rang his wife. 'Where's Bernie?' I asked.

'He's on Seabex. Why?' she said.

'Great. When did he get off Byford?'

'Three weeks ago. Why?'

I then told her about the accident.

What had happened on the Byford Dolphin was horrific. It deeply shocked me. Two divers I'd known were dead. When I'd worked with them as a complete novice, they'd both been extremely careful to ensure that I knew exactly what I was doing.

I decided there and then that I was not going to have any truck with any nonsense offshore. Coming as it did after a period in which I'd been becoming increasingly concerned by the senseless hazards faced by divers in the North Sea, this unnecessary tragedy made me determined to do what I could to stop anything similar ever happening again.

I was all too aware that there wasn't sufficient honesty in the diving industry to own up when such tragic mistakes took place. Indeed, as I'd seen with my involvement in the Professional Divers' Association, any efforts made by employees to be professionally involved in the safety of their industry were actively discouraged.

I'm not an aggressive or militant person by nature, but I don't like to see injustice and don't see why we should tolerate it in any way – whether it's merely the way we speak to each other or conduct our routine affairs. Human beings are immensely resourceful. If we can send men to the moon, we can certainly sort out how to work with each other. I don't see why we should have this kind of nonsense going on with employers at loggerheads with employees. I wasn't going to jump up and down waving banners, but I was determined to do what I thought was appropriate.

I'd been off work for a few weeks when Bill Bain from Comex phoned. 'Do ye fancy Christmas and New Year on the *Odin*?' he asked, in his dry Scots accent. 'They're crewing up and I hear ye can do with some work, Ed!'

I didn't know anything about the *Odin*, but I accepted readily. Any job was better than none.

Vicky wasn't very happy. She'd been looking forward to us spending Christmas and New Year together. But she drove me to Truro railway station.

I was quite keyed up, looking forward to being back at work. At the station, I met Guy Collins, one of the other divers on the team. As we hailed each other gleefully, our respective girlfriends stood by looking glum. We were then joined by Mick Sullivan, whom everybody knew as 'Stumpy'. He was going to be the diving supervisor on the *Odin*.

Every time the train stopped, people we knew got on. So we ended up having quite a party. We stayed overnight in a hotel in Morecambe Bay.

The next morning, we flew out by helicopter to the *Odin* – an enormous, dirty crane-barge that was a converted oil tanker. The crane was gigantic – its hook was as big as a fair-sized room. The four-man cabins were very grubby, as were the toilets and showers at the end of a long corridor. The tubular-steel bunk beds were less than comfortable.

The diving job was a peculiar set-up. The barge operator usually used divers from another company, K. D. Marine. We were expected to use their equipment, which was very different from the stuff we normally used. There was also a K. D. Marine diving team sitting there on stand-by, because they hadn't been demobilised. There was also a saturation diving team on board. It was all very odd, because when we got there the only work that was required initially was air-diving.

Our job was to fit riser clamps on to the steel jackets (or legs) of two unfinished platforms so the pipelines could be connected. Then the saturation team would do all the pipeline welds.

Before we started diving, the crane lifted up a huge mobile dive-spread, the size of a garage forecourt, and placed it on the lattice-work of the jacket. It was then held in place with chain-pulls.

Every day, we'd get up and try to eat a god-awful breakfast – the caterers were not very good. Then we'd go out on to the deck and make our way to the dive-spread. Sometimes a bridge was connected, so we could just walk across. On other occasions, we'd have a basket-transfer, where the crane hoisted four men hanging on to a rope net connected to a large ring. It's a system people either love or hate. It depends if you're into fairground rides – as I am – or if the instability makes you nervous.

As we weren't given any drawings, we were expected to find things in nil visibility, only to discover that instead of the one piece of tubular steel we'd expected, there'd be a dozen or so sticking out. As we could dive only at certain times of the tide, we made very slow progress.

The superintendent got very pissed off with us. So I said to him, 'Why don't you give us some drawings? Then we'd have some idea what the hell we're supposed to be doing.'

'You mean,' he said, 'you haven't been given any drawings?'

'No, we haven't. And it's ridiculous trying to work without them.'

So they found some drawings and we began to make some progress. But to make things go even quicker, the divers in the saturation team were informed they'd have to do some air-diving to help us with the work.

It'd been a long time since some of them had done any air-diving and they were unused to its more hectic pace. When you're air-diving, you don't have the luxury of an eight-hour bell run. After a limited period, the air-diver has got to come up to the surface. So while he's in the water, he tends to be like a ferret, scurrying from one place to another.

Unfortunately, the saturation diving team had a most horrific time. In approximately fifty dives, they had two type-two bends and an air embolism, which is a very serious accident.

It was surprising there weren't even more disasters. I'd never before seen such bad working practices. One day, I walked on deck and to my absolute horror saw bundles of scrap cable just being dumped into the sea. It went on for hours, until the whole lot had been cleared.

The deck crew consisted of badly paid, unskilled Spaniards. Teams of them were walking along the bare members of the unfinished platform, with no handrails, dragging welding cables.

They were also running the winches when we were setting the clamps. These were unwieldy things, weighing a couple of tons each. To direct their movement, the diver speaks over the intercom to the supervisor who then relays the message over his walkie-talkie to someone who doesn't speak any English and who's operating the winch. So we worked with the continuous fear of being crushed to death by a swinging clamp. Despite this, we eventually managed to get most of them fitted without mishap.

On Christmas Eve, to our intense surprise, we were provided with a festive meal. The first course was a booze-drenched soufflé. Assuming that this would be the only alcohol available, all the divers took three or four of these things each and squeezed them dry. Then the wine was served! By the time the third course arrived, everybody was absolutely drunk. Then we were given cans of beer! Before we knew it, people were dancing on the tables, singing away at the top of their voices. The poor guys who were serving up the meal were wandering around trying to hand over plates of turkey. It was a riot.

At the end of the meal, somebody had the bright idea that we should have races through the two risers – the pipelines lying on the deck. They were about a metre in diameter and twisted so it was impossible to see the end. After scurrying up and down them for a while, a few of us decided we'd sit in the middle of one of them and finish off the remaining cans of beer.

We all went to bed that night extremely drunk. The last thing

I can remember was being sick into a wicker wastepaper basket and being disappointed by the results.

Fortunately, we weren't supposed to be working on Christmas Day. I awoke eventually to see an enormous wooden crate by the bunk. On it was a label, saying, 'Must be delivered on Christmas morning. For the attention of Ed Punchard.'

I prized the crate open with a crow-bar. Inside was a note from Vicky wishing me a happy Christmas. There was also a television and an enormous Scalectrix set. That was my Christmas present!

Everybody was very excited and we'd just laid out the track when the superintendent walked in and said, 'We're diving.'

'You're joking!' I said.

'No, no,' he replied. 'They want us to dive.'

'But we're all absolutely wrecked.'

'Don't worry about the rest, Ed. You're the first to dive.'

We staggered over to the dive-skid. While we were waiting for the tide to slacken, I put on all my gear. I was feeling so bad that I lay down in the dive control, clamping to my face one of the oxygen masks from the decompression chamber. I could only pray that we weren't going to dive after all.

Then the supervisor arrived and said, 'It's all right. They've cancelled it!'

Phew!

A couple of weeks later, when it was time to set the risers, the crane lifted one of them up horizontally and then swung it into the vertical. As it turned, a shower of beer cans and wine bottles came out of the end and splattered all over the deck! It'd been a hell of a party!

Early in 1984, the weather became really bad. Late one night, a group of us went out to watch the waves. We stood on a walkway that went round the crane and was some fifteen feet above the deck. Suddenly a giant wave crashed against the stern of the *Odin* and we were up to our knees in green water. If we'd been standing on the deck, we'd have been washed overboard. So we quickly rushed back to the accommodation.

In the morning, the walkway where we'd been standing had been ripped away. Nothing was left of it. At the rear of the barge, there'd been a couple of containers used for the diving support. They'd both been smashed open as though they'd been paper bags. Nothing was left inside. Another container had been pushed back into the oxygen quads. These big steel frames had been flattened and the oxygen bottles shoved together.

All this took time to sort out and although the weather improved, Stumpy, as the diving superintendent, felt that diving could not commence. But he was put under an immense amount of pressure by the client to get on with the job. It was an absurd situation. Diving is not something that can be carried on willy-nilly, regardless of the weather or other hazards. It's too dangerous a job.

On 4 February – my birthday – I left the *Odin* to go on leave and headed home to Vicky, assuming I'd be back on the barge in a fortnight.

When I arrived in Falmouth, the newspapers were filled with reports of illegal nuclear discharges from Sellafield, which is on the margins of Morecambe Bay. I became rather disquieted. While I'd been diving, I'd seen a green slick all around the platform. The following day, all the marine life had disappeared.

The two things might well not be connected, but I didn't like what I heard. So I picked up the phone and spoke to Greenpeace. I told the chap who answered where I'd been diving.

'You're diving *where*?' he said. 'Haven't you heard about the radioactive slick that can't be found?'

That was enough for me. I phoned up Comex and scrubbed myself off the crew change.

CHAPTER SIX

TAKING ACTION

It'd been a very nasty job on the *Odin* and many dodgy things had happened there. It wasn't how I felt things should be. So I went through some serious rethinking. I wanted to continue working offshore – I also intended to keep on diving. But I was in something of a quandary.

Having had such long discussions with Paddy on Murchison, I began to think more about the inspection side of things and whether it'd be possible for me to spend some time working topsides, as well as working in the water. The idea was much encouraged by the knowledge that company reps were earning £120 a day, while as a diver I was earning half that.

There was no way I could move straight into such a job. But there might be the chance of becoming a data recorder, who acts as an assistant to the inspection controller. So I phoned Comex and spoke to a few people in the inspection department to drop the word that I'd be very happy to do such work if an opportunity arose.

While I was waiting for something to happen, Vicky suddenly announced, 'I'm getting really pissed off with you working offshore. You're nearly always away and so we're hardly spending any time with each other. If you're going to keep on with it, I'll have to do the same thing.'

I thought it was a great idea and she started looking at available diving courses.

Early in March, before she'd had time to do anything about it, I received a call from Comex, telling me that my name had been put forward to BP for approval and that my C.V. had been accepted as an inspection diver.

'There's a job on the diving-support vessel *Sulair*, working in the Forties field,' the guy said. 'Are you interested?'

I left Falmouth a few days later and flew out from Aberdeen on a Bristow's Sikorski to Forties Alpha, where I was transferred by basket to the *Sulair*. It had the most fantastic air-diving spread I'd ever seen. It was like Aladdin's cave.

The only problem with the facilities was that divers weren't allowed to eat with the ship's crew. This caused us to suspect that they were eating better than we were. We noticed, for example, that we never had any fruit. So the diving superintendent complained to the cook.

'If I put the fruit out,' the cook said, 'the divers will eat it!'

I spent a couple of weeks on *Sulair*, working as a diver. Then suddenly a spot arose for a data recorder. I was asked if I wanted to do it and, as BP gave their approval, I started work topside.

It was immensely hectic, mainly because of the approach adopted by BP to inspection. They wanted every report in such great detail that it seemed to me a little over the top. But it was in fact the best possible grounding I could have been given.

The supervisor I worked with was a man called Titch Halsall, who'd just returned from working in the Middle East. We got on like a house on fire. We clicked as a team and got through an immense amount of work. I was really enjoying myself.

After a month on *Sulair*, I went with the boat to Aberdeen for a crew-change. There were the usual mutterings on board about pay. But I really wasn't fussed. I was quite satisfied with the rate I was getting for the data recording. So I didn't pay much attention.

When we arrived in Aberdeen, we all went for several beers and a trip to the local strip-joint, Crazy Daisy's, down by the docks. Afterwards, we were sitting in a pub when one of the diving supervisors rejoined the group and said, 'Well I've done it!'

'Done what?'

'Told Mike Chew at Comex that we're not going back on the ship until we get a pay rise.'

'Oh, no,' I thought. 'Phoning from a pub! Christ, that's no way to do business!' I tried to ignore the whole thing.

He was going to and from the telephone quite a lot. I knew he was talking to Comex and that the situation was rapidly getting out of hand. With the last bit of logic left in my drunken head, I strolled off down the road and went to a call box. I tried to track down Graham Bagley, who was running the Professional Divers' Association. I eventually discovered he was at the Comex base. I had him tannoyed and then explained what had happened.

'It would be an immense service to everybody,' I said, 'if you could involve yourself and apply a bit of sense to the situation.'

'All right,' he said. 'I'll see what I can do.'

I really didn't want anything to do with the affair. The circumstances were totally wrong. So I went back to the bar. Shortly afterwards, a telephone call came through to say that Graham was on the way to have a chat with us all.

When he arrived, he asked everybody what their rates were and it turned out that several were very badly paid. So Graham phoned up Comex and said, 'Look, we've got seven guys here and considering their experience several of them appear to be underpaid. Perhaps you ought to consider some improvement.'

And that's exactly what Comex did. They phoned back to say they'd improve the rates. I got nothing out of it and hadn't wanted to be involved. But I was later told that because it was known I'd been there, some people at Comex assumed I'd been responsible for the whole thing.

I did a second month's stint on *Sulair* and was due to go on a fortnight's leave. As my annual diving medical was out of date, I left a day early so I could go to Offshore Medical Support, an excellent place where they do an incredibly thorough check.

'You've got blood in your urine, I'm afraid,' the doc said. 'We'll have to do something about that.'

They did more tests and told me it might be some time before the results were through. When I told Comex what had happened, they were brilliant and said, 'OK, no sweat. We'll send somebody else offshore. You can work in the office till everything is sorted out.'

After my leave, I worked in the Comex office on their bid for that year's inspection of the Mobil platforms. When the test results came through, the doctor informed me that I'd a bladder infection that would respond to treatment.

About this time, I walked into the office of the Professional Divers' Association with an old diving friend, Chip Scott. I just wanted to say hello, because I'd recently been put on the

Association's executive. As Graham Bagley was offshore, a guy called Brian Lane was looking after the office.

'Things are really going mad here,' Brian said. 'A whole bunch of K. D. Marine guys have just joined the association and now they reckon they're going on strike. They say there's some problem with their pay.'

We'd been talking about their grievance for a while, when a bunch of senior executives from K. D. Marine walked into the office. They were obviously very anxious about what was happening and wanted to talk to a representative of the Professional Divers' Association. Brian and I were the only officials there.

'We're awfully fresh to this,' I said, 'and we don't know exactly what's going on.'

'Well, can't you instruct them not to go out on strike?' one of the K. D. Marine chaps said.

'Of course not. They may all have just joined the Association, but if we give them any instruction they're as likely as not to ignore it and go out on strike anyway. Surely it's more sensible if we try to keep a level of involvement – talk to them to see if we can sort something out.'

The next day, Graham returned. By then, it was obvious that the men had a genuine grievance and, no matter what the PDA said, they intended to go out on strike.

We discussed the matter for a long time. It was clear that if only the divers working for one company went on strike then that particular company would be damaged. The PDA had no quarrel with an individual company. What it was demanding was a national agreement on pay and working conditions. The standardisation that would result would prevent diving companies undercutting each other to the point where they felt obligated to pay divers low wages. The cost of divers would become a fixed charge made by every company. So it was decided that it would be best for the Association to call for a two-day stoppage by divers throughout the industry in support of its demand.

It was clear that our decision meant there'd be a hell of a lot of work. So I found myself in the embarrassing position of having to telephone Comex so I could explain the situation and ask to be excused from working in the office. To give Comex credit, they immediately gave me permission to take leave of absence so I could spend my time organising a stoppage that'd include their divers!

Without a doubt, the administrative task of contacting all the divers working in the North Sea was the most difficult I could have ever tackled. There were some 130 offshore structures in the UK sector. There must have been fifty separate diving operations taking place. And we had only two telephone lines.

That morning, I went into town and did two things. First I bought a suit, because I knew I'd be speaking to such people as the directors of diving companies. Then I phoned up Vicky and said, 'I need you here in Aberdeen.'

'Why?' she asked.

'I need your clarity of thought.'

'What are you talking about? I can't just drop everything and fly to Aberdeen. I'm doing my sculpture and tomorrow I'm off sports diving.'

After putting the phone down, I felt disappointed that she hadn't agreed to come, but I went back to the office. A lot of chaps were helping there, including some divers from a ship called *The Ugland*, which was in harbour waiting to go off on a Mobil job.

We started phoning around all the diving operations, asking them to support the stoppage. It was instantly obvious that we needed more than our two telephone lines if we were going to get round them all. Telecom refused to supply any extra lines. So somebody was dispatched to send telexes through the Imperial Hotel. That worked for a while, until the management got snotty and said we couldn't send any more. Things were looking desperate.

Later that day, there was a knock on the door and Vicky walked in.

We greeted each other warmly. 'What made you change your mind?' I asked.

'Ed,' she said. 'if I told you I needed you in Aberdeen, I would say it only if I meant it. So I thought, as you'd asked me, I'd come straight away.'

She'd dropped everything and jumped on a plane. It was great. She immediately started to get things organised.

An hour or so later, there was another knock on the door. Three Telecom guys were standing there. Two had telephones in their hands and the other was holding a telex machine.

'Who's Vicky?' they asked.

'Oh, yes,' she replied. 'We'll have two telephones here and the others there. Put the telex in the corner.'

The rest of our mouths dropped open. It was tremendous. We might not have been in control of the situation, but at least we had communications.

Our intention was not to disrupt the oil industry in the North Sea, but to draw attention to how badly divers were being treated – to put the issue into the public arena. We were quite sure that we were doing the right thing, even though the strategy had not really been worked out, as it had arisen unexpectedly from the action of one group of divers.

We felt that the stoppage was a success. Twenty-five diving operations shut down for either all or part of that forty-eight-hour period. That was despite the phenomenal pressure placed upon divers to continue working. Diving companies were telexing their divers to say that nobody was going on strike. Because it was impossible for them to contact other rigs, the divers didn't really know what was happening. So the fellows who actually went on strike were in an extremely vulnerable position. It had always been difficult to make any protest offshore. A contract worker has to be approved by the operator and anybody labelled as a trouble-maker would usually find he was no longer required back.

At the end of the two days, a message was sent to the diving companies saying that, unless discussion on a national agreement had begun within twenty-eight days, there would then be another two-day stoppage.

What happened then should perhaps have been foreseen. The other organisation that had been representing divers was the National Union of Seamen. They'd already published earlier in the year a statement demanding a very modest improvement in pay. During the twenty-eight days, the NUS got together with the diving companies and agreed upon a pay rise similar to that outlined by the PDA. And it was substantial. My own pay rate, for example, was almost doubled. So the problem was solved. But the PDA was effectively left out in the cold.

After the strike, before Vicky went back to Cornwall, we went out for a meal with Chip Scott to a delightful bistro. Chip talked to Vicky about what she wanted to do.

She told him she'd taken the Part 4 diving course and was desperately keen to get her full ticket, but she simply couldn't afford it.

Chip reached into his pocket, took out his wallet, wrote a cheque for three thousand pounds, and handed it to Vicky. 'Give it me back when you've got it,' he said.

Vicky's mouth dropped, but she had the good sense to accept it. She went back to Cornwall and booked into the full professional divers' course at Prodive.

A week later, I returned to the Offshore Medical Centre. The doctor said, 'Well, the good news is that everything's turned up clear. The bad news is that the final thing we have to do is to make an internal visual inspection of your bladder, just to make sure.'

'How the hell do you do that?' I asked.

I was soon to find out. They took me into hospital and under a general anaesthetic shoved a fibre-optic tube up through my penis into my bladder. When I came round from the anaesthetic, I felt I'd been trampled on by a herd of cows. For days, my private parts were excruciatingly painful. It really was like peeing razorblades!

But, having passed my annual diving medical, I went back to Comex. When I went in to see the Inspection Manager, Tom Aldridge, I said, 'Let's not beat about the bush. Am I going to get back on the *Sulair*? I want to continue with my job.'

'Ed Punchard, you above all people,' he said, 'should know that Comex doesn't have a policy of discrimination or retribution. Are you available now?'

'Yes.'

'Well, be ready at twelve the day after tomorrow for the flight back to *Sulair*.'

When I arrived there, Titch Halsall, the diving superintendent, said, 'I've been waiting for you to stop piss-arsing around in Aberdeen. We've needed you here. I want you to run the inspection.'

'What? As inspection co-ordinator?'

'Yes.'

'You must be joking. I've only been doing data recording for six weeks, for Christ's sake.'

'I don't care. You leave it to me. I'll get it all sorted out.'

And he did. I became the inspection co-ordinator, liaising directly with BP's diving representative. I was immensely busy all the time. Not only was I involved in the inspection but also with co-ordinating some fascinating construction work. An extensive hyperbaric welding repair had to be made to a cross-member twenty feet below the surface, at the centre of the plat-form. To do this, we installed the first ever one-atmosphere cofferdam – a giant shell that was clamped in place and provided with its own shaft to the surface so that the weld could actually be done inside it.

Towards the end of the year, the work on *Sulair* finished and we were all demobilised. As I'd lost a chunk of work through failing my medical, I took a job working in the Comex office on the BP report, thinking it might provide valuable experience. The rate of pay was lousy and the experience proved conclusively to me that I wasn't cut out for working in an office.

Around this time Vicky completed both her diving and inspection courses. She then came up to Aberdeen for the 1984 Association of Offshore Diving Contractors' Conference. It provided her with an excellent opportunity to meet people in the industry. Although as a woman qualified to dive in the North Sea she had considerable novelty value, the name of the game is contacts.

I introduced her to several people at Comex, including George Arnoux, the Safety Manager, who promptly decided that she could be his assistant at the conference. As he was the Chairman of the Safety Committee for the Association of Offshore Diving Contractors, it was an excellent introduction to the important people in the industry.

While she was walking round the exhibition, Vicky was accosted by one of the old school of American divers from McDermott Construction. He looked at her name-tag, which said she was a diver, took his cigar out of his mouth, and said, 'My Gawd. It's happened!'

After the conference, Vicky went round the offices of the diving companies looking for work. At K. D. Marine, a chap told her to sit down and then said, 'Are you sure you can hack it out in the North Sea?'

'I don't see why not,' she replied.

'What about sharing cabins with men and things like that?'

'Why should that matter? I'm not trying to make a point about women. I just want to improve my bank account like everybody else.'

'And how would you react if faced with this kind of behaviour?' he said, producing a batch of photographs taken of divers in various states of undress.

'I've seen it all before and don't find it shocking. So I can't see why it should bother you.'

He then pointed out that, even if she was acceptable to a diving company, her credentials would still have to be approved by the oil companies.

When I finished in the office I returned to Cornwall. As Vicky and I were coming out of the station, we bumped into Stumpy, the supervisor I'd worked with on the *Odin*.

'What are you doing here?' I asked. 'Where the hell are you going?'

'Ah, I'm going to a funeral, mate,' he said.

'Whose?'

'Willy Carr's, my bell partner.'

'What happened?'

'He lost his helmet.'

'How?'

'I don't know. It apparently just came off.'

'What kind of helmet was it?'

'A Kirby 17.'

'But they have a pin that keeps them on.'

'I know. But we weren't using the pins.'

Because of accidents like that, divers using Kirby 17s were not only made to use the pin to secure the helmet, they now have even started strapping them down with elasticated bungy cords. So much for the high-tech of diving!

After we'd returned to Falmouth, Vicky was told that Britoil had approved her C.V. and she was offered work on a vessel called the *Moray Harstad*, starting just before Christmas. I was offered work at the same time by another company. But I turned it down, telling Vicky that it was her turn to have a crack at it. So off she went. For the second year running we spent Christmas apart.

Vicky came back in January. While she'd been away, I'd been giving much thought to my own career. My experiences led me to decide that I should work independently of the diving companies. Having had a crack at diving-inspection co-ordinating, I believed I should work directly for a specialist company such as Orca, the one for which Paddy worked. So I approached them and they said they'd be happy to employ me if they could get my C.V. approved.

Meanwhile, I continued to be involved in the Professional Divers' Association. As it had been somewhat eclipsed by the NUS, it was obvious that the association could flourish only if it had more resources and a stronger clout. So the executive decided we should contact the ASTMS to discuss the possibility not of a merger but of a working association. This was agreed by both sides at the start of 1985. A press conference was called and photographs taken of all the representatives present.

Soon Orca informed me that I'd been accepted as the field co-ordinator by a major oil company to work on their gas fields in the Southern Sector of the North Sea. The job was to monitor and review the way in which the inspection work was carried out on three diving vessels, each of which had their own diving representative.

I was set to start, when suddenly there was a hitch. A photograph of me at the press conference called by the PDA and the ASTMS had appeared in *Roustabout*, an industry magazine. It had been spotted by somebody at the oil company and an assurance was required that Ed Punchard wasn't a trouble-maker. The situation was fully explained to me and it was made clear that unless something was forthcoming I'd be unable to work.

I was upset by the whole incident. I was aware that once anybody is in any way put into the public eye, there are consequences. But I knew that I wasn't a trouble-maker. I was not that sort of person. I just did what I thought everybody should do—regardless of their background—when faced with crass stupidity and things that endangered life. In such circumstances, I believed, I had every right to be angry and to take sensible action. But I'm not stupid. I knew I had to buy the groceries.

So, on the headed notepaper of the Professional Divers' Association, I wrote a letter resigning from the executive. That apparently was good enough. I was able to carry on working.

CHAPTER SEVEN

RUNNING INTO PROBLEMS

After that nonsense was sorted out, both Vicky and I went up to Aberdeen, prior to starting work in the North Sea. She was taken on by Comex for a BP job on *The Sheerwater Aquamarine*, which was going to Fortes Charlie. I went off to the Southern Sector.

Working in the Southern Sector for the first time was a considerable shock – there was such a difference in everybody's attitude. The whole approach was far more casual. When the first job was mobilised, there wasn't even a proper dive control. The supervisor hung all the panels and intercom boxes on a bulk head and started talking to the divers.

'Where are you going to take down the data?' I said.

'Well, I just sort of make notes,' the man said.

'But to do that you need a table, a chair, a pen, a piece of paper and things like that!'

'Well, this is the way we've always done it!'

'Not any more,' I said.

The three representatives, who were all new, and I kicked up a hell of a fuss and after overcoming initial reluctance we managed to get proper dive controls established.

I was also surprised to find that the condition of the platforms seemed rather poor. One day, when I was out in a Z-boat, I spotted a great split, about an inch wide, in one of the main steel-members on one of the platforms. I called up the Offshore Installation Manager and told him about it.

Admittedly, all platforms are designed to have what's called 'redundancy' in them. So, even if a major defect did develop, there would be sufficient support elsewhere to prevent the platform falling over. But I was still shocked that nobody seemed perturbed by a split main-member on a platform.

I also came across several other niggling problems. I discovered from one of the data controllers that the divers sometimes recorded data underwater with chinagraph on a scratch-board, rather than using a proper controlled system of data recording on the surface.

One of the small air-diving vessels being used was a brand new conversion from an old Great Yarmouth supply boat. They hadn't quite managed to sort out the anchors, because they were attached by chains rather than wires. This had caused lots of problems. One day, the ship moored up against one of the installations in the field. This is done stern-on when diving is going to take place. So the port and starboard ropes are looped around legs of the platform and tightened up on capstans. The two forward anchors, which have already been laid, are then adjusted. So, between the tension created by the anchors and the capstans, the right position is maintained.

It's normally fine, but the ship's crew had never before worked in the oil industry. They were fishermen in a newly converted boat and I was constantly worried that they were going to plough into the platform.

We'd been anchored up for a few hours. I'd been up on the bridge and everything appeared to be all right. I went down to my cabin and then set off for the recreation room down a long corridor which looked out across the diving area. Over the end were fitted large aluminium diving ladders that were about fifteen feet long.

I looked out, over the stern, and saw these heavy ladders just slowly being concertinaed. Then I realised that we weren't anchored off the platform. We were actually bashing into it stern-first. The anchors had obviously slipped and the stern rope had coiled around the leg.

I went dashing into the recreation room, because I knew Mark Webster, the representative, was in there watching television.

'We're bashing into the back of the platform,' I shouted. 'What the hell's going on?'

Without taking his eyes away from the set, Mark said, 'Oh, yes. The skipper popped in here a couple of minutes ago and said, ''Where's the chief engineer, because we've got to switch the steering back on?'' My God!' he exclaimed, as the penny dropped. He jumped up and went shooting off to see what had happened.

I followed him up to the bridge. By that time, we were well and truly wrapped around the platform.

'What the hell's happened?' we asked the skipper.

'We had a bit of a problem with the power generation,' he said. 'We're a bit short of supply. So we turned off the steering so we could switch the air-conditioning back on!'

We eventually moved off and recovered the anchors. Mark and I then set off in a Z-boat so we could have a word with the Offshore Installation Manager on the platform. We were truly embarrassed and thought that all hell would break loose.

When we saw him, the OIM was totally relaxed. 'This happens all the time,' he said. 'Don't worry about it.'

A few weeks later, one of the supply boats ploughed straight into one of the Southern Sector platforms. The story has it that the skipper had just fallen asleep. I worked on the inspection of the damage the boat had caused. The first diver down reported back, 'There's some debris down here. It's new. I wonder what the hell it is? Hang on, what's this? Oh, it's a bit of the ship's bow!'

Indeed, I found that the whole atmosphere in the Southern Sector was peculiar. The platforms were the first to have been installed, having been there since North Sea gas was introduced. Many people had been working there from Great Yarmouth for years, and a certain cliquishness had developed. A long-running cosiness had been established between some of the contractors and the oil companies. On the other hand, outsiders, especially those coming down from Aberdeen, were regarded with a considerable amount of hostility.

After working through the year in the Southern Sector, the inspection contract came to an end. I then spent a couple of weeks over Christmas in the office in Aberdeen, preparing new procedures and revising the company's planned maintenance manual. It was a task I thoroughly enjoyed. Writing clear and detailed procedures was, I felt, one of the better ways I could encourage safe and accurate working conditions. This I tried to do, for I was dealing with such useful safeguards as hat-mounted underwater television cameras and a process called real-time recording. This involves a bank of fifteen or so video tapes which are used in sequence to record all underwater video work. So any particular transmission is stored and is available for checking by anyone – including company representatives and divers.

The task completed, I returned to join Vicky in Falmouth. Her work in the North Sea had also ended, but she'd been so disgusted by many of the malpractices she'd witnessed that she'd decided she would never work offshore again.

During the summer, however, my eldest brother, Dave, had decided he was fed up with being a civil engineer and wanted to become a deep-sea diver. Both he and Vicky's elder brother had taken the professional diving course. Dave went to work for Stena, a Swedish company that was starting up in the North Sea. So our families were still well represented in the industry.

For the first time, Vicky and I spent Christmas together – in the house we'd just bought.

I fully expected that I'd be asked again to work on the same Southern Sector job, but in January 1986 I was informed by Orca that this wasn't part of the plan. No formal reason was given, but unofficially I was told that during the previous season I'd been too dilligent and so was seen as somebody likely to increase rather than decrease the oil-production company's expenditure.

It was a real nuisance. Because I'd thought I'd got work for the 1986 season, my name hadn't been considered for other contracts.

I was finally placed with Chevron as the inspection co-ordinator on a diving-support vessel called the *Dynamic Constructor*. When I arrived at the docks at Peterhead, I thought, 'That's familiar!' It was the *Seabex* painted blue. It was great. I'd been very fond of it. Apparently, the German dentists had sold the boat and it was being operated with SubSea.

When I started walking round, I found all the old Comex equipment, including my old diving suit with 'Ed' written on the back. I even found things I'd made, such as a bench I'd welded for the divers to sit on. It was a bit like being on the *Marie Celeste*!

We sailed off to the Ninian field. Most of our work was at Ninian Southern, which two years earlier had suffered a serious structural failure – one of its members had snapped. While it was being repaired, the workers on the platform were on permanent stand-by ready for evacuation. They were living on a flotel, a floating hotel moored alongside.

The apparent cause was the propagation of a defect from a weld on a manway, an oval hatch cut in the member to allow access for a welder to complete the main internal structural welds on the member. The opening is then closed and welded. These welds had never been inspected before, but subsequently they were included in the programme. As there were something like two hundred of them, it was time-consuming work and many hours were spent inspecting these welds, both visually with MPI, and with ultrasonic equipment and radiography.

A problem we encountered at Ninian was that on occasions the drillers would, without warning, dump drilling mud over the side. One afternoon, I was on the bridge when this started to happen. At the time, a chap was changing a high-pressure line on the deck, which suddenly was covered in a fine white dust. It was just as though cement powder had been thrown everywhere. The chap too was covered and tried to finish the job as quickly as possible. Unfortunately, he mistakenly hadn't bled the line. It was still under pressure. As he got to the end of the thread, the fitting fractured and shot back into his face, puncturing a hole in the middle of his forehead. His skull was fractured and he looked horrific. He was helicoptered off to hospital. Luckily, he survived.

During this time, my brother Bernie was working in the Norwegian sector of the North Sea on the *Safe Regalia*. Having passed his hyperbaric welding course, he was qualified to do underwater welding in a habitat – an underwater chamber with a monitored atmosphere in which the weld is carried out.

One day while he was on the ship, a fire broke out in the engine room. It didn't endanger the ship itself, but it did melt all the cables from the engine to the computer. So, although the engines could still function, they lost the dynamic positioning for the vessel.

At the time, there were two divers working in the habitat 440 feet below. All the control had time to tell them was, 'There's a serious problem. Get your helmets on and get out of the habitat immediately.'

Before the divers could move, there was another message: 'Forget that. We're going to be off. We'll be back as soon as we can.'

With that, the divers' helmets were dragged straight out of the habitat. The lights went out and there they were, abandoned at the bottom of the North Sea inside a little box.

Fortunately, there were emergency back-ups in the habitat, including a supply of gas. The main danger was the temperature, because it was extremely cold down there. So they got inside the emergency sleeping-bags and put on the masks that allowed the heat from their breath to be recycled.

As they were still able to talk to the *Safe Regalia*, they were informed the *Stadive* had been contacted, was on its way and would be with them as soon as possible, but it'd be at least four hours.

The two poor divers just had to sit it out. Eventually, the *Stadive* arrived, picked up the signal from the habitat's emergency beacon, positioned itself above it and lowered its bell into the water. A diver was sent across to the habitat with a helmet and an umbilical, which he gave to one of the trapped men. He was brought back to the bell and the diver went back for the other man. The four of them were squeezed into the bell, the door was shut and they were brought up to the surface where they were decompressed in the following days.

The two divers from the habitat were then asked to fill in the standard boarding-card for *Stadive*. One of the questions was, 'Reason for visit?' They filled in, 'Nowhere else to go.'

At least that was one occasion when a diving accident didn't end unhappily! I heard the story of it from my brother, Bernie, while I was home on leave from the *Dynamic Constructor*.

I continued working there until the end of the season. But, from everything I heard and saw during 1986, I knew that a complete change was taking place throughout the whole oil industry.

When the Americans erected the first oil platforms off their own coast, they hardly bothered to inspect them. They knew from experience that the rigs had been put in an environment where they'd last fairly well. But when the North Sea platforms were erected, it was soon obvious that they were deteriorating rapidly, because of several structural failures. So the specialist diving companies were called in to do the repair and inspection work. They also did all the original research. They developed underwater magnetic particle inspection – the oil companies didn't. So, for the first ten years, all the oil companies did was to call in a diving company and say, 'We think there's a problem. Solve it for us.' And that's what the diving companies did. There were only about half a dozen of them and they made fat profits, but they did get the work done.

But then a certain oil company began changing the rules. It insisted that divers had certain qualifications which it believed would improve the quality of inspection. Nobody seems to have questioned whether this was really true. But as a result, the diving companies couldn't get sufficient people. It was absurd. When you want a washing machine repaired you call in a specialist, you don't ask for a bank statement and a copy of the engineer's qualifications. Yet that's the kind of information an oil company demands before it will allow divers from a contractor to work on the platforms.

Divers aren't stupid. Yet, as professional people, they're each expected to spend a thousand pounds or more a year on keeping their qualifications up to date. That amount can represent ten per cent of some divers' incomes. You start to wonder why this is necessary, when there's no consistency in the methods or requirements of the different oil operators.

In the original, dynamic phase of the North Sea oil industry, the priority was to get the oil out. If it cost an extra fifty million pounds to build a platform, it'd be paid. But when the construction work ended, the oil industry became much more like other manufacturing industries. Costs and budgeting became the major concerns. That also inevitably resulted in a change in personnel. The original oil pioneers were replaced by cost-conscious accountants.

In 1986, this new breed of oil executive really came into its own. At the beginning of the year, there was a sudden, dramatic drop in world oil prices. It had the most devastating effect on Aberdeen. Suddenly, there were thousands of redundancies as the accountants moved into action. House prices plummeted. There were tales of people becoming destitute overnight. Unfortunately, the lower oil prices also affected the offshore work. Because inspection programmes are organized on a five-year rolling basis, it was possible for them to be instantly reduced, in one case from some six months to forty-five days. Also, some contracts were not put out to tender as before and had to be bid for on a lump-sum basis.

Some of the work carried out in the North Sea began to be rushed through. On one occasion, when a diving job was coming to an end, a representative pointed out that a particular weld had not been inspected. There were no divers left in the saturation system at the correct depth. It would have cost the diving company another £40,000 a day to keep the vessel there. Because of the cost-cutting atmosphere that prevailed with the fixed-priced contracts, it was decided to send an empty diving bell down to make it appear as though the inspection was being carried out. So that everything seemed authentic, the voice-monitoring recorder was switched to play instead of record so that the voices of divers talking and breathing were coming over the intercom, so if the representative walked into the dive control it'd sound as though there were actual divers in the water!

This almost universal change in attitude was remarkable. Everybody came to know that they were supposed to do things cheaply. This had the most disastrous effect on the diving industry. The diving companies began squabbling between themselves. Teams and equipment were cobbled together for each specific job. Virtually all research and development stopped.

The whole thing had gone completely out of control – there was no sense there any more. Yet, it should be obvious that doing good work and making a profit are not incompatible. It's not just about safety; it's also about the long-term costs. If the correct work isn't done at the correct time, it will cost a damned sight more in the long run.

But with the drop in oil prices, everybody's mind seemed dominated by the principle 'make it shorter and make it cheaper'. I remember wondering how long this was going to last and, if it did go on, how long it was going to be before it caused a serious problem.

CHAPTER EIGHT

IN SEARCH OF A PARADISE

Towards the end of 1986, Vicky and I were sitting around feeling generally disgruntled. Suddenly, Vicky said, 'Here's a piece of paper. Here's a pen. Write down what you'd need to make your life perfect. We've been spending all our time considering what we've got and trying to make it better. Enough of that. Let's start from what we'd really like. Then we'll work out ways of getting it. So just make a list of the three things you'd most wish to do.'

It seemed a brilliant idea. I wrote down on my piece of paper: '1. Continue living with Vicky; 2. Work as a marine archaeologist on shipwrecks; 3. Live somewhere nice.'

Vicky wrote: '1. Marry Ed; 2. Write books; 3. Live in the sun.'

'Right,' Vicky said. 'How are we going to get these things?'

'I don't know,' I replied.

'Well, we'll start with mine first. Marry me!'

'OK.'

'When?'

'Next week.'

'Fine. Where shall we live?'

'Where would you like to live? Where is "somewhere nice"?'

'I don't know. I just fancy an island paradise.'

'Right. Well now, we must find one.'

We took out the atlas and started to look for islands.

The following Friday, we were married at Falmouth Registry Office.

Our first choice for our island paradise was the Seychelles. We spent a couple of weeks investigating that. But then we decided it wasn't the place where we'd like to live permanently. Vicky's brother told us he'd visited the Azores and that it was a splendid place. So we decided we'd tootle off there for our honeymoon.

We loved the place, met people we liked and decided that somehow or other that was where we'd live.

A few days after we arrived back in Falmouth, we bumped into a chap we knew who was a maritime archaeologist.

'What are you up to?' he asked.

'We're just back from the Azores. We've decided we're going to move out there to live.'

'What you going to do there?'

'Well, when I'm not offshore, work on some wrecks,' I said airily.

'That's interesting. I think we ought to have a chat.'

That evening, he told us he was working on a marine archaeology project recovering artefacts from Manila galleons in the Philippines. 'I know you've got a lot of contacts in the North Sea diving industry. Would you be interested in the project?'

'If it's got any substance, of course I would,' I replied.

I spent much of the winter working on the project. I was immensely busy, commuting from Falmouth to London and Aberdeen, talking to all kinds of people – the special project team at Stena Offshore who'd recovered the American space shuttle; maritime lawyers; merchant bankers and other potential investors.

Unfortunately, the project came to a sudden end when American lawyers pointed out that, even though the licenses had been endorsed by the new government in the Philippines, they'd been issued by ex-President Marcos and there were certain to be problems. But it wasn't a waste of time. I had obtained an immense amount of useful information about maritime archaeology.

But I didn't immediately want to go back offshore. Vicky was pregnant and I wanted to be at home when the baby was born. Vicky was convinced she was going to give birth early in February, but February passed without any sign of the baby. So I continued to turn down work and to wait. Meanwhile, we'd applied to the Portuguese authorities for permission to reside in the Azores and the friends we'd made out there were looking for a house we could buy.

Vicky had decided that the baby should be born at home. At the time, we had something of a menagerie – a cat, a dog and two rabbits, all of whom lived in the house. The rabbits always had done, ever since I bought them in a moment of madness in Truro market. Usually they'd sleep on either side of our bed at night. They'd pop in and out of the cat flap. The garden was their salad bowl, but we also gave them additional food, although the only thing they'd eat was Tesco's wholemeal muesli at £2 a bag. As I poured it out into the bowl, I'd always take out the Brazil nuts. I couldn't bring myself to allow them that expensive luxury.

Eventually Vicky went into labour. The cat, the dog and the two rabbits trooped one after another into the bedroom and sat down in a line in the corner. When the midwife arrived, there was a frantic scene while she tried to chase all the animals out. She managed to expel the cat and the dog, but the rabbits steadfastly refused to leave. They were still there when our daughter was born. We called her Suzie and she's wonderful.

A few weeks later, I had a call from Orca, asking if I'd be interested in taking a job as a representative on a diving-support vessel working out of Great Yarmouth that I'd been on previously in the Southern Sector. This time I'd be working for Philips Petroleum on the Hewitt field. I accepted gladly. It was exactly the work I wanted at the time.

I got on well with the people at Philips and had no problem of any kind with them. But the work was another reminder of how different things were in the Southern Sector.

When I first went on to the bridge of the ship I had great difficulty in working out who the skipper was. There were six chaps there, all good-old-boys from Norfolk, rolling their own and looking identical. I told one of them that I wanted the boat moving and he said, 'Yew should 'ave a word with the skipper. He be over there. I'm just an able seaman.'

It was very confusing.

After that contract, I went on leave and Orca asked if I'd be willing to transfer to Murchison, working as inspection controller for Conoco. It was delightful to be back there.

As there was no point in Vicky waiting around, we decided she should go off to the Azores, even though all the paper-work wasn't complete. About two weeks later, I flew out to join her.

In the early evening, as the plane prepared to land, I could see stretched out below the nine islands that make up the Azores. On the island of San Miguel, the town of Ponta Delgada was outlined in lights. At the airport, Vicky and Suzie were waiting to welcome me.

We drove in a hire car, through the narrow, dusty backstreets of the old town, where thin-faced women dressed in black peered at us over the bottom half of their doors.

For a week, we stayed with friends, while agents tried to find us a place we could rent. They showed us house after house; all were poky and totally unsuitable. Then we were reluctantly persuaded to look at a place in the village of Caloura, twelve miles out of the town, along the coast.

We set off in the agent's Fiat Uno, and at Aqua de Pau – a settlement euphemistically called a town – we turned right, down a slight incline towards the sea. It was exquisite. On either side were vineyards and before us was a spectacular panoramic view of the bay, where the still, blue sea met the azure blue of the cloudless sky.

Half-way between Aqua de Pau and the harbour of Caloura, we pulled into the drive of an astonishing colonial house. We knew immediately that this was the place of which our dreams were made. In front was a pond and a disused fountain. In the garden was a giant fir-tree, over a hundred feet high.

Built at the turn of the century, the house still had its original furniture and decorations. So it had a slightly faded, but totally captivating beauty. There was a kitchen, dining-room, two sitting-rooms, a couple of bathrooms and four bedrooms on the first floor, and four more on the floor above.

We moved in a few days later. Unfortunately, we were a trifle short of funds and cars were extremely expensive. So for three hundred pounds, I acquired a sadly dilapidated MG 1300. As I'd had a similar car at university, I knew them inside out and assumed I'd be able to make do and mend. I failed to realise that in a country where there are no MOTs and cars are kept on the roads well beyond their reasonable working life, a three-hundred-pound car was not worth having. I've never been so defeated in all my life. Despite my tender and perpetual care, the wretched thing rapidly ran itself into the ground.

But life had its compensations. For what seemed no more than a pittance, we hired a young maid who doted on Suzie. And

The fittest I've ever been at the end of my diving course in Falmouth.

Fully dressed in diving gear, hot water suit, Kirby/Morgan 17 with TV camera and light, the div is in his element.

Piper Alpha the day before the disaster. The navigation platform is seen below the cellar deck on the nearest corner, the site of our escape to the spider deck and away. (Mike Toy).

The *Maersk Cutter* pumps water into the conflagration.

On the Piper the Tartan riser explodes, releasing huge quantities of burning gas. (Robert Gibson)

Back deck of the *Silver Pit*. Andy Carroll, Stan Macleod, myself and others tend Eric Brianchon prior to his lift into the helicopter. (Paul Berriff/STV 1988, Rescue TV series).

nchman M.A.L.M. Bob Pountney bringing aboard Robert Carey, attended by winch operator ght Lieutenant Pat Thirkell above the *Silver Pit*. (Paul Berriff/STV 1988, Rescue TV series).

Vicky and Suzy meet me at Newquay Airport later in the day.

All that remained of Piper Alpha after the disaster. (Occidental Petroleum).

a brisk walk away was a crystal-clear sea where we could swim and snorkel the day away.

The house, however, was not for sale and it would have been too expensive for us even if it had come on to the market. It would have been sensible to stay on there, but our plan had committed us to buying a place of our own.

Eventually, in Lagoa, a place between Aqua de Pau and Ponta Delgada, we found a house that we decided to buy. It was huge, with a lot of character. Downstairs, the ceilings were supported with tree trunks and their spreading branches. There were large arches made from beautiful volcanic stone. On the two floors above was an enormous number of rooms. We decided that, with not a great deal of work, we could turn the downstairs into a pleasant bistro, which would provide us with at least a supplementary income.

With the value of property in Britain rising so quickly, we decided to keep our house in Falmouth. We'd arranged to remortgage it so we could pay the deposit on a place in the Azores. The rest of the money we'd obtain from a local loan. The agent agreed that until our finances were worked out, we could rent the house. He even managed to find us some furniture that we could borrow until ours had been crated up in England and sent out.

So we packed up our things and prepared to move. Suzie and Vicky went on ahead in a taxi. By this time, the MG 1300 was just managing to keep clear of the scrapyard. Its big-ends objected noisily whenever the engine was switched on, oil was leaking everywhere, and the front of the car had started to separate from the rest of the body. You could put your little finger into the crack which spread from where the sub-frame was attached up through the wings.

I loaded up this virtual write-off to the roof with all our belongings. Then I found a space to accommodate the two bad-tempered kittens we'd acquired. Vicky had called one Rolling Day, because I was in the habit each morning of saying, 'We've got to get the day rolling.' The other was called Fast Walker. Then there was just room left for me to squeeze in.

I set off at a crawl, praying that during the five-mile drive the incredible weight in the car wouldn't split the wretched thing in two. Much to my amazement, we arrived in one piece. I unloaded the car and drove it to the garage. For all I now, it's there still, slowly sinking into an ever-growing pool of oil.

With our somewhat spartan furnishings, the house was less than comfortable. But life was not unpleasant and we were happy, especially Suzie. With her blonde hair and blue eyes, she was the centre of attention wherever we went. One day, I was in the small supermarket with Suzie in the pram. I went to pick something off a shelf, turned round and Suzie had gone. I spotted her immediately in the arms of a gaggle of local women, who to her delight were bouncing her up and down as they cooed over her.

Early in November, Suzie fell ill with a chest infection. We took her to the local doctor's surgery and were asked to sit in the waiting room. All the windows were shut fast, even though the sun was blazing in and it was a very warm day. Obviously, the local people didn't find it so. They were all wearing thick woollen jumpers, while we baked in our thin cottons.

After an age, the doctor called in Vicky and Suzie. First, he asked Vicky to sit down and then he said, 'I speak very good English. Tell no one I speak English. Nobody knows I speak English. I listen to the BBC World Service. Tell no one. These are dangerous times!'

Vicky ignored this unexpected display of histrionics, and explained carefully what was wrong with Suzie.

The doctor examined Suzie and said, very deliberately, 'I shall write you out two prescriptions – one in English and one in Portuguese. Take the Portuguese one to the pharmacy. Show the English one to nobody. It is for you to understand what I am giving your child. Show it to nobody. These are dangerous times!'

We concluded that his dire warnings arose from the complex political situation that had existed in the Azores since the revolution a decade earlier. It was something about which I was not going to learn more at first-hand. A few days later, we received a letter saying that the mortgage in England had fallen through.

It was impossible to do anything about it from the Azores. So I flew back to the UK to rearrange the remortgage, buy a car, sort out the paperwork, crate up the furniture we needed, and drive it in a borrowed lorry down to Lisbon. I also needed to chase up some work. It was clear we could only live in the Azores if I worked offshore as usual.

What I thought should have taken a few days ended up taking much longer. Eventually I'd made all the arrangements. Early in the morning of the day I expected to pick up the lorry to start loading it, I received a phone call from the man who owned it saying he'd changed his mind and I couldn't drive it down to Lisbon. That really delighted me.

A few minutes later, the phone rang again: 'Would you like your name to be put forward for a three-year contract doing a bit of everything, with married accommodation in Sarawak? You're not guaranteed to get it, but you're very well placed. Are you interested?'

'Yes,' I said.

Shortly afterwards, I had a third call. It was from Stena Offshore, the company for whom my elder brother, Dave worked: 'Are you interested in working for the year as an inspection controller on Piper Alpha?'

'Yes,' I replied. 'When does it start?'

'Shortly. But you are committed to this job? You're not thinking of doing anything else, are you?'

'Of course I'm not.'

'Fine. We'll be in touch.'

Being unable to borrow the lorry seemed to be the last straw that broke my resolve to return immediately to the Azores. I knew I had to find a job with a diving contractor. All my noble thoughts about working independently and being able to change the way things were done had got me nowhere. As the restrictions being placed on inspection battered my spirit, I decided to concentrate on more diving. I would take some more courses. All I needed was cash to pay for them. Going back to work for a diving contractor, such as Stena, seemed the most sensible thing to do.

So I phoned up Vicky in the Azores. 'Hear this,' I said. 'I've been let down on the lorry. So there's no way I can get out as I'd planned. I've been offered a long-term contract in Sarawak. I'd like to do it. So we must talk about it. I'll know for sure in a week or so if it's definite. If I don't go there, in a few weeks I'll be on Piper Alpha. The only way I'm going to see you before either of these jobs come up is if you fly home. Get on tomorrow's flight.'

There was a stunned silence at the other end of the phone. Poor Vicky had by that time given up all hope of my ever returning. Every week I'd kept on phoning to say I'd be with her in a fortnight. I'd been spending every day on the phone trying to get everything worked out. It'd been a nightmare.

The next day, I went to pick Vicky up from Heathrow airport. It was wonderful to see her and my daughter again. As we were driving back to Cornwall, she said, 'If you're going offshore all season, I'm not going to live in the Azores. I know we need the money, but it's bad enough you being away from home when I'm living in Falmouth. So the Azores is off.'

As our house had been closed up in preparation for our move, we had to rent somewhere else. Fortunately, a diving friend was off to a job in the Middle East and so we moved into his house. After a couple of weeks, I was informed that I hadn't been given the Sarawak job. But Stena rang to inform me that my C.V. had been approved by Occidental.

Within days, I left Falmouth for Aberdeen so I could start work on Piper Alpha.

PART TWO

OUT OF THE INFERNO

CHAPTER NINE

ON PIPER ALPHA

Before I went out to Piper Alpha, I had to spend a couple of days in Aberdeen.

At Occidental, I was given a day's briefing. It was exceptionally pleasant. The lunch was splendid and I met several men from the top management of the underwater department. One person I knew was Doug Renwick, the project engineer, who initially called me about the job. We'd met when previously he'd been working for Comex.

I was also shown all the files and forms I'd need as an inspection controller. As I'd never worked for Occidental before, I had to acclimatise myself to the approach of a new oil company, because they're all different. It wasn't a difficult thing to do. The problem was that you had to put to one side your own experience and philosophy of your work. Everything had to be learnt again. So you knew there'd be times while you were working that you'd have to stop and say, 'Now, am I in Oxy-think or BP-think?' The Occidental approach was comprehensive, but I'd never seen so much paperwork in my diving career.

Later at Stena, I was introduced to the office staff. The company had expanded so rapidly that they'd had to move into a huge office in the Westhills Industrial Estate.

The next day, I went offshore.

At the airport, Occidental had its own check-in, with a small lounge and reception area where I was asked to fill in an offshore registration form. Because Vicky and I were living in a friend's house, I wrote down the wrong address. The mistake was later to cause problems.

A security man then searched my bags – looking, as always, for booze. He was slightly bemused to find I was taking my personal computer with me. Experience had taught me it was an invaluable means of collecting and storing the data in my job.

'What are you going to do with this?' he said. 'Play games?'

I ignored him. After being frisked, I went into the departure lounge. Ten minutes before we were due to leave, a television was switched on and the group of us waiting to leave watched Occidental's video about how to escape from a ditched helicopter. We put on our survival suits and were taken by a minibus to the Bristow's Sikorski. As usual at Aberdeen airport, there were helicopters everywhere, taking off and landing.

After about an hour's flight, we landed on Piper Alpha, a hundred miles south-east of the Orkneys. Compared with the other platforms I'd been on, it seemed dirtier and much more cramped. At reception, we had to stand in line in the narrow corridor. There certainly weren't any comfortable chairs to sit on.

The first thing that I was told was, 'Keep your survival suit.'

'Don't we hand them in?'

'No. Keep it in your room.'

No explanation was offered. But it was most unusual. I'd never been asked to do that on any other platform.

Then I was told about my cabin. 'It's not in the main accommodation block. It's back outside where you just came in. Walk across the little deck area along the companionway in front of the pipe-deck and you'll see the block there.'

It was a small additional accommodation block, with six cabins on each of the three levels. When I arrived in my room, the chap I was to share with was already there. Called Brian Lithgow, he was the photographic technician. So he was known by everybody as 'Lens'. A Glaswegian, he was a bit of an oddball. He sported a tight little pigtail and wore circular National Health spectacles.

After we'd introduced ourselves, I said, 'What's all this with the survival suits?'

'Ever since the explosion on Piper back in '84, they make yew keep it in yer cabin – just in case yew need it. Didne Stena tell ye, we all have to wear fireproof overalls as well?'

'You're joking?'

'No, I'm not.'

'I thought it was pretty unusual to be given free overalls. That's the first time that's happened to me for years. So what the hell happened in '84?'

'Nothin' much. It wasne a big deal. A big bang and a bit of excitement, ended up in the bar at the Skean Dhu Hotel.'

I started unpacking my gear. The cabin had obviously recently been refurbished, but as I commented to Lens, it was a bit small. For the past three years, working as a representative for an oil company I'd almost always had my own cabin.

'Christ!' he said. 'Yew should see those on Claymore. They're six times as bad. There isne a shitter or a shower in your room. Ye have to go doon the end of the corridor.'

When my gear was stowed away, Lens took me back to the accommodation module to show me around. After passing reception, you could go either left up into the billiard room or to the right either down a stairwell to the cabins or straight on to the galley.

Entering the smallish galley, I walked past a row of soft-drink and ice-cream machines on long steel counters. Immediately in front were the tables and in against the far wall was the refrigerated display for sweets, gateaux and cheesecake. Above it was a huge mirror with a highland piper engraved on it. On either side was a rather mucky looking fish tank. To the left were the serving areas, including one with a range of salads. Slightly to the right were laid out all the cheese and biscuits. Beyond was the tea and coffee. As it was a little before lunch, the food was still being laid out by the catering staff.

Lens and I sat down with our coffees and Chris Rowan, the diving superintendent, walked in. He was an active, cheerful guy who was an ex-Royal Engineer. We introduced ourselves and he told me to go down to the cellar deck after lunch. 'You'll have plenty of time to sort yourself out,' he said. 'It's going to be a couple of days before the divers go into the water.'

Later, I had a bite to eat and met several guys from the diving team. On the way out Lens insisted that I saw the snooker room. He spent a lot of time there. He was a real snooker freak.

We returned to the cabin and put on our overalls and hard hats. Outside, we put on our rig boots. We then walked to the enclosed stairwell which led down the side of the platform. At the top we paused and Lens identified for me the distant rigs, including Tartan and Claymore. Close by was Tharos, the semi-submersible support rig.

As we started going down the stairs, Lens pointed out the lifeboat we were supposed to use. As we passed the crane pedestal, I was struck by how much noise there was on Piper. We walked past the oil and gas separation module. From there, we continued on through the well-head area (A module), which was full of extremely noisy pumps and throbbing machinery. As we went outside, there was a great blast of heat.

'What the hell's that?' I asked.

'Och, those are the John Browns,' Lens said. 'If we'd gone doon the north face, you'd a seen 'em. They're great big gas turbines, like aircraft engines. They're made by John Browns and have huge exhaust systems. When the wind comes from the north, it sends the heat under the platform and up here. So if yew think this is hot, yew wait till there's a north wind! There're times in the dive module when yew can hardly breathe.'

'So how do you cope?'

'If yew can get your hands on a fan for yer office, it'll just make life tolerable.'

'Why don't they do something about it?'

'It's bin like it fer years. So they're no goin' to change it noo. They just say, "Everybody's bin workin' in these conditions for years. So you can too." '

As we went down the lowest level on to the cellar deck, I suddenly noticed that my hands had picked up a coating of white dust from the rail. The stuff was everywhere.

'What's this?' I asked.

'Oh that's the salt. It's from the John Browns. There's a seawater-deluge system which sprays water into the exhaust in an attempt to cool it doon. So a film of seawater is spread over everything. As it dries, it turns to salt.'

'The perfect corrosion environment,' I said. 'No wonder everywhere looks so rusty.'

We walked along the deck into the diving control module. Just inside, there was a double air-locked door into the dive module. Then there was a small area with a tea and coffee machine. Lens introduced me to a couple of the riggers who were standing around. Turning left into the corridor, we passed the small darkroom where Lens worked. Just past the door to the left was the hole in the floor for the vertical ladder that led into the dive control. I turned right and on the right there were two offices.

The far one was for Barry Barber, the Occidental representative who was the overseer of the whole diving operation. He shared it with his clerk, Dick Common.

The other office was the one I was to share with Chris Rowan and later Stan MacLeod, the diving superintendents responsible to Stena for the diving team.

Inside the door of the office, on the left hand side, was a bench for inspection equipment. Above were shelves. On the top one were the files containing the inspection data and reports. These files went all round the room. In front of the door was another bench with a cabinet beneath. On the right were a couple of filing cabinets and two desk areas.

Chris pointed to one of them and said, 'This one's all yours, Ed. For the next half an hour or so, get yourself sorted out and see what's what. Then I'll show the dive skid to you and the other new guys.'

'Can I bring my computer down later?' I asked.

'You've brought your own computer? That's great,' he said.

'Yes. I thought it might be useful for doing reports and things.'

'Sure. Bring it down.'

I sat down and started getting my bearings, going through the drawings of the rig and the work-scopes. It was extremely important that I studied them. As the inspection controller, I was responsible for planning much of the divers' day-to-day activities.

A short time later, a man of about fifty came into the room. He had a shock of white hair and was the spitting image of the father in *Bonanza*.

'Hi, I'm Barry Barber, Occidental's rep,' he said with an accent that had a slight colonial edge. 'Come and have a chat.'

As we walked out, he said, 'Let's have a coffee first.' Then jokingly he added, 'When you make me coffee, it's very black with two spoons of coffee.'

'When you make me coffee,' I replied, with a grin, 'it's white with no sugar.'

With our coffees, we went into his office which seemed encased in box-files. Barry introduced me to Dick Common, his clerk – a tall, almost gangly, lightweight, bald man who was about my age. When he spoke he had the soft burr of an educated Edinburgh accent.

'Dick does my daily telex to Occidental,' Barry said. 'You'll have to provide him with a full list of all the tasks that've been completed. So you'll see quite a lot of him.'

The three of us chatted away for a while.

I took an instant liking to Barry Barber. He was open and obviously on top of things – a thorough professional. He clearly never flapped or was nervous in any way.

'Have you ever worked for Occidental before?' he asked me.

'Never.'

'Well, the one thing you have to understand with Occidental is that there's an enormous quantity of paper generated. It's far more than any other job you'll have come across. You have to be on the ball all the time. They really don't like it if your paperwork is in the wrong order or if anything's incorrectly completed. It'll take you a while to get used to it, but Dick and I will ensure you know the score.'

He then ran through the forms that had to be completed in quadruplicate – the material transfer sheets for when data or other material was sent in; the photo logs; the video logs; inspection sheets for close visual inspections and so on.

'You don't collect the data,' Barry said. 'That's done by the diving supervisor. There isn't a data recorder here. The supervisor does the lot.'

'That's unusual, isn't it?'

'Yes. But it's the way we've always done it. It seems to work out OK. But it does mean they're rushed off their feet. So your job is far more one of supporting him so he's relieved of the paperwork when it's been completed. Just keep everything organised. For example, if it's a weld inspection, don't send it in until the whole thing's completed – the visual, the photography, everything. Then bring the whole pack of data in to me. I'll see it's up to Oxy's requirements. Then I'll sign it. Nothing leaves here without my signature. When we get rolling, forms come out of your office faster than off a printing-press. There's plenty of stationery in here, but if you need anything else, we'll order it.'

Although I was impressed, I felt more than slightly daunted by the massive quantity of paperwork and filing. Having been an oil-company rep, I knew roughly what to expect. If I fucked up, I expected to be stepped on.

After I'd gone back to my office, Chris said, 'Big Colin's coming to show you round the system.'

An obviously very fit South African arrived and quietly drawled, 'How yer doing? I'm going to show you the gear.'

I went with Colin Tapsell out of the dive module. Immediately in front on the deck were two decompression chambers, which we looked around. Next to them were the quads where the oxygen bottles were stored. I was a bit surprised to see a hose playing water on to them.

'What the hell's that for?' I asked.

'It's keeping them cool.'

'Why?'

He led me out on to a projecting skid area and pointed up to the gigantic gas-flare. 'That's why,' he said. 'We don't have anywhere else to store the oxygen bottles. As that's likely to make them bloody hot, we spray water on them all the time.'

'That's a bit primitive, isn't it, for Christ's sake?'

'I know, but that's what they've been doing for years. Don't worry about it. Just keep on taking the money!'

As we walked back, Colin pointed out the Kellys which ran along the inside of the dive module. They were thirty-foot long steel cylinders for storing supplies of high-pressure air.

To the north of the deck was the grit shack, where all the slurry equipment was stored for the high-pressure grit gun. Behind the dive module were the stores in an old, blue container. All the suits were hanging up there and various items of equipment. Unlike many of the jobs I'd been on, the stores were certainly no Aladdin's cave.

We walked on from the stores into the mechanical and electrical workshop, which was full of hydraulics, compressors and lots of working machinery. On the left side was a workbench and many tools. On the opposite side was a much smaller office space, with many plastic storage bins stacked against the wall.

I was introduced to Alister Mackay, the electrician. Then, pointing to another guy, Colin said, 'And this is Wendy.'

'What d'you mean, "Wendy"?' I asked.

Wendy laughed and said, 'My name's really John Wood, but I've always been known as "Wendy" – it's a name that's just stuck.'

'These guys have been here for years,' Colin said. 'So if you've got a problem with any of the kit, they'll sort it out. They're really good.'

We then went back, past the dive module, and turned left immediately before the decompression chambers and climbed down a little stairwell on to the dive skid – a largish platform that was much like most other dive skids, with air-winches everywhere. But there were also *two* wet-bells.

'As you can see,' Colin said, 'we've two independent diving systems here. So we can run two teams simultaneously. All the controls are also duplicated in the dive control.'

'So you have two air divers in the water at a time?'

'That's the way we do it.'

I realised then why Barry Barber had said the information would be coming in thick and fast. There had to be the planning and supervision of two divers at a time – with an accurate recording of the information they both submitted. It was double the usual work.

Colin pointed out the various equipment on the dive skid – the controls for the hot water and air supply. The diving bells were unlike the Comex ones I'd used. They had Perspex canopies on them to let in a certain amount of light. All the umbilicals were handled by hydrdaulics, so they didn't have to be coiled by hand on deck. Instead, they were hung underneath the deck in rope nets.

'It all looks to be in good shape,' I said.

'Yes,' Colin replied. 'The diving equipment on here's always been excellent. By the way,' he said, pointing to a huge pipe going right over the dive skid, 'this is the main oil line. If you ever get cold, you can always warm your hands on it.'

Then he slid open the door of the small shed where divers could shelter from the weather. 'This is the Wendy Hut,' he said. As we walked in, I noticed on the walls the usual arrangement of coms-boxes so that the supervisor could call the divers out on deck.

Inside, Chris Rowan, the superintendent, was talking to two of the divers – Keith Cunningham and Joe Wells.

After we'd chatted for a while, I asked, 'What's all this about having to wear flameproof overalls after the '84 explosion?'

'That was something else,' Joe said, in his laid-back American accent. 'At the time, we were down on weather. There was no way we could dive. Man, there was a huge sea running and thirty-knot winds. So we were all hanging out in the rec. room. Then there was a godawful explosion. Some of the windows came crashing in and everything fell over.'

'Yes,' said Chris. 'I was watching this guy playing table-tennis and he leapt across the table being hotly pursued by a flame. It was really outrageous! As most of the divers were in the rec. room, I got the team together and we went along the corridor to the exit door. There was a lot of smoke and flame outside.

So we grabbed a firehose and switched on. Then we advanced behind it. But when we saw how fierce the flames were, we threw the hose down and sprinted back inside!'

'Didn't you go to the lifeboat?'

'That's the next place we went. But, after a quick look over the side at the state of the sea, we could see that was a dead loss. So we made our way back up to the reception and the helideck. They brought in a Chinook without seats. There was a hell of a wind blowing anyway and we were all hanging on to the handrails. But the blast from the helicopter sent one guy rolling across the helideck towards the edge. Big Colin here managed to grab him before he bounced into the sea!'

'Poor sod!' Colin said. 'He thought he was a beach-ball!'

'We all piled into the Chinook', Chris continued. 'There were dozens of us crammed in there. But the pilot managed to take off. He went to land on Tharos but the sea was running so badly it was bobbing up and down like a yo-yo. He tried to land there three times and then gave up. So we were flown to Aberdeen. As soon as we arrived, we were taken to the Skene Dhu Hotel. It was great! There was a free bar and we all got pissed.'

'Then some guy from Occidental arrived with a whole wad of cash,' said Colin. 'He asked us how much we needed to get home and to keep us going till they'd sorted out all the problems on Piper. So we all filled our pockets and buggered off home.'

'It was a real laugh,' Joe said.

'Wasn't anybody hurt?' I asked.

'Not really,' Chris replied. 'I think three or four of the guys were slightly injured.'

'So what caused the explosion?'

'Haven't a clue,' Chris said. 'It apparently started in the gas-conservation module and was soon dealt with. Since then, we've had to wear these fire-resistant overalls – but I don't know if they'd be worth a damn if there really was a fire.'

'And the survival suits?' I asked.

'Yes. We've got to keep those in our cabins in case we have to get off Piper in a hurry.'

'What excitement!' I said. 'It sounds great.'

From the Wendy Hut, Colin and I went back up the stairwell and past the decompression chambers into the dive module. We walked by the tea-room and the dark-room, but this time instead of going right to my office, we turned left and climbed down a vertical ladder. It led into the dive control, which was called 'the gondola', because, as if it were the gondola of an airship, it was slung under the dive module. Facing the dive-skid was a long row of windows, giving an excellent view of everything taking place there.

I'd never seen an air-dive control that looked so good. There were brand new colour monitors up on the wall. Everything was duplicated for the two diving systems. The two supervisors faced each other, across a table with their coms-boxes. On the wall beside them were all their controls. All the gas supply was encased in hard piping, just as you'd find in the saturation control of a dive-support vessel. There wasn't a piece of grey duct tape in sight.

I was impressed. Having thanked Colin for showing me around, I climbed up the ladder and returned to my office and continued going through the paperwork.

After a little while, I went back into Barry Barber's office.

'I've been hearing about the explosion here in '84,' I said.

'Yes. That was a nasty business.'

'I don't know. Sounds as though the chaps think it was a bit of an adventure.'

'I'm sure they did. But I think we were bloody lucky. D'you know anything about this platform?'

'Not much. I heard that when it was built in 1975, it was then the heaviest platform and was operating in the deepest water.'

'True. But there's a lot more to it than that. I enjoy working here. But there are those who believe Piper Alpha's jinxed and always has been.'

'How come?'

'Are you sure you want to hear?'

'Of course.'

'Well, Piper Alpha had a bad start. It was built in two parts – one at the McDermott fabrication yard at Ardersier and the other at the UIE yard in Cherbourg. Both parts were united at Ardersier. When the French section was being towed across the English Channel, some half a mile behind its barge, its heavy towrope caught a coaster and dragged it into the platform. One of the crew men on the coaster was killed.'

Barry Barber went on to tell me more about Piper Alpha's unusual and disturbing history. In 1975, at the height of the oil book, the giant frame, or jacket, was finished off in a hurry. It was launched during a storm, hit the sea-bed with unexpected force, and was damaged. So, right at the start, Piper Alpha needed to be repaired.

The platform was designed to be one of the first to use large scale impressed current cathodic protection to defend it against corrosion. But Piper Alpha had been in the North Sea for nine months before the system was commissioned. So during that period, its bare steel jacket stood unprotected in seawater that is estimated as two and a half times more corrosive than the Gulf of Mexico.

The underwater inspections revealed so many significant defects that a vast complex of reinforcing clamps had to be installed underwater. Piper Alpha had one of the most repaired jackets of any offshore oil installation. It wasn't surprising that some experts agreed with Jack Donaldson, Occidental's former safety expert, who claimed that Piper Alpha was the most dangerous platform in the North Sea.

Although nobody died in the '84 explosion, there had been casualties on Piper Alpha. In October 1982, three men plunged seventy feet to their deaths from a gangway that had been incorrectly installed between the platform and Tharos. In September 1987, an oil worker slipped on a deck of Piper Alpha and fell to his death.

Even more alarmingly, there had apparently been, over the years, attempts at sabotage on Piper Alpha. For example, at the end of 1986, a compressor in the gas-conservation module was shut down for refurbishing. After the repair work had been completed, an engineer decided to make a final check. When he reopened an inspection hatch, he found that a batch of ballbearings had been placed inside the compressor. He opened up other hatches and found more ballbearings. If it'd been switched on with the ballbearings inside, the compressor would have blown itself, and anybody around, to pieces.

So far, Piper Alpha had managed to contain its jinx.

CHAPTER TEN

THE NIGHT SHIFT

On my first full working day on Piper Alpha, Lens and I had a morning coffee together in his small dark-room. We chatted away for a while about ourselves. When I asked him where he lived, he laughed and said, 'Believe it or no, in the posh part of Edinburgh.'

'You're joking!'

'Aye. I've got this flat in the posh part of Edinburgh. No' that they like it. I drive round in an old London taxi. The local rate-payers are gettin' up a petition to have me moved!'

'Do you live on your own?'

'Nae. I live wi' me girlfriend. Me marriage didne work oot – but we've got a wee boy who's a real smasher.'

'Have you been on Piper long?'

'A guid few years. It's fine oot here. I spend a lot of time playing snooker.'

'So your girlfriend doesn't mind you working our here?'

'Aye. I dinne work in the winters. So I have plenty of free time. When I'm oot here, I try to phone her every night at aboot nine o'clock.'

That was all right when Lens was working days, but within a fortnight of my arrival, there were a couple of changes to the work schedule and, like the rest of us, he had to work nights.

The first of these changes was that, just after we'd started diving, somebody at Occidental decided we ought to have only one diving team. So half the divers were demobilised and I'd lost half my workload. The second change was introduced because Piper Alpha went into what is known as 'the shut-down phase'. This didn't mean that the oil production stopped – as can sometimes be the case – but that all the planned maintenance and construction work was carried out. So the rig was full of extra fitters, painters, blasters and riggers. As the construction had high priority and scaffolding could be erected only during the day, the diving was pushed on to the night-shift. This was necessary for safety reasons. If a scaffold pipe is dropped, it travels at high speed through the water and could pierce a steel plate. So it could easily transfix a diver.

As soon as we started working nights, Lens had a word with me.

'If it's all the same wi' yew, Ed,' he said, 'any night when there's no' much work to do, I'd like to go up to phone my girl at aboot nine o'clock.'

'That's fine with me, Lens, providing you let me know where you'll be so I can get in touch with you if you're needed.'

Almost every evening from then on, if Lens was on shift, he'd nip up to the recreation room just before nine to phone his girlfriend and, I think, have a quick game of snooker. Everybody knew it happened – and nobody minded. Lens was hard working and well liked.

After a couple of weeks, Lens went on leave. While he was away, it was decided that, as part of the general inspection, we'd take photographs of the risers in the splash zone.

The diving team wasn't concerned only with what is happening underwater. We also inspected the risers and clamps for at least twenty feet above the water-level. So on Piper, divers could often be seen on the spider deck, inspecting bolts and welds.

For us to take the photographs we required, it was necessary to use a Zodiac. There wasn't one on Piper, as there is on many platforms. So we had to use one from the stand-by boat which, as a statutory safety requirement, is permanently stationed close to the rig. These boats, as part of their emergency rescue equipment, always had a Z-boat on board.

On the day we were to take the photographs, Barry called up *Euan*, one of the stand-by boats, on the radio and asked if a Z-boat could be brought over. When they agreed, Barry, as he was required, informed the control and radio rooms on Piper of what would be happening.

I decided I'd go with Paul Vaughan, who was Lens's relief, on the photographic trip. As the Z-boat with its two-man crew headed towards us, Paul and I went down on to the spider deck. We walked on to one of the boat-bumpers and climbed into the inflatable rescue craft.

We were intending to take photographs of the main oil line and the Claymore riser. Unfortunately, because of the John Browns blasting away, it was nigh-on impossible to get in close enough. The Z-boat crew tried their best, but we were being suffocated by the most unpleasant mixture of exhaust fumes, steam and sea-water.

After we'd done what we could, we decided it'd be a good idea to take a few stand-off photographs of the rig. Shortly after we'd set off, the engine of the Z-boat coughed, started again, spluttered, coughed, went 'Phut' and died as a large cloud of black smoke drifted upwards.

While the crew tried unsuccessfully to restart the engine, we began drifting into the heat beneath Piper's gas-flare. Because the fault seemed terminal, one of the crew radioed the stand-by boat to come over and pick us up.

While we were waiting, the two crewmen told us how useless the Z-boat was and how impossible it was to get any spare parts sent out for it.

'Why's that?' I asked.

'If ye dinne supply cash fer guid enough geer, it inne goin' to work.'

'What about the spare boat?'

'What spare boat? There's only this one. And it's often bin oot of action for days at a time.'

I was appalled that at any time the stand-by boat should be without a fast rescue boat.

After the stand-by boat arrived to pick us up, I went up on the bridge and asked the skipper if I could radio the diving superintendent, who at that time was Chris Rowan. I explained that the Z-boat had broken down.

'Aye, aye,' he said. 'Enjoy the party and make sure you're in a fit state when you get back!'

'Honest, Chris. It's not like that. The Z-boat has broken down and we'll get back as soon as we can.'

'Fine story. Z-boats are supposed to rescue people – not break down.'

When I left the bridge, the Z-boat had already been hauled aboard on davits. Paul and I went down into the crew's rec. room, which doubled as a hospital. It looked extremely barren. The only facility seemed to be a couple of old video tapes.

'Christ!' I said. 'Is this all you've got?'

'Aye.'

What about newspapers?'

'We dinne get newspapers. We dinne get anything'.'

'Right,' I said. 'From now on I'll see you get ours. Our company sends a batch out every day. I'll arrange for them to be handed on to you.'

They were extremely grateful. As we chatted, I discovered how badly paid they were and how little was provided for them. I found it difficult to believe that the crew were expected to live in such poor conditions, bobbing up and down for hours on end in the turbulent North Sea. These were the people who were supposed to respond instantly to any emergency!

After a couple of hours, it became clear that they weren't going to be able to fix the Z-boat and take us back to Piper. So I persuaded the skipper to allow me to ask Chris Rowan to organise a basket-transfer. Usually, they're very reluctant to do so. They're thought to be somewhat dodgy. But I'd no intention of staying longer than I needed in such inadequate and uncomfortable conditions on the bleak stand-by boat.

The rope-net attached to the huge ring was dropped by the crane from the helideck on to the stand-by boat. We hopped on to it and were hoisted the two hundred or so feet to the top of the platform. It was a relief to be back on Piper!

I found the work on the rig most enjoyable and soon got into the swing of it. Although there were times when it was hectic, there were also occasions when we could relax.

After a few weeks, Chris Rowan went off to Claymore and was replaced as superintendent by Stan MacLeod. Barry Barber, Dick Common, Stan and I got on very well together.

We all liked doing the *Telegraph* crossword. As soon as the first diver was in the water and the shift had started, one or other of us would photocopy the crossword and hand it out as though it were a piece of work. Depending on how busy we then were, we'd each have two to three hours in which we'd have a go at completing the daily crossword. In truth, none of us was very brilliant at it, but eventually, by pooling our resources and with the help of any diver who called into the office plus a good dictionary, we'd usually manage to finish it.

Because the shift was so long, there was always some time to spend on our special interests. Barry Barber's was currency exchange. I'd occasionally call into his office and find him puffing away at his menthol cigarettes, while poring over the pages of *The Financial Times*. He became fascinated by my computer and we spent some time discussing how it could be used to record and predict changes in the money market.

Barry was a most interesting man who had a deep affection for his wife and family. He was particularly proud that his eldest son, Charles, was just off to university to study law. For years, Barry had done much foreign work for Oceaneering. He was the supervisor for the diving work carried out on the *Lucitania* and had many fascinating stories to tell. I chatted about all manner of things to him and in time came to regard him almost as a father.

I also got on well with Stan MacLeod. Although he was very mild-mannered and pleasant, he was excellent at his work. He expected people to get on with their own job; if they didn't, he'd want to know why. Stan loved fiddling around with things. For some reason or other, there was a UVA lamp in Barry's office. Stan planted orange and apple seeds in a flowerpot beneath it. He was delighted when the small green shoots started springing up.

Although we worked from six in the evening till six the next morning, I found it extremely pleasant, working nights with Stan, Barry and Dick. Unlike during the day, when everybody else was up and about, there were very few other workers around.

The only really tedious thing about working nights was the inadequate and inappropriate food we were served on Piper. On better rigs, there's never a problem. The kitchen staff always put on a decent meal whenever people finish a shift. But, for some reason on Piper, they were very reluctant to provide anything at seven in the morning other than bacon and eggs. Because it wasn't the main meal of the day for anybody important, nobody would do anything about it. With only greasy food to eat, I started breaking out in spots. Only after Barry had threatened to put all the divers back on the day shift, were the kitchen staff ordered to put out a bowl of salad at breakfast time for the divers who were coming off their twelve-hour shift.

There were also a few other problems about working on Piper. Every two or three weeks, the diving team would get together after a shift for a safety meeting. We'd go through any points that had arisen during the work. It seemed a good idea but, if something that had gone wrong was raised, it wasn't always dealt with. At consecutive safety meetings, I pointed out that the stairwell from our accommodation block had a great deal of gunge jammed into the grating. Although it wasn't always slippery, it certainly became so as soon as it was wet. I once noticed that somebody had made a half-hearted attempt to clean out the grease, but they'd only done so from places where it wasn't really a problem. Most of the stairwell was never properly cleaned. It was a small thing, but I tired of asking about it time and time again.

Another cause of problems was that the wells were being deepened and so there was a great deal of drilling taking place. After I'd finished my breakfast, if it was a nice day, I'd sometimes walk out of the galley on to a narrow walkway. From there, in the warmth from the gas-flare, I could see right across into the drilling deck, where the drill was spinning like a turntable with the drill pipe being brought up in batches and stored into the derrick so that it could be added to allow the drill to descend deeper into the rock. The drilling mud, which acts as a lubricant, was gushed through a hose into a header, which sits on the top of the spinning pipe, from where it was pumped down to the drill.

The drilling was not only noisy: it also created a great deal of vibration. I'd been on platforms where there had been a certain amount of vibration, but never to the extent it was on Piper. It'd frequently wake me up. Sometimes, it'd be vibrating so much that, when I opened my eyes, the curtains across the bunk would be swinging backwards and forwards. On a couple of occasions, I was woken up and the sensation was so disturbing that I got dressed, went to the side, and tried to see how much the 700-foot structure was swaying. It was quite unnerving, because one felt it shouldn't be happening. Piper Alpha wasn't a floating structure: it was stuck firmly into the sea-bed. But the vibrations went on every day. If anything, they even seemed to get worse.

Working offshore is a stressful enough environment at the best of times, but when you're trying to relax by watching a film and then you find the whole cinema shaking it's disturbing. Several times it was so bad that I walked out of the film. Once, the vibrations actually tripped the cinema's video projector. Often I was in the galley when the coffee started shaking in the cup.

Things got so alarming that one day I said to Barry Barber,

'This is crazy. The drill bit's going to stop and Piper is going to start spinning round!'

Fortunately, for most of the time, we were kept too busy to be overconcerned about the conditions on Piper Alpha. And, as on any rig, entertainment was always provided by the many colourful characters who worked there.

One of these was Mick Short, the day-shift rigging foreman. He was a great guy, who'd worked for diving companies on Piper for several years. Having gone through a divorce, he'd decided to change his lifestyle. He worked offshore during the season and spent his winters living like a king in Bangkok. With his dark hair and black moustache, he was obviously quite a ladies' man. Every now and then, he'd receive letters from two cockney mates who owned a bar in Bangkok. They always enclosed photographs of beautiful Thai go-go dancers. His proved to be the most popular mail received on Piper!

Another regular feature of life on a rig is the wind-up. In any closed society, the slightest peculiarity in anyone's character is instantly spotted and people will go for it every time. It's great. You either learn to lose your foible or your life's made a misery.

Joe Wells, the American diver, was always being wound up by another diver called Kev Daber. He was an ex-naval diver who'd done a saturation course on the way to the Falklands – after the Navy had discovered it hadn't enough deep-sea divers to do all the necessary recovery work!

As Joe had a prodigious appetite, he'd always bring down to the dive module from the galley a piece of pie or cake, which he'd stick on a shelf in my office. Then a couple of hours later he'd warm it up in the microwave. Kev took to opening up whatever Joe brought and coating the inside with mustard. So Joe took to hiding his snack. But every time, Kev would find it. The saga of their childish but astonishingly good-natured game of hide-and-seek provided the rest of us with a long-running source of entertainment.

I spent a lot of time in my office, working with my computer. It was immensely useful for co-ordinating information and making sense of the mass of paperwork I had to get through. At the end of each week, for example, I had to compile a status report, which involved me in going through all the dozen or so job-packs of different inspections or construction work. Normally, it would have been written out in longhand, before it was sent off to the project manager at Occidental. Rather than write it out every week, I put it on the word processor and at the end of each week I could run off the additions that had taken place to the work and the anomalies that had arisen. The result was a much better document that took far less time to compile. It gave a complete status report on the work schedule, the anomalies discovered and the remedial action taken.

Also, because I'd become unhappy about the qualification courses for divers, especially those issued by the Welding Institute, I decided to write a proposal to Stena for a course that could be held at the end of the season to requalify the divers working for Occidental. Although it would be up to the standard required for the North Sea, it would deal specifically with Occidental's procedures – so, as much as anything, it was an orientation course.

So with one thing and another, I was kept extremely busy on Piper. After five hard-working weeks, I went home for ten days' leave.

Vicky, of course, wanted to know what the platform was like.

'It's a standard, tatty old rig,' I said.

'In what way's it tatty?' she asked.

I gave her some examples and then added, 'Apparently, when Red Adair was involved with the design of Tharos, he saw Piper and said, "There's bound to be a major blow-out in the North Sea one day and it's more likely than not to be on Piper Alpha." I don't know if it's true or not, but that's what people on the rig claim he said. There's so much vibration on the thing that one day it'll probably shake itself to bits.'

After my return to Piper for my second five-week stint, most of the diving work continued to be concerned with the inspection of risers, welds and the many clamps that had been introduced over the years to strengthen discovered weaknesses. These were totally adequate repairs, although so many clamps had been attached to the Piper jacket that they'd significantly increased its weight.

In previous years, a number of minor cracks had been discovered that needed to be regularly monitored. It was fascinating to be able to see these defects. Usually, when you're inspection diving or co-ordinating, the vast majority of the time you don't find anything. But that wasn't the case on Piper. Also, because we had a particularly fine colour video system, we could see the defects in dive control, especially when the diver was doing magnetic particle inspection. The 'black' UV light showed any crack clearly.

We were interested and excited by finding the defects – it was, after all our job. We were inspectors. The defects didn't particularly shock us. Piper was a rig with many known defects, although we kept on coming across a number of these that had become significantly worse.

When we were inspecting the thirty-inch oil line that carried all the oil from Piper to Flotta refinery, we had to examine a known defect at transition weld no. 3, which was at a depth of sixty feet. It was the point where two lengths of the riser had been joined together and where the protective sheathing for the splash-zone terminated on the riser. When we looked at the weld, it appeared as if the defect had propagated. In one of the toes of the weld, there was a crack that went all the way round. Information about this major defect was immediately passed back to Occidental by telex. This was quickly followed by a fax of the data sheet, showing the exact position of the defect. We expected that this would lead immediately to some remedial action. Not only was it a more significant defect that I'd seen anywhere, it was on the main oil line.

In the documentation we sent to Occidental, we'd said it might be possible to provide a video of the defect. It was an extremely difficult thing to obtain. If you want to video a weld, you use white light so you can see it clearly. But when you're doing magnetic particle inspection, you use UV light, which can show the defect effectively on video, but only if the diver sticks the camera on his helmet right up against it. When that's done, it's impossible to see all the weld. So there was no video technique to show both the crack and the weld. It was even more difficult in this case, with a crack extending all the way round the riser.

In a fairly short time, we received instructions from Occidental to send them a video of the defect. We had a go and produced something which showed the defect but not its relation to the weld.

A few days later, Barry called me into his office and said, 'I've got Oxy's senior engineer on the phone. He's not very happy with the video we sent in. I told him we'd done our best and he really couldn't expect any more. But maybe you could have a chat with him. See if you can fill him in with how difficult it was.'

I'm a very polite person when I talk to people, so I said, 'Hello. What can I do to help?'

'I'm really not very happy about the video you sent,' he said.

'There's no commentary with it. We can't see the defect in relation to the position of the weld. What have you got to say about it?'

'You've got to understand it's really a bonus that we've been able to provide any kind of video at all. It's not like doing a visual inspection. There's no technique for it.' I also felt like pointing out that Occidental had been provided with the video only because of the excellent system provided largely at Stena's expense. (Oxy having steadfastly refused to provide one because of the cost).

'Fine,' he said. 'But why isn't there a commentary?'

'Because we made several attempts at videoing the defect and sent you the best one as quickly as possible. This is a dive control – not a video studio.'

'Don't you think that's a bit complacent?'

I take a pride in my professional attitude. So I was shocked by his comment. I held the telephone at arm's length, put a hand over it and said to Barry, 'Who is this idiot? Why's he giving me a hard time?' Then I thought to myself, 'This is a career decision!' I just wanted to tell him he was a jerk. When you're a diver, you know just how heavy and unwieldly it is to have on your head a Kirby 17 with a video camera mounted on top of it. If he thought filming under those circumstances was easy, he was away with the fairies.

Barry said, 'It doesn't matter. Just keep him happy.'

I swallowed my pride and said, 'No, I don't think it's complacent. You've got to appreciate the difficulties. We try very hard here and it's always our intention to do the best job we can.'

That didn't seem to satisfy him and he whined on for a while. Eventually, we agreed that we needed to get more information about this major defect.

The problem with any crack on a rig is that it becomes a site for all the stresses and vibrations which, instead of passing on through the metal, stop there and cause the crack to propagate. When a crack is first found, the normal procedure is to grind it with a hydraulic grinder. The actual loss of metal isn't significant. What is important is the shape of the defect. With a crack in the toe of a weld, there is a harsh profile: the grinding smoothes it down so that the defect is effectively removed.

In this instance, the crack went right the way round the riser and the crack had already been ground several times over a period of years. But it was obviously propagating more significantly than it ever had before. It was impossible to keep on grinding the defect – eventually the grinder would go straight through the metal.

So it was essential to establish the depth and extent of the crack to see how significant it was. This can be done by two means – ultrasonic testing, which is effective but expensive, or a technique called Alternating Current Potential Drop (ACPD). This measures electrically the distance between two points on a metal surface. A probe is used with a contact attached either side of the crack. A high frequency electrical current is passed between the two contacts along the surface of the metal. As the current follows the contours of the metal, when there is a crack, it has to travel further. The diver then uses the probe and takes a resistance reading on a good piece of metal close to the crack and one across the crack itself. The difference between the two measurements will show the depth of the crack.

However, it is impossible from the readings to differentiate between a single deep crack and a depression caused by grinding. Both may, in fact, represent exactly the same distance the current travels between the probe's two pins. So the depth of the grind has also to be separately measured.

To do this, I had suggested in my initial report that we brought in an expert, called Pat Chambers, for the ACPD and then used a relatively new technique called BP Aquaprint. Vicky had done much of the trial work on this in Falmouth harbour and I'd used it a couple of times. So I was well aware of its benefits – and the difficulties of the procedure.

Using ACPD, readings are first made every 25mm round the crack. Then aquaprint is applied to the area to make a cast, which is then cut into sections at the exact points where the ACPD readings were taken. It's very exact, but aquaprint is about the fiddliest, nastiest job that can be done underwater. It comes in a large mastic twin-pack tube, which is fitted to a compressed-air gun with a special nozzle. When the trigger is pressed, the gun pushes the mastic piston down, the aquaprint is mixed in the nozzle and comes out like a big glob of toothpaste. This has then to be positioned in the correct place.

It was agreed that this process would be used to measure the crack in the main pipeline. But it was decided that instead of BP Aquaprint, we'd use a new compound that was supposed to be similar.

When the equipment arrived, I saw that we'd been sent only a certain number of tubes.

'This isn't enough,' I said to Barry.

'Well, it's about sixty pounds a tube,' he said. 'They don't want us to waste the stuff.'

'Barry, there's no way we're going to waste it. This is a major defect in Piper's main pipeline which is a major pipeline in the North Sea.'

'I know. I know. Just do what you can. Brief the guys. I know they'll do their best.'

It's impossible to imagine, until you've actually tried, how hard it is to do anything underwater. Despite the difficulties of the conditions, to be useful the work had to be done exactly. Preparation has to be fastidious, because there's a limited time in which to work. In this case, magnetic identification marks with dymo tape had to be put on the pipe, because all the work had to be referenced. Because the weld was tucked under an overlap between two pieces of metal on the riser, it meant the diver had to work from underneath. A special platform had to be built for him to stand on. The case had then to be made in sections, because it was impossible to do more than a foot at a time and the pipeline was three feet in diameter.

Eventually, everything was ready. Only a couple of the divers had ever used aquaprint before. But all the diving team had to be briefed.

The first time it was used, everybody went into dive control to watch on the monitors what happened.

The diver pressed the trigger of the compressor gun. The mastic came out and he started to push it into place, working his way round the riser. It was looking good. Then it started to drop off. The diver quickly pushed it back with his fingers and it stuck like treacle to his hand! He ended up virtually covered in the goo.

'All right,' I told him over the coms. 'Don't worry about it. Ditch that one. Put a new pack in. Fix a new nozzle. Get your magnets out and your plastic sheeting. Now fix it over the weld. Then pull it back a bit at a time, so you can push up the aquaprint under the plastic sheet.'

Sometimes this works, sometimes it doesn't. After casts were brought back to the surface, I inspected the results, comparing them to the photographs we already had of the entire weld. In these, every position where Pat Chambers had taken an ACPD reading was marked with a black chinagraph line. Unfortunately, some of the casts turned out to have air bubbles in them and others had stretched slightly and not picked up the imprint accurately. So I then worked out which specific sections had to be redone. It was a long, tedious, but essential business.

Because, in these conditions, the compound we were using wasn't as adhesive as BP Aquaprint, it wasn't as effective in this job where it had to be pushed up from beneath over the weld. So it was decided to swap the whole batch, which meant sending back all the guns and remaining tubes and getting in the BP equipment.

That created much whining about cost. There'd been enough fuss when we started about the desirability of using something that cost sixty pounds a tube. But now Barry was getting continuous earache about the cost of the work.

It provided a perfect example of how budget conscious oil companies were, even though in this case we were dealing with the most serious defect in the most serious location I'd ever seen. If the pipeline failed, not only would there be a loss of twelve percent of the UK's oil production, but there would be major pollution in the North Sea.

CHAPTER ELEVEN

THE FINAL DAYS

On 3 June 1988, it has been reported, there was a fire on Piper Alpha. Apparently a plater had been using a blowtorch to mend a handrail, forty feet above sea-level. A spark ignited gas that was being discharged from a waste pipe and had built up under the platform. For nearly half an hour, there was a blanket of flame of some hundred square feet. It was eventually put out by the fire-fighting team, using water cannon. Fortunately I did not see this.

On 23 June, a mattress caught fire in Room C11 in Piper's accommodation block. Apparently, the room's heat and smoke detectors were not set off by the fire, which was discovered only when a steward arrived to make the beds. The damage was small and a spokesperson from Occidental claimed it had been started by a cigarette, even though the occupants of the room didn't smoke.

Because of these fires, it was pointed out at a safety meeting that, unlike the newer platforms, Piper Alpha didn't have status lights to display its state of alert. This could be relayed to the crew only by the loudspeaker system, which was difficult to hear if men were working close to noisy machinery.

Yet, despite its deficiencies and its age, the use of Piper Alpha as a production platform was scheduled for further expansion.

From the time it was erected, Piper had been a major producer in its own right. In its heyday, it had produced more oil in a day than any other rig anywhere in the world – some 317,000 barrels a day in 1979. So it'd been the biggest money-spinner ever. But in addition to all the work it did in its own field, it processed gas from other platforms. Piper was connected by pipelines with Claymore and Tartan. So Piper was like a giant junction box.

In the summer of 1988, a pipeline from the new Chanter field was also being brought to Piper and connected through a new riser. The diving team was involved in the preparations for the installation of this riser. Towards the end of June, the construction work involved was given the highest priority.

The divers' task was to install two clamps within the air-range where we were working – at depths of fifty and one hundred and twenty feet. Clamps at lower depths were to be installed by saturation divers from Tharos.

Before the installation could take place, rigorous preparations had to be made. A taut wire was rigged above and below the working area so it followed what would be the central line of the riser when it was in position. This provided the point of reference for cleaning the member and marking it up to establish exactly the right place for the riser clamps. These were then installed, using specially prepared spirit levels with wedges. Finally, the bolts were put into position.

The special process used for tightening the bolts is known as 'Hydratighting'. A hydraulic jack is attached to each nut. Then rather than twist the nut to tension it, the bolt is hydraulically stretched so no twisting force is applied. As the bolt is stretched, the diver uses a little tommy bar to tighten the nut. The pressure is released and then reapplied to see if the bolt will move any more.

Using the same process, we also installed a third riser clamp above water at the twenty-foot spider-deck level. Another job was installing the Skagit winch – a huge construction which was part of the rigging needed to install the new pipework.

This work had been going on for several weeks. During that time, Stan MacLeod went on leave. When he returned, I walked into the office and found him working at his desk on what appeared to be an antique brass piece of equipment.

We chatted away for a while about his leave. Then he asked me when I intended taking mine.

I'd been trying to plan my next crew change to coincide with

The Alexander Kielland overturned in 1980 with the loss of 126 men. Here it is shown in Stavanger Harbour after being righted and inspected by my colleagues in 1983.

The steel jacket of Piper Alpha, over 500 feet long, being towed out prior to its installation. (Aberdeen Journals).

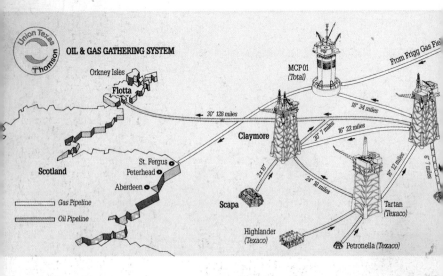

Piper Alpha with adjacent rigs and onshore terminals showing connecting oil and gas pipelin (Occidental Petroleum).

Some of the survivors from the *Silver Pit* walking from the helicopter at Aberdeen Royal Infirmary. From right to left: Steve Middleton, Dick Common, Mahmood Khan and Alistair Mackay (Aberdeen Journals).

Arriving at the Skean Dhu Hotel, having been checked over at the hospital. Left to right: myself, Joel Ralph, Stan Macleod, Brian Jackson. (Aberdeen Journals).

Robert Carey and Robert McGregor. The bravery shown by the injured survivors was staggering - (Aberdeen Journals).

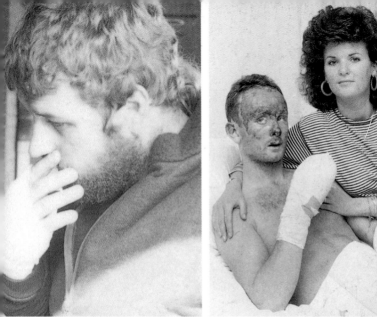

(left) Ian Letham, who survived the explosion and loss of his rescue craft in one of the major blasts. Sadly his crewmates Malcolm Storey and Brian Batchelor, together with others in the boat, did not survive. (Aberdeen Journals) (right) Mark Reid, whose honest account of his escape is one of the most moving. (Aberdeen Journals).

Prince Charles shaking hands with George Carson, medic and engineer of the standby vessel the *Silver Pit*, who worked so diligently during the rescue. Behind are others from the *Silver Pit's* crew. (Press Association).

The main accommodation module rises from the depths. (Occidental Petroleum).

Inside the accommodation module the police, divers and other workers had the solemn and difficult task of recovering many of those lost. They did this well in difficult conditions. (Grampian Police).

Myself with survivors (from right to left) Bob Ballantyne and Derek Ellington at the press conference called by Frank Doran MP (on my left) to discuss the interim technical report. (Aberdeen Journals).

The public inquiry chaired by Lord Cullen, with its daunting array of QCs and experts. (Aberdeen Journals).

Lord Cullen with the model of the jacket remains and seabed debris pile. (Press Association).

the examination I needed to sit so I could renew my in-water inspection certificate. I wanted to ensure it was in order, because I intended to take the saturation-diving course at the end of the year. But the examination date had just come through and so I said to Stan, 'I want to leave Piper for my leave on 7 July. The exam's ten days after that.'

Once that had been agreed, I glanced at the brass object Stan was so assiduously polishing. 'What on earth's that?' I asked.

'Oh. It's an old lung-tester,' he replied. 'It's what they used to test divers' breathing in the old days.' (As part of their annual medical examination, modern divers undergo tests to measure the total capacity and strength of their lungs.) 'It's something like a hundred years old,' he went on. 'It's stamped with the name of the maker – Siebe Gorman.'

He handed it to me and I examined it carefully. There was a brass mouthpiece, a long pipe with a pot on the end, a couple of jets, and a small fan-shaped wheel that would obviously spin round when you blew into it.

'Have a go!' Stan said.

I was just about to when I stopped and said, 'You must think I was born yesterday! There's no way I'm going to blow into this thing. Get somebody else to do it.'

So I handed it back to him. He shrugged and continued polishing it.

Pat Chambers then walked into the office. He had a similar conversation with Stan about the lung-tester.

'So what d'you do?' he asked.

'What you must do is blow really hard to get the wheel spinning,' said Stan. 'Without that sudden burst it won't work. Look, I'll show you.' He blew into it and the wheel whirred round. 'There! You have a go.'

Pat picked it up and blew away. The wheel didn't spin but from the two jets came a shower of talcum powder that went all over him, turning his dark beard white!

'How the hell did you do that?' Pat said, dusting himself down.

Stan then showed us the trick. The machine didn't have a normal mouthpiece. If you blew it like a trumpet, out came the talcum powder. To make the wheel spin round, you had to put your tongue over the obvious hole so that the wind was diverted into a smaller, hidden hole under the rim of the mouthpiece.

From then on, we had a lot of fun with Stan's patent lung-tester. Every time anybody new came by, they were encouraged to have a go, while everybody who'd been caught before lurked in the corridor waiting to gloat.

By the beginning of July, Stan was running out of victims. Then he announced a new one was arriving and would be sharing my cabin.

The *Lowland Cavalier*, a diving-support vessel, had come out into the field to do some work laying Coflexip pipe, a flexible control pipeline. Its DP beacon was fixed to a small projecting deck on Piper and, to maintain it, their technician was being sent over. He was a man in his early sixties, called David Wiser. Inevitably, everybody referred to him as 'Budweiser'.

When he arrived, we were diving and so Stan asked me to go up and look after him, as he was going to have the third bunk in my cabin. Although he'd been offshore a long time, he hadn't spent much time on a rig and so I showed him around.

'What's it like here?' he asked.

'It's really all right. I'm quite enjoying it. The platform's tatty, but the guys working here are a half-decent bunch and very friendly.'

I took him down to dive control and Stan, seizing upon a new arrival, managed to catch him with the lung-tester.

Budweiser was going to be around for four or five days. But he had very little to do – just keep his eye on the beacon and adjust it every now and then. So he spent a lot of the time down in my office or in the cabin.

The day after his arrival, I was sitting in the dive control when suddenly I became aware of a very strong smell.

'What the hell's that?' I asked Stan.

'Some sort of gas, I suppose.'

I phoned up safety to report it. They sent somebody down to check it out.

Shortly afterwards, I had a blinding headache and so I decided to go upstairs to take some aspirin. As I went up the enclosed stairwell, I came across a chap standing on one of the small protruding platforms. He was using a flare gun to try and light the flare. (On Piper, there were two flare stacks to burn off the excess gas. They used to swap them around, depending on which direction the wind was blowing, so there weren't waves of heat blowing across the platform.)

I stood and watched him. It took several attempts to light the thing. Afterwards, he told me that when they swapped over the flares, gas had to be bled out of the one that was to be lit, and in the few minutes it took for there to be a switchover, it was likely that methane gas would be smelt on the rig.

Two days later, there was a similar smell of gas.

As my leave approached, I knew that, because we were working nights, I'd find it difficult to get back into a different work and sleeping pattern. There was just a chance, however, that I might be able to finish early on my final shift and so be able to get some sleep before setting off for Aberdeen in the morning.

I'd be able to do that if the only work that had to be done was simple and straightforward, like underwater cleaning. There was some; it was grit-blasting a small member at the fifty-foot level that we'd found was partially flooded – which might mean there was a crack. On the other hand, it was possible that work would start that night on installing the Chanter riser. Everything was all set for this. Tharos, which was going to carry out the installation, had moved in close to Piper.

Tharos was a semi-submersible, just like an exploration rig, but its sole function was to act as a massive support vessel for construction and diving. It had a mobile diving unit (or flying diving bell), which had hydraulic thrusters that allowed it to be manoeuvred by a pilot sitting in a one-atmosphere chamber. There was also on Tharos an extending bridgeway that could be used in an emergency to connect it to a rig.

Trying to change my sleep pattern and hoping I'd be able to get an early night, I got up at about eleven o'clock on 6 July – the day of the final shift before my leave. I'd had only four hours sleep since the previous shift.

I wandered down to the dive control. The day-shift riggers finished work at twelve and so they were just changing over with the night-shift. But in the offices, apart from Barry who was always at his desk, there was nobody around. So I went into my office to finish off all the paperwork and prepare the hand-over notes for my relief, a man called John Brooke. He also lived in Falmouth, but as he'd just bought a surfboard shop in Penzance, he'd given up working offshore regularly. He'd agreed to stand in for me as a special favour.

I'd almost sorted out all the forms when I discovered I'd mislaid a data sheet. It really annoyed me. I'd never lost a data sheet in the whole of my professional life. Hoping that it'd turn up, I continued with my work.

After I'd finished the filing, I looked at the clock. It had just gone three and so I settled down to start revising for my inspection examination.

Almost immediately, Barry walked in. He was a man without any conception of working hours who'd happily do his job for most of the day. 'Ah, Ed,' he said. 'Can you spare a moment?'

He went through an aspect of the work and asked if I'd do a drawing. 'Doesn't he realise,' I thought, 'that I'm not supposed to start work until five o'clock?' But as I liked him and we had such a good working relationship, I didn't say anything. I went back to my office, put away the textbooks and started working on the drawing.

About half an hour later, Stan walked in and said, 'What the hell are you doing down here?'

'I came down to do a little studying, but Barry called in and asked if . . . '

'I'm going to have words with Barry,' he said, making for the door.

'No, you're not. Don't worry about it. I'll have it done in half an hour.'

So Stan sat down and started reading.

'What's the book?' I asked.

'The *SAS Survival Handbook*. I was given it for my fortieth birthday.'

'Good God! Looking for another job, are you?'

I finished the drawing and then did about an hour's study. At five o'clock, the time I normally started the shift, I went into Barry's office. We decided that the first dive would give a final look at one of the clamps on the Chanter riser. The next diver would then start work on the flooded member. We'd continue with that until we heard from Tharos that the underwater rigging had to be in place for installing the riser.

Barry told me that the scaffolding foreman had been in touch to say that it might be essential to continue working and so the dive team had to be prepared to stand down if necessary.

After talking to Barry, I prepared the dive plan with alternatives should any contingency arise. I then drew from my files all the drawings that would be needed and made photocopies of them and the dive plan for Barry and Stan.

Just after six, Keith Cunningham made the first dive. I then realised I still hadn't found the missing data sheet. An inner battle of wills followed, while I debated whether to make it up – something I'd never done before – or speak to Barry about it.

Just as the dive was about to end, the phone rang and we were informed that a heavy lift was about to be carried by the crane on Piper. So the divers had to be stood down. A few of them wandered upstairs to find out how long it'd be before we could start again.

'I don't know,' I said. 'All I've been told is it could be anything between one and three hours.'

Several of the divers then decided they'd go up to the billiard room in the accommodation module to wait until they were called back.

John Barr, the diving superintendent then phoned me. 'Where's the pump-status report?' he asked.

'Oh, no!' I exclaimed. 'I'm sorry.'

It'd been part of my daily routine at quarter to five, before going on shift, to walk out of my cabin into Piper's control room at the centre of the rig to collect this report which showed how many of the fire pumps were in operation. Because I'd gone down to work early that day, I'd forgotten all about it.

So I went dashing up to the control room which was on the top deck, in the centre of the rig. Full of dials, it was like a cramped control room in a rather tatty power station. As on an old ship, all the panels were painted with gloss paint, rather than having the original cellulose-finish.

'You're late,' one of the guys said.

'I know. I've been busy down below.'

'Well nothing changes. It's exactly the same as usual.'

He went to a filing cabinet and pulled out a blank form. Then he looked at the lines on the panel immediately behind the desk to check the status of the pumps which can be used to suck in water should they be required for the fire hydrants. Two were switched to manual, so in an emergency they could be operated from the control room. All the others were switched off.

The reason for this was that, in the past, water pumps on rigs had suddenly been switched on and a diver working close by had been sucked into the intake. It had apparently once happened on Piper, when a diver called Happy Day had been partially pulled in and had badly hurt his shoulder.

Of course, it needn't be necessary for all the pumps to be switched off. If the whole system had been a different one, we could have informed the control room where the diving was going to take place and only the pumps in the immediate area need then have been switched off. Even that then isn't strictly necessary.

Large metal cages over the inlet will prevent a serious accident.

I dashed down to the dive-control and handed the pump-status report to John Barr with my profuse apologies.

At about a quarter past eight, we were informed that the lift had been completed and that we could recommence diving. Andy Carroll made the second dive, and was followed by Chris Niven while Gareth Parry-Davies remained in the Wendy Hut dressed as his stand-by diver.

By the time everything required for the restart had been completed, it was a quarter to nine. Lens drifted into the office to ask if it was all right for him to go up to the accommodation block so he could telephone his girlfriend. I nodded and off he went.

I decided I couldn't wait any longer to have a word with Barry about the missing data sheet. So I went into his office.

He was in radio communication with the *Lowland Cavalier*, which had moved close into the Piper platform. It was using a remotely operated vehicle (an ROV) on the sea-bed.

When he'd finished talking, I said, 'Their ROV sounds like a pretty swish piece of equipment.'

'It is,' he said. 'Apparently it cost eleven million quid. So there's no way they'd want to lose that!'

'Well, Barry, I've got a confession to make.'

'You haven't gone and lost the *Lowland Cavalier*'s ROV all on your own, have you, Ed?'

'No. But I am missing a data sheet. I can't find it anywhere.'

Barry had a good look round to see if it was in his office, but couldn't find it. 'Don't worry,' he said. 'Just go back and have another look. Start at the beginning and look through all your things.'

So I did. This time, I went through my filing cabinet and found it. It'd simply been dropped into the wrong file. I was delighted. I wandered out on to the cellar deck to have a look at the *Lowland Cavalier* which was moored close by. There was a moderate swell, and the ship bobbed up and down lazily. It was a most pleasant summer evening.

At twenty past nine, Gareth entered the water in the diving bell to clean the flooded member with the grit gun.

Shortly afterwards, the phone rang. It was Vicky, wanting to check when I'd be arriving home. We chatted away happily for about ten minutes. Things began to feel much better and I felt extraordinarily optimistic. Just before she put the phone down,

I said, 'I've got the feeling that something big's going to happen. It's really going to change everything!'

I felt great. I reflected that the worst thing that can happen when you're working offshore is to have a bad telephone call from home. There is nothing more disheartening, because you can't do anything about it. I've always found that I could only work effectively in an offshore environment when I wasn't worrying about my home life.

As my watch had stopped working a couple of days before, I asked Stan the time. It was nearly quarter to ten. I had hoped I might have been able to finish the shift about that time but, because the divers had been stood down for over an hour, I wasn't going to be able to get away for a while.

Just then, Barry called Stan and me into his office to have a chat about how the shift was proceeding. He and Dick Common were sitting behind their desks. Stan leant with his back against a filing cabinet and commented on how fast the apple and orange seedlings were growing on the windowsill. I stood just inside the doorway, my arm resting on the other filing cabinet.

We were talking away, when suddenly, for a split second, all hell broke loose . . .

CHAPTER TWELVE

AN ACCOUNT OF THE ACCIDENT

The chain of events that led to the first explosion on Piper had already been put in train long before it actually happened.

For weeks, there had been intense activity on the platform. In addition to everyday production and processing of oil and gas, it was the mid-summer maintenance period and a considerable amount of construction work was being undertaken. This included fitting the new riser from the Chanter field and installing an additional fan cooler for the instrument air system. Because of all this work, there were even more men and equipment on Piper than usual.

On 3 July, Piper was switched to Phase 1 gas production, which meant that the gas recovered was not exported, but used in other ways or flared off. Oil production continued as normal. No written instructions were issued to the operators on how the plant should be run under this mode. Apparently, most of the men were considered to be experienced, even though the only time since 1979 there had been a Phase 1 operation on Piper Alpha was for sixty days after the explosion in March 1984.

One of the many tasks undertaken on 6 July was maintenance on the pipework around the gas condensate pumps. These pumped the condensate (a mixture of natural gas liquids removed during the purification of the gas) either into the main oil line or back into the reservoir.

A technician working for a sub-contractor removed the pressure safety-valve (psv) on condensate pump A and blanked off the open pipe-ends with the existing gaskets and blank flanges kept for that particular purpose. After the valve had been serviced, it could not be replaced because the crane was busy elsewhere and so was unavailable. The work permit was then suspended and returned to the control room, where according to normal practice, it was passed on to the safety department.

When the shifts changed at 18.00, it appears that the night-shift production-operators were not informed that the psv had been removed from condensate pump A. Nor, as the work permit wasn't in the control room, had they any way of discovering that the psv was missing. When the shift started, everything appeared to be normal.

At about 21.45, there was a major disruption to the gas processing system. The south-west gas flare began to roar and the flame was much larger than normal.

At 21.50, condensate pump B tripped and shut down, setting off a buzzer in the control room. Because of this, several men, including Erland Grieve, were called by radio to start either of the condensate pumps on the 68-foot level, below C Module. They managed to restart one of the pumps, but it immediately tripped again.

Fifty feet below sea-level, the diver, Gareth Parry-Davies, was working at a depth of fifty feet on the partially flooded member. Chris Niven, the previous diver, had finished his decompression, changed and joined the stand-by divers in the Wendy Hut, where they waited instructions from the diving supervisor to tend the diver in the water.

Way above the dive skid and module B, Vincent Swales in the mud module was watching the gas flare. No longer just larger than normal, it had grown enormously as the greatly increased volume of gas was forced out of the stack. Between the tulip and the flame was a surprisingly large gap. Suddenly, the flare died for a moment and then with a roar renewed its exceptional intensity.

In the cinema, men from the day shift had their enjoyment of the film 'Carrie' disturbed by the angry roaring of the flare.

In the control room, there was the sound of more buzzers. In quick succession, the drum holding condensate reached a high level and there was a shut-down of two out of the three centrifugal compressors. Seconds later, the third centrifugal compressor shut down. Suddenly, three low-level gas alarms were indicated in quick succession. This was followed by a high-level alarm near a compressor. Frantic instructions were heard being passed between the control room and the operators as they tried to establish what was happening.

Inside the Wendy Hut, Keith Cunningham, the diver, had earlier noticed the noise of the extra gas being flared off as a result of the Phase 1 operations and thought little of the now-excessive flare noise levels audible on the dive skid. Amid the usual divers' banter, he chatted and joked with Tony Payne and Steve Middleton about their fortunate escape from the explosion and fire on Piper in 1984.

A high-pitched scream, like metal ripping on metal, was heard in the mechanics' workshop. Immediately afterwards, at 21.58, there was a massive and violent explosion. There had been a huge leak of gas in C Module. The explosion started fires and caused massive damage to pressure vessels and machinery in various parts of B and C Modules. These caused leakages of diesel oil that further fuelled the fires.

In the control room, next to C Module, Geoff Bollands was flung across the room, injuring his arm. Alex Clark was also badly hurt. Badly shaken, they peered around through the wafting smoke and dust. The large double doors were hanging from their hinges. They could also see that the multitudinous electrical control panels were hanging off the wall, leaving their maze of wires exposed. All the platform's communications systems had been destroyed. Without these, there was no way of issuing instructions or warnings. Also destroyed were the controls for the containment systems, including the fire pumps. At the time, none of these were on automatic. They had been switched off, apart from a couple which were on manual, as a precaution while diving was taking place. As none of the pumps could be switched on from the control room, there was no water available for fire-fighting. What sprinklers did briefly operate were using the remnants of water left in the system.

From then on, it was simply a matter of time before a conflagration developed. With the massive shake-up the platform had experienced, there would inevitably be other gas leaks to cause further explosions. The fate of Piper Alpha was sealed.

In the workshop, next door to the control room, there was similar damage. The bulkheads were buckled and the ceiling had collapsed.

In the tiny Wendy Hut, the strip light fell and was left dangling on its wire. The divers rushed out to see a stream of oil pouring down from the main oil pipeline and spreading rapidly over the dive skid. As John Barr, the supervisor, gave the instruction to recover the diver, fires were starting all around them.

'Well, I can tell you, Ed,' Joe Wells told me later, 'it was pretty fucking difficult getting the diver out and staying there to man the winches with fires breaking out all around you!'

In the accommodation module, the cinema emptied as men ran to their cabins for their survival suits before hurrying to their muster point in the galley.

In Aberdeen, the Maritime Rescue Co-ordination Centre intercepted a Mayday signal from the *Lowland Cavalier*, which was still alongside Piper Alpha. (David Kinrade, Piper's radio operator sent Maydays for as long as he was able before the flames forced him from the radio room.) At Flotta, the operators of Occidental's oil terminal noted a marked reduction in the supply coming from Piper that suggested it had ceased production.

On platforms throughout the North Sea, radio-operators were picking up the sounds of a developing disaster. Initial Mayday calls were being replaced by an increasing, confused traffic of rescue vessels and nearby ships. Slowly, the offshore radio rooms filled with passers-by who listened in silent horror, knowing the accident could easily have involved them.

My old friend, Titch Halsall, was the diving superintendent on the Murchison platform. He was called into the radio room there to listen to the flurry of ominous messages. Several times during the previous few days, he'd tried to call me on Piper to find out how Vicky and I were getting on. So Titch was all too aware that I was still on Piper. Alarmed, he didn't stay long in the radio room. It was getting increasingly crowded.

On Claymore, Piper's sister platform, many workers stopped what they were doing to stare at the massive smoke cloud rising twenty miles away. A clearly discernible glow showed that there was a major fire. Keith Ellis, a rigger, watched helplessly, knowing that his brother David was one of the men on Piper Alpha.

In the mud module, everything that hadn't been bolted down had been punched upwards. Vincent Swales could see that the flare was roaring to its fullest extent, indicating that the whole production process was being bypassed. To the west side of the platform, flames were shooting up around A and B Modules past the skid deck. He turned around and smashed the fire alarm. Nothing happened.

All over the rig, people were instinctively following their training and emergency instructions. In the absence of any form of announcement, most were trying to make their way to the galley to muster, have a head count, and take instructions. After all, that was what they were trained to do.

Inside the accommodation module, emergency lighting flickered on for a while and then failed. Men made their way through the darkness to the galley. Some carried the torches that'd been clipped to their bedsides. Initially, there was little smoke there, but it soon began to fill up. After twenty minutes, it was thick and black.

Harry Calder had been woken in his cabin by the explosion. Eventually, he abandoned the inside to take a chance among the smoke and flame outside. Before he left, he heard colleagues call on their hand radios: 'We need breathing apparatus. What's happening? Is anybody getting out? We are all going to die!'

Many men were now lying on the floor of the galley or in the stairwells, keeping low to reach some air. They were dipping towels in the fish tanks and wrapping them around their faces to help them breathe.

Mark Reid poured juice from the drinks machine over his head. The bedlam inside the galley affected him badly. He later admitted that at one point he lost control and has said:

'I shouted, "Is there anyone here from Bawden drilling?" I thought I was going to die and wanted to be with somebody I knew.'

Jeff Jones shouted back, 'I am over here,', and shone a torch. Mark went over to him.

They tried a door at the back of the galley. Mark held onto his friend's waist, as he led the way shining his torch through the smoke and darkness.

The men next to the double kitchen doors said it was impossible to go out. Mark replied that men were already dropping dead in the galley so there was no point in staying.

Outside, they hid from the heat next to a shipping container full of fruit. Men were inside and passed out tomatoes which Mark and Jeff squashed over their heads and faces to keep cool.

They dashed away to find more air. Afraid of the helicopter fuel store above, they refused to venture up and when water from an adjacent ship's water cannon cascaded on the deck they lapped it up like dogs. It enabled them to get their body fluid back up again.

'I remember being grateful for that,' Mark said later.

Bob Ballantyne had donned his survival suit and spent some time checking cabins to see that they were empty. Then he found a way out to B deck and on to the drill deck.

Harry Calder made his way with Ian Fowler towards the helideck. From there, five men were to jump the 175 feet into the sea and survive. They included Joe Meanan, Billy Clayton, David Lambert, and Ian McKenzie.

Roy Carey was with Erland Grieve, trapped in the north-west corner at the 83-foot level. Two operators wearing breathing apparatus arrived and told the three men to hold their breath and follow them quickly to the level below. When they had all reached clear air, the two operators said they were returning to try to start the diesel fire water-pumps. They disappeared back into the smoke. Neither was seen again. They were Robert Carroll and Robert Vernon. Before descending the knotted rope left by the others, Erland waited while Roy first removed his life-jacket. It was ridiculously bulky.

Vincent Swales had joined Steve Rae. After several tortuous journeys to and fro through the smoke, they eventually went to the one place they wouldn't normally have chosen – the wellhead deck and the 'Christmas trees', the blow-out preventors on top of the wells. Then they went down the ladder to the beacon platform, just below the south-east corner. From there, they could see men climbing down the rope on the north-west corner. This group effecting their escape included Joe Wells and others from the dive team, workers from the control room and mechanics' workshop, and those who'd been by the condensate pumps at the time of the explosion.

Both Vincent Swales and Steve Rae kicked off their boots. Vincent stopped to have a pee and, just in time, both men jumped into the sea.

Seconds later, at 22.22, the conflagration was multiplied tenfold. As there'd been no fire-water deluge either to contain further leaks or cool the massive quantities of machinery, the heat from the fires had compounded the severe failures resulting from the first blast. At the centre of the cellar deck, just above the dive skid, the Tartan gas-import riser blew – eleven and a half miles of eighteen-inch-diameter gas pipeline started to release hydrocarbon gas at a pressure of 1,800 p.s.i. The effects were devastating. A fireball shot out from below the centre of the jacket, enveloped the platform and rose to a height of some seven hundred feet. The roar was blood-curdling and it was not to stop for the next four hours.

On the 64-foot level, Roy Carey had removed his lifebelt and was about to descend the rope with Erland when he saw the approaching fireball. He later said, 'I just straightaway pivoted, with my back to it, and just crouched right down. In doing so, I think I saved myself a lot of burns. I covered up with my hands and then the flame was on us. At that moment, we were just on fire. So I went through the railings. I just decided that I had to leave the platform at that time and I went straight through the railings – just pushed myself through and dived into the sea.'

Somehow, Erland also made it into the water.

Unknown to them, Dusty Miller, one of the dive team riggers, who'd been watching them from a tiny smoke-free space on the 100-foot level, was also falling towards the sea through the same fireball.

Mark Reid had made his way to the west side accommodation roof, next to the helidecks. He later said:

'The explosion was like a massive mushroom effect from the guts of the rig . . . it just engulfed us with a deafening bang. I felt the searing heat chasing me all the way.

'I was walking around bewildered as if nothing was left and I felt the fireball come up and hit me on the face. I had my hands up and they got severely burned.

'I didn't decide anything. I just thought I was burning alive and I took a run and jumped off the helideck.'

Mark Reid was the fifth and only other person to survive the jump from the helideck. Jeffrey Jones did not escape.

Crashing into the sea he opened his eyes before re-surfacing and expected the water to be on fire. It was not, but his heavy boots filled with water and he struggled in his twisted life jacket. He saw another man who appeared to be drowning and he clung to him in agony as his skinned hands were bitten by the salt water.

Other men who'd been seen desperately waving from the helideck and even out on the flare-stack were seen no more. Nobody knows if the two Telecom engineers who'd been trapped above Dusty Miller also jumped. Neither of them survived.

Also in the sea, but at the south-east corner, Vincent Swales and Steve Rae were praying that the *Maersk Cutter* would neither drown them with its huge fire-water monitors nor cut them up in its thrusters before they were seen. For agonising minutes and despite the intense heat, they couldn't decide if they were actually any safer being in the water. Then the giant plumes of water coming from the *Maersk Cutter* were suddenly switched off and they could see the crew of a Z-boat pointing towards them. They were saved. Mark Reid and his companion were to wait another hour.

Harry Calder and Ian Fowler had somehow managed to hide from the heat of the blast. Amongst the chaos all around the rig, they met and made their way to the pipe-deck and lay under a table in the fabrication shop for protection. They could hardly breathe. Falling in and out of consciousness they turned to each other, shook hands and said goodbye. They never believed they would now survive. Suddenly, the floor collapsed and they were lying at an angle. Having a clear view through the smoke, they crawled along scalding-hot pipes that burnt their hands. Then they jumped the hundred feet into the sea, missing the flaming water. After swimming for what seemed an eternity, a light on a supply boat flashed at them. For a time, it seemed as if the boat was moving away, but then it returned and picked Harry Calder up.

Another ship came along to rescue Ian Fowler. The *Maersk Logger* picked up John Menzies, Dean Naylor and Bob Paterson.

Back inside the accommodation module, the thick glass windows started to crack. Some of the men collapsed on others already lying unconscious on the floor.

On Tharos, a radio message from Piper was received at 22.33 on Channel 9. It said: 'Most people in the galley. Tharos come. Gangway. Hoses. Getting bad.'

Jim McDonald was still amongst the suffocating men in the accommodation module, hoping that a helicopter would arrive. Earlier, he'd asked the safety officer which escape route he should follow, but the man had just shrugged his shoulders. Trying to find a way to the outside, he summoned together the last of his strength and in the stifling heat and through the thick, oil smoke he descended the stairwell. Several times, he had to clamber over bodies. In the total darkness, he had only his sense of touch to guide him. Later, he said, 'It was as simple as this – you either stayed where you were and burned to death or you tried to get out. I knew I was making for the fire, but it was useless making for the helideck.' Finding a way out at the office level, he met three of the Bawden crew. The four then made their way to the drill deck and eventually lowered themselves into what Jim called the 'red-hot' sea.

In the water, Bob Ballantyne was clinging to the south-east leg, hoping to be rescued. He had clambered down steelwork on the jacket leg just prior to the second explosion.

At 20.52, the remaining gas pipelines connected to Piper erupted in a further and even more gigantic fireball. Millions of cubic feet of gas in miles of pressurised steel tubes fed the fire with awesome intensity.

Some vessels in the vicinity sped away to avoid being engulfed. A Z-boat from the *Sandhaven* was beneath the rig, rescuing survivors. The blast tore it apart, throwing Ian Letham into the sea and killing the others. In the unbelievable heat, he swam as best he could. As he drifted by, Bob Ballantyne grabbed him and pulled him to the rig's leg. As he did so, he saw that Ian's lifebelt had disintegrated and his hard hat had melted on his head. Both men were eventually picked up and taken to one of the Maersk ships.

Jim McDonald and his three companions were also picked up and, as they sped away, Jim looked back at Piper. 'I saw the crane jib melt with the intense heat,' he said. 'There was only flame coming out of the water. The rig was away. The only thing I could see was the drilling derrick. I couldn't see the accommodation, the rig, the helideck – just flames shooting out of the sea.'

CHAPTER THIRTEEN

ESCAPE

Having climbed down on to the spider deck, I tried to find a way to the sea. I looked at the north-west leg we'd just come down, but I couldn't see a vertical ladder. I started to walk towards the next leg (B4), where I could see one. But as that took me towards the flames, it didn't seem to be a sensible move. So I turned back to the north-west corner, but I still couldn't find any way of getting down to the sea. (I discovered later that there was a vertical ladder, but it was on the opposite side of the boat-bumper, obscured from view.)

I decided there was nothing for it but to turn round and walk straight back to B4. As I was walking in that direction, I looked out towards the stand-by boat, the *Silver Pit*, which was about a hundred metres from the north-west corner. Its Z-boat had been launched and was speeding towards the rig. I waved and pointed to the B4 boat-bumper. The crew gave me the thumbs up and headed towards it.

I walked straight to the leg, out on to its boat-bumper and climbed down the vertical ladder to almost sea level. Within a second or two of my getting there, the Z-boat arrived and I climbed in. I was possibly the first person to escape from Piper Alpha. We then started hauling in the others who'd followed me. Each time we managed to get a couple on board, the swell pushed the boat inside the jacket. Having been under the platform, taking photographs in a Z-boat, I was very conscious that even in a slight swell there was a danger of suddenly coming underneath one of the members and being knocked out by a riser-clamp. So I was constantly shouting, 'Watch your heads, fellows. Watch your heads!'

A more obvious danger was the pieces of flaming debris falling into the sea all around us.

There was a small explosion up above. The Z-boat crew didn't hang about, but headed back to the *Silver Pit*. There were nine of us who'd been taken off the rig – Gareth Parry-Davies, who was still wearing his diving-suit, Joe Wells, Andy Carroll, Stan MacLeod, Derek Ellington (a Wood Group fitter), Brian Jackson (a Stena rigger), Noel Ralph (another rigger), Davey Elliott (the night-rigger foreman) and myself.

As soon as we were clear of the platform, we turned round and gazed back at Piper. Surprisingly, it wasn't totally ablaze, as I'd expected, although there were enormous flames erupting from B Module immediately above the diving offices. From this area poured a cloud of black smoke several hundred feet high that billowed away from Piper to the north.

After a few seconds, the Z-boat reached the *Silver Pit*. The only way of getting on to it was by clambering up the rope-netting hanging over the side. It really was a most tortuous way of transferring from a small rescue boat on to a large ship.

As I'd been the first one on to the Z-boat, I was at the back and was the last one off. I leapt on to the net, so the Z-boat could get straight away. My left leg was dangling down, trapped between the Z-boat and the *Silver Pit*. Everybody was shouting down, 'Ed, mind your leg! Mind your leg! Move it!'

I desperately tried to free it, but couldn't. I just had to pray the Z-boat wouldn't take my leg with it. But nothing happened to me. I wasn't injured. My leg didn't even hurt. So far, my luck was holding!

We were the first people to be taken to the *Silver Pit*. It was a large boat, about 150 feet long. Just forward of the bridge was a large open space which was the rescue area. The nine of us stood there, gazing over the starboard side at Piper where the fire was getting ever bigger. As we were only about a hundred yards away, we could clearly see men everywhere – still climbing down the ladder on the north-east corner and many more running around amidst the smoke on the helideck.

We just stared, open-mouthed. For a while, apart from a few

muttered exclamations, nobody said anything. We were just all so relieved not to be still there. It looked so bad.

'Did you see what happened to Dick Common when we were in the Z-boat?' Joe Wells asked me. 'He was climbing down the rope and suddenly he fell off and bounced off the boat-bumper into the sea.'

'Christ!' I said. 'That's the end of him!'

A few minutes later, at 22.17, the Z-boat returned with a second load of men rescued from Piper. I was delighted to see that among them was Dick Common, soaking wet.

'Are you all right, Dick?' I asked.

'Fine.'

'But you hit the bloody boat-bumper when you fell!'

'I know. But I'm fine.'

'Where did you hit it?'

'Right in the middle of my back.'

He pulled up his shirt and there wasn't a mark!

Dick was a clerk, very lightweight and anything but athletic. So I said to him, 'You had a lot of guts, setting off to climb down that rope.'

'I didn't want to go, but Barry Barber said, "Don't tell me it's fucking difficult. Get down that bloody rope." So I set off.'

The fire seemed to be gradually increasing in intensity. We could feel its growing heat.

At 22.22, there was a huge explosion and a roaring sound as one of the gas-risers exploded. A massive, all-engulfing fireball ripped from the underside of the platform, hit the sea, shot back up, surrounded the platform and rose to a height of about six hundred feet. Where previously there'd been a cloud of smoke, there was now a raging inferno. Off the north-east corner, the sea appeared to be on fire.

It was the most staggering sight. Even though it was happening before our eyes, I couldn't come to terms with it. What was happening seemed beyond comprehension. Yet I felt no surprise. 'It's happened at last,' I thought. 'How odd I should be here!'

But as I looked at the handful of us on the *Silver Pit*, I had the sickening realisation that there was going to be a massive loss of life and that we might be the only survivors. Faces flashed through my mind that I might never see again – Barry, Lens, Tony, Chris, and John Barr. I couldn't envisage any way in which people could escape the holocaust. I knew, only too well, that there must be many men trapped inside the still-visible accommodation module. What on earth must be happening to them?

Stan MacLeod turned to me and said, very quietly, 'I'm glad you got off, Ed.'

At that point, I decided it was essential to make a list of those of us who'd survived. It was important it was sent back to the shore as soon as possible. I didn't want any of our families to suffer any more grief than they had to.

The decision made, I immediately shifted into my normal, organised mode. I went up to the bridge and obtained a notepad and a pen. I then began writing down the survivors' names and the companies they worked for.

Then, to my surprise, I saw that the Z-boats were still picking up people from the sea. They were even going right under the platform, where there seemed to be fewer flames.

Above, the inferno still raged. This time, there was going to be no mass evacuation of Piper by helicopter.

The *Silver Pit* moved a little closer. A Z-boat arrived with another clutch of survivors who were helped aboard. One of the crew appeared on deck with some mugs and a jug of tea. I moved around, taking people's names. The men stood in groups, talking quietly to each other. It was a lull – an unnatural period of calm.

At 22.52, a third, even more powerful explosion shattered what peace there was. A white, clear pall of heat surrounded the platform. Immediately, the intensity of the radiated heat increased. A gigantic fireball mushroomed into the air and swept, almost in slow motion, towards the *Silver Pit*. It became unbearably hot and it was difficult to breathe. A rope close to me began to smoulder.

The *Silver Pit*'s starboardside was facing the western edge of the rig. We were all standing in the large rescue area, forward of the bridge. I was on the port side, furthest away from the rig, leaning against the side-bulkhead of the ship.

A couple of men darted inside and I could see Stan MacLeod and Joe Wells with a whole huddle of other men sheltering from the heat behind the stairwell leading up to the bridge. I hurried towards them, but I could see there wasn't any space left. It was packed with people. There wasn't any cover there for me.

I glanced up at the fireball. It was getting hotter and hotter. I looked around for somewhere to escape. Then I saw the man who'd been standing a little forward of me climb over the side on to the rope netting, putting the ship between himself and the conflagration. Just behind me, to the right, was an open rescue gate. Hanging down next to it was a rope.

There was no point in staying on deck to be burnt. So I hopped through the open gate and hung on to the rope with my feet dangling in the water. It was an immense relief to be out of the intense heat.

As the ship was in some danger, it suddenly set off at full speed. The man on the rope netting, Mahmood Khan, was well clear of the water and so he just clung on. I tried desperately to leap forward so I could join him, but I couldn't quite make it to the net because I was still wearing my heavy rig-boots. As the ship gathered momentum, I was dragged down into the water and began aquaplaning like a waterskier without skis.

Nobody knew either of us were over the side, hanging on for dear life. So I hollered as loudly as I could. I kept on shouting for what seemed an age, although it was probably only a couple of minutes. Eventually, a head with orange ear-muffs on appeared over the side. The man smiled at me.

'Stop the ship!' I shouted.

He smiled again.

'Stop the ship!' I shouted again and the head vanished.

Then other heads appeared. I saw Andy Carroll and Stan MacLeod. They looked extremely puzzled, obviously not expecting to see me being dragged through the water at high speed.

I was finding it harder and harder to keep holding tight. The further I slipped down the rope, the more time I spent under water. Eventually, instead of skimming over the surface, I was, for increasing periods, being scooped through it.

After taking in a few lungfuls of water, I seriously contemplated the possibility of letting go and swimming away. But I was reluctant to do so. It wasn't sensible to be swimming in rig-boots and I didn't want to be chopped up by the ship's propeller.

So I decided I'd hang on for as long as possible. But my strength no longer matched the force of being towed through the water. My arms were numb. Every so often, I'd feel myself slip another two or three feet down the rope. Each time, I expected to run out of rope, but it seemed impressively long.

In my desperation to hang on, I pictured Vicky and my daughter, Suzie. And it worked. When I thought of them, my hands gripped tighter and I'd stop sliding. I'd long lost the ability to shout. Most of the time, I seemed to be underwater. Every so often, I'd catch glimpses through the bow-wake of a world tinged with green where faces peered at me over the speeding hull of the ship. At other times, I'd bob momentarily out of the water and try to fill my lungs with air rather than sea.

Once, I saw Gareth Parry-Davies leaning over the side in his diving-suit. He was waving his fist at me and I could see his lips saying, 'Fucking hang on! Fucking hang on!' It really got through to me. His expression was so intense. There was no way I was going to let go.

All the time, I was trying to kick off my rig-boots. Because they were old, I always found it difficult enough on the rig, but in the sea it was nigh on impossible. At last, I managed to get rid of one, but the other wouldn't budge.

Throughout, I'd kept my legs wrapped round the rope. Then suddenly I felt a searing pain in my crotch. The back part of my body was being lifted up. I realised that the other end of the rope wasn't loose. That's why I never came to the end of it. It was attached to somewhere further back in the ship and from there somebody was trying to haul me out of the water. It wasn't working very well. The further up my rear end was lifted, the deeper my head was plunged into the sea.

Then almost instantly, from doing ten knots or so, the ship stopped. The bow wave rushed completely over me and then it was perversely calm. I had no strength at all in my arms. They felt just like jelly. I feebly and slowly pulled myself back up the rope to the open gate where Andy Carroll and Gareth were waiting to pull me in.

'Are you all right?' they said. 'Are you all right?'

'Yes, I'm fine. But you're going to have to pull me in. There's no way I can get up there.'

So they grabbed hold of me and manhandled me on to the deck. I was so obsessed with getting my remaining rig-boot off that I knelt there, like a dog, saying, 'Get my rig-boot off. Just get my rig-boot off. Please get it off.'

The instant it'd been pulled off, I felt much better.

'Don't you frigging guys know,' I said to Andy and Gareth, 'that I may have passed my diving medical, but I don't want to go back into the water!'

After a cough and a splutter, my strength came back. Once more, I felt the same rush of adrenalin I'd been experiencing since the moment of the first explosion.

As I stood up, I was greeted by the man in the orange ear-muffs who'd smiled over the side at me when I was in the water. He turned out to be George Carson, who was both the ship's only medic and its engineer.

I then went to look again at the blazing inferno that once had been Piper Alpha. It was no longer a rig on fire: it was being consumed. From the cellar deck downwards, the steel members were red-hot as though they were in a furnace. Beneath, the water was steaming. The sky and the surrounding sea were bathed in a brilliant orange and the raging fire's constant scream of anger obliterated all other sounds. A thick pall of black smoke framed the picture of total devastation.

Eddie Amaira, another of the divers, said, 'There'll be nothing left – nobody left.'

The *Silver Pit* had moved in a large arc from the north-east of the platform round the west side to some four hundred metres off the north-west corner of the platform. Tharos had moved away to a safe distance, having been virtually hit by the fireball.

'A terrible thing happened to one of the Z-boats,' Eddie said. 'It must have been from the *Sandhaven*. When there was that massive explosion, it was just heading away from the rig with some survivors. The fireball must have ignited the fuel tanks and it was blown to bits. It just disappeared.'

Just then, a Z-boat arrived with a couple more survivors. Once again, the dive team, assisted by a few others, snapped into action. As trained divers, we were used to behaving in an extremely disciplined way in the most difficult of environments, so we carried on working as the usual well-oiled machine. Because Stan was the superintendent and I was the co-ordinator, the divers continued to ask us if we'd do this or that. Then we'd go off to organise whatever was required.

As one of the new arrivals had injured an arm and his back, we took him down to the hospital, which was very bare. There was only one medical examination couch and a couple of chairs. The man was laid out, covered with a blanket and made as comfortable as possible.

Minutes later, several of us simultaneously spotted three or four men hanging on to a drifting piece of wreckage.

I dashed up to the front of the bridge, called to the skipper, 'Sail over towards that wreckage,' and pointed it out to him.

That didn't seem to get me very far. The skipper didn't acknowledge me in any way. He just appeared to ignore me.

I rushed round on to the bridge. The skipper seemed totally

overwhelmed by what was happening. Obviously, his hands were full manoeuvring the ship. There was no way he was also able to take the responsibility for any form of rescue co-ordination. But we needed him and I knew I had to get the best out of him. As patiently as I could, I repeated the instruction. Then, at last, he responded.

So I'd be able to see more clearly and be able to give the skipper instructions, I went out in front of the bridge. Three times, the ship moved close to the wreckage. But each time the skipper insisted on being downwind of the survivors so, as any weekend sailor could have predicted, we drifted with the wind past the wreckage.

This made the rest of us furious. Gareth Parry-Davies – still in his wet-suit – tied a piece of rope around his waist and called up to me: 'Ed. Tell the fucking idiot I'm going to leap into the sea and get those guys out. Just make sure he knows what I'm doing.'

So I went back onto the bridge and said to the skipper. 'We've got a diver in the water. He's there. I'm going to keep on telling you exactly where he is so you can manoeuvre the boat.' I then shouted through the window. 'Go for it, Gareth.'

He climbed over the side, leapt into the water and started swimming towards the wreckage, which turned out to be the charred remnants of a lifeboat.

All the time, I kept up a commentary for the skipper: 'OK. We've got a surface diver in the water . . . He's off the port side . . . He's ten feet away . . . He's fifteen feet away . . .'

The *Silver Pit* was a stand-by ship that was supposed to be equipped to deal with an emergency. But the skipper didn't seem to know what to do and once again took his ship downwind of the three obviously badly injured men. Gareth was swimming like crazy. He got within a few feet of the men, but then he ran out of rope.

I shouted down to the men on the rescue deck, 'Find some more rope and tie it on.'

People were already searching desperately, but none of them could find any spare rope. In my view it was becoming crystal clear that the *Silver Pit* was woefully ill-equipped to deal with a serious emergency.

As the men drifted further away from Gareth's reach, a Z-boat fortunately arrived and plucked the three men off the wreckage. They were Erland Grieve, Roy Carey and Eric Brianchon, a Frenchman. All three were badly burnt.

When the Z-boat arrived at the *Silver Pit*, the three men had to climb up the rope netting. It was a cruel, useless way to bring aboard badly injured men, even when the weather conditions weren't bad and there were many willing hands there to help. And these three men were badly shocked and traumatised.

Jim Craig, Donald Thompson and Neil Cassidy were among those leaning over the side trying to haul in the men who were so preoccupied with hanging on that they wouldn't climb up. Gareth clambered down to help them. Fortunately, there was only a gentle swell, but even then the men's cumbersome life-jackets kept on being caught up in the rope.

One of the injured men held on to the net so tightly that six men were unable to pull him on board. Every time Gareth managed to prise open a finger, the rest would clamp on even tighter. It took a good deal of Gareth's gentle coaxing to persuade the man to let go of the net. Jim Russell's survival suit was so full of water it had to be sliced open to drain it before he could be lifted in with great difficulty by Charlie Lamb.

I felt as though I'd become part of an old wartime newsreel showing the oil-smeared, blackened faces of men being rescued from the flotsam of a wreck. And these survivors had exactly the same expression – the dull blankness of pain and horror.

The three men were brought on deck, their lifebelts were removed, and they were wrapped in blankets. The top of Roy Carey's head had been burnt away. There was no hair or skin. Just his skull was showing.

Eric Brianchon, the Frenchman, was in an even worse state. Apart from an occasional strip, all his clothes had been blown off. The whole of his body was very pale, apart from a few firedarkened patches. Huge shards of very fine skin hung from him. They weren't pieces of flesh. It was just like somebody suffering from severe sunburn.

Before Eric could be carried into the hospital, we had to move the injured man already on the couch. I helped carry him to a bunk. Then I went back outside to help Andy Carroll with Eric. It took an age to get him over the step of the watertight door. *Silver Pit* was supposed to be a stand-by boat for emergencies that could take the whole complement of a rig. But it took us minutes to get one seriously injured man in through the door. It was unbelievable how badly designed the ship was. I later learned it was built in 1947.

We managed to get Eric into the hospital and on to the couch. He kept on saying he was cold. He was very stiff, his knees were bent up and he was hardly moving at all. We put a blanket over him and said soothing words: 'You're all right now, Eric. Don't worry. You're safe.'

George Carson, the medic did everything he could. He was superb. He rose completely above the disaster. His calmness when he spoke to people immediately lifted them. Unfortunately, he was totally hampered by lack of equipment. As divers, we knew that a man with bad burns needed a saline drip. But we were told there were no saline drips aboard the *Silver Pit*. There weren't even any painkillers. It was appalling.

When the medic went to attend to the two other injured men who'd been sat down on the deck, I was left alone with Eric. I could see him drifting away – he had a thousand-yard stare.

I knew he spoke very little English. Once when he'd been in Barry's office, we'd with some difficulty conversed about Grand Prix racing and about Jaguar winning the Le Mans 24-hour race.

So to try and bring him back, I said to him, 'Eric, do you remember we talked in the office about Alain Prost?'

He stopped gazing into the distance and his eyes focused on me. 'Alain Prost,' he mumbled. But as he came back and began to warm up, he started to feel the pain. He was deeply distressed and kept on trying to pull the blanket round him.

I had to force myself to stay there. Although I felt guilty about it, I didn't want to stay to witness his agony. I left as soon as I felt I could do no more. I wanted to get out on deck to help with the other survivors.

Roy Carey was the next to be taken into the cramped hospital. His wet clothes were removed, he was wrapped in a blanket and sat on the floor of the hospital.

It would be impossible to encounter a man with such spirit as Roy Carey. All the time, he kept on saying calmly, 'Don't worry about me. I'll be fine. No problems. Just leave me here. You look after the others now.' And I'd look at him sitting there smiling, with the top of his head missing. He was amazing. It'd already been a night where acts of horror had been intertwined with acts of heroism. But nowhere did I come across anything to match Roy Carey's strength of character.

Erland Grieve was then brought in and taken to sit on a bunk in one of the cabins – with two people in it, the hospital was already full!

One of the injured men asked me if I could give him a cigarette.

I don't smoke. So I went back on deck and said to one of the crew, 'Where's the bond?'

'Oh, it's round the corner there.'

'Go and get some cigarettes then.'

'No. I can't do that.'

'Why the hell not? An injured man wants a smoke.'

'But the skipper's got the key.'

'Well get the key from the skipper, open the bond and get some cigarettes.'

'Oh, no. I couldn't do that.'

That incensed me. 'Look. A seriously injured man wants a cigarette,' I said. 'Give me an axe and I'll open the bloody bond!'

I would have done it too, but one of the other crew members said, 'Here you go,' and handed me a packet of cigarettes and a lighter.

I went back to the cabins and started handing around the cigarettes. When I called into the hospital to see how Roy was, the medic said to me, 'Look at your foot.'

I looked down. The white sock on my left foot was drenched in blood. I pulled it off, had a look, couldn't see anything wrong, and put the sock back on again.

'No, no,' George said. 'My cabin's just round the corner. Go in there, take those wet clothes off, and help yourself to some of my kit. Then come back and see me. I don't want any unnecessary casualties – like you catching pneumonia.'

So I did as he said. George had a look at my foot, but there wasn't a cut or a graze. How the blood got there was a mystery.

I went out to go back on deck and, as I was passing somebody's cabin, I saw a pair of rig-boots. So I put them on. It seemed stupid to keep on walking around in socks.

When I arrived back on deck, Andy Carroll came up to me and said, 'Our Z-boat's been caught by some underwater explosion that's broken the drive and punched a hole in the boat.'

'Are the crew all right?' I asked.

'Yes. They're being picked up by one of the stand-by boats. But now we've got no Z-boat. Things are bad, Ed. We've just passed through a large area where there were both dead bodies and men hanging on to pieces of wreckage. We picked a few up, but the ones further out were waving frantically to us. I waved back from the stern to acknowledge them, but I soon lost them in the dark. It was heartbreaking,' he said. 'It's insane to have survived the fire and then to be lost in the sea. The *Silver Pit* isn't picking them up. So tell the skipper to get on the radio and say there's all these men in the water and we've got to have some help around here right away.'

I went back to the bridge and said to the skipper, 'We need to get on the radio to call more small boats.'

Once again he didn't respond. I wanted to shout at him, but I knew I couldn't afford to upset him. We needed him and he was doing his best. But the radio message was also vital. So to stay calm, I counted up to ten and then said, 'We need to get all the ships around to launch their lifeboats. There are men in the sea. I'll operate the radio. Is that OK?'

When the skipper nodded, I picked up the handset. There was a constant radio traffic between the ships. I jumped in and said, 'Break, break. This is *Silver Pit* calling all ships in the vicinity. There are many survivors floating on the surface between *Silver Pit* and Tharos. That is between the north-west area and the south-west area of the platform. Any ships with Zodiacs, lifeboats or small craft of any description, launch them and come to this area. There are many survivors in the water.'

As soon as I stopped talking, the constant hubbub or radio traffic continued. Amongst the multitudinous messages, I suddenly heard to my great delight that Dusty Miller, one of our riggers, had been picked up by the *Maersk Leader*. Another of the diving team was a survivor!

Shortly afterwards, Stan MacLeod came on to the bridge. Calmly but firmly, he said to the skipper, 'If you maintain your present position, we're going to be under that flame coming from Piper. There's a hell of a lot of poisonous, combustible gases coming off the rig and you're putting the ship in danger. Move west. Move away from under the flare. If it starts leaking H_2S, we're all going to be dead.'

So the skipper hove to.

It was crazy that we were having to do such things. There didn't appear to be anyone issuing any instructions to the crew or anybody else. Apart from the courageous sailors in the Z-boat, the only person in the crew who seemed to be taking any responsibility for organising the rescue effort was the medic. The brunt of the work was left to the dive team and other uninjured survivors.

I kept on calling into the hospital to have words with Eric, but every time I went in he was obviously in more pain. As there was no medication, the only thing we could do to make him more comfortable was to say the odd soothing word and readjust his blanket. He needed intensive care and should have been in a proper hospital. But as yet, over an hour after the first explosion, there was no sign of the first rescue helicopter.

CHAPTER FOURTEEN

THE LONGEST NIGHT

Z-boats arrived several times with more survivors. They were all suffering from burns and shivering with shock and cold. Some had suspected broken bones. As each one was brought on to the *Silver Pit*, he was wrapped in blankets.

It seemed that, apart from the first dozen or so who'd escaped from Piper uninjured, everybody else needed attention. Some were fit enough to stay in the galley, but those in a more serious condition were taken to cabins. A few were almost unconscious, while those who'd breathed in large amounts of smoke were coughing a great deal and were likely to vomit.

Because of this, I wouldn't allow anybody to be left alone in a cabin. All the divers and others were terrific, including Steve Middleton who'd had a pretty bad time. They took it in turns to sit with people and didn't leave until somebody came to relieve them. It wasn't a pleasant job, but it was really worth doing.

George Carson, the medic, continued to be superb. By his manner, he provided immense comfort and support to all the survivors. He sometimes even managed to raise a smile.

Erland Grieve, who worked for Occidental, had bad facial burns and was sitting in the cabin next to the hospital. George had earlier examined him briefly, but had been forced to move on because there were people with injuries that seemed worse. When he came round again, somebody said to him, 'What about Erland?'

The medic looked at him and said, 'Don't worry about him. He's only stayed in the sun too long anyway!'

It might easily have seemed like an uncaring thing to say about a man who'd had most of his face burned, but it helped lighten the tension. Erland looked at him, smiled broadly, and took another slow drag on his cigarette.

I continued to compile a list of all the survivors who'd been brought to the *Silver Pit* and was constantly on the look out for anybody I'd missed.

As I was dashing across the deck, one of the crew came up to me and said, 'Excuse me. Are they my boots you've got on?'

It was bizarre. Perhaps I should have told him to run away and do something useful, but instead I was very British about it and said, 'I'm terribly sorry. I'll hand them back when I've finished with them.'

'That's fine,' he said. 'You see, they cost a lot and we don't get much pay.'

Such a trivial thing at such a time seemed somehow full of pathos. But I remembered the conditions they work under and I promised him I wouldn't leave the ship wearing his boots.

About half past midnight, as there was nothing for me to do at that moment, I went into the galley to grab a cup of tea. Then I started to check through my list.

I noticed for the first time, John Barr, the diving supervisor, sitting with a blanket wrapped around him. He was with two of the divers, Tony Payne and Chris Niven. Chris had blisters on his forehead and scalp. The three men had apparently been on the *Silver Pit* for quite a time, but for some reason I hadn't noticed them.

John Barr was coughing a lot and didn't seem very well. He was, in fact, much worse than we thought, having taken in a great deal of smoke. But, because he was so disciplined about it, he wasn't being treated as one of the seriously injured.

I went over to him and said, 'Are you all right, mate?'

He nodded. I could see he was having some difficulty with his breathing.

I then said to Chris, 'What happened to you three?'

'When that second explosion came, the three of us were still on the twenty-foot level. So we jumped into the water.'

'Jesus! What the hell did you do?'

'We hung on to the bottom of the leg and just kept pushing our heads under the water for as long as we could. Then we saw one of the Z-boats. So the three of us swam off towards it.'

'I'm bloody glad to see you,' I said. 'It means there's only a handful of the dive team still missing. Did you see anything of Keith Cunningham and Barry Barber? They were both with us on the north-west corner.'

'I think Keith swam off. So I don't know where the hell he is. Barry was with us in the water. I last saw him hanging on to a rope.'

'Was he all right?'

'He appeared to be.'

As I was writing their names down, there was a prolonged groaning noise outside. Bill Lobban and Roy Thomson rushed with others to the portholes to look out. Still wrapped in flames, the whole mass of Piper was collapsing on one side. It hadn't fallen apart. The legs at the north end were giving way and so it was slowly bending over. The accommodation module was virtually touching the water. It was obviously soon going to sink into the sea. I didn't want to see it happen. I went back to work on my list.

Then I walked round checking the cabins and found that several more people had been brought on board. Bob McGregor and Mike Jennings were in bunks. Both were coughing badly. In another cabin, there was a man with chest injuries; it was Iain Duguid.

As I'd found a couple of empty cabins, I went back to the galley and said to John Barr, 'Come on, John. Come and lie down. You're better off somewhere else.'

So I led him into a cabin and took off all his wet gear.

As I was walking along the corridor, I bumped into Andy Carroll, who'd been looking after the injured. 'Did you know,' he said, 'there's a Z-boat in the stern? The crew reckon its outboard can't be started.'

'Bloody hell!' I exclaimed. 'I'll go and see about it as soon as I've sorted this out.'

When I'd finished, I went along to George and said, 'The helicopters are soon going to be lifting people off. We must liaise with Tharos to ensure our seriously injured men get away. I need to know from you who're the priorities.'

We worked out a list of about a dozen and said that the three most urgent cases were Eric, who was still drifting in and out of consciousness; Roy Carey who, despite his cheeriness, was clearly in a bad way; and Erland Grieve, who had a badly burned face and hands.

I took the list to Stan, who was on the bridge.

Then I walked round the back of the bridge and found the other Z-boat. The hull was badly blistered from the heat of the explosion, but the boat was still inflated.

So I returned to Stan and said, 'We've got another Z-boat back there. We need to get the thing launched.'

'Don't worry about it, Ed,' he said. 'I've already looked at it. The engine's useless.'

Stan then tried to raise Tharos on the radio, but the two channels – 16 and 8 – were constantly jammed with the ship traffic involved in the rescue. He jumped in as soon as he could and said, 'Tharos. We've got three seriously injured survivors who need immediate evacuation. They have burns and lung problems. Insist on priority evacuation by helicopter.' He then told them he also wanted to pass on a list of all the survivors as soon as possible.

They said they'd get back to us. But they never did.

Just then, an oil line burst in the main engine and it had to be shut down. *Silver Pit*, Piper's emergency stand-by boat, was without power and began to drift slowly towards the still-raging remains of the rig. For a time, it looked as though we might all have to jump into the sea and swim for it. Fortunately, we passed by at some distance. But the shut-down meant that George, the only medic, had to leave the sick and attend to the engine. Fortunately the survivors, Derek Ellington, Ian Ferguson and Willie Young were fitters and able to help.

We did our best for the people brought aboard, assessing their condition, and trying to organise the evacuation of those who were seriously injured. The initiative for most of this organisation continued to come from the diving team.

Stan and I discussed what we should do when the helicopters arrived. The skipper announced that he wouldn't allow anybody to be taken off from the rescue deck. So the sick would have to be carried on stretchers on to the back deck, which was the place officially designated for helicopter evacuation.

It was terrible. It meant the injured men had to be taken up and around stairs that were covered in oil from the hydraulics of the Z-boat's launching davit.

I went down into the galley and said, 'Who's able-bodied? We need to strap each of the seriously injured men into a stretcher.'

Two of the volunteers were the injured divers, Tony Payne and Chris Niven!

To my disgust, I discovered that there were only two proper

stretchers on the *Silver Pit*. So only two men could be prepared at a time. Eric, the Frenchman, was to be the first.

There then followed the time-consuming process of getting the injured men out of the cabins where they'd been installed. The design of the *Silver Pit* was ridiculous for such an emergency. A man on a stretcher is rigid and it's as difficult to move him as it is a coffin. Yet the corridors were extremely narrow and full of obstacles. So it took a lot of effort – once again, mainly on the part of the survivors and George Carson.

Somebody came running down to tell me that a helicopter was on the radio. I ran up to the bridge and took over the handset. 'This is *Silver Pit*, I said. 'We've got nine men who have serious injuries and need urgent evacuation. But there are three who're a priority.' I then told the pilot what each man's injuries were.

I went back down and checked that the first two men were being put into stretchers. Then I rushed up to the back deck – a smallish area with a yellow spot painted on it which was supposed to let the helicopter pilot recognise where he was.

The helicopter steadily came in and hovered. The winchman suddenly appeared and started descending with an orange glass-fibre stretcher. He was swaying quite a bit and bounced off the guardrail before he landed. Then, kneeling down, he pulled at the cable to make sure he'd plenty of slack.

I went up to him and said, 'The first man'll be out any second.'

When I turned round, they were already trying to manhandle Eric in the stretcher through the narrow passageway alongside the bridge. We transferred Eric to the helicopter's stretcher and strapped him in. As he was being hoisted up, I said, '*Bon voyage*, Eric. Good luck.'

I dashed back down and found that the second man, Roy Carey, was already being eased through the narrow corridors in the stretcher. He was followed by Erland Grieve, on a stretcher brought by the helicopter. The fourth man was almost ready.

As Roy Carey was being winched up, I saw a television camera pointing at me. 'That's astonishing,' I thought. 'What the hell is that doing here?'

I later discovered that Paul Berriff and a Scottish TV crew had been spending some time with the helicopter-rescue services. They just happened to be around that night when the call went out from Piper. When I eventually saw the video they'd made, I heard the pilot say at one point, 'Can't raise *Silver Pit*. Their radio doesn't appear to be working properly.' It's just as well we didn't know that at the time!

The winchman had told me that as they'd already picked up other people, there was hardly any room left in the helicopter. He was very good about it and extremely apologetic but, by the time the fourth man, Alec Rankin, was brought on to the back deck, the helicopter had gone.

Andy Carroll went to get some more blankets and we laid Alec down on the yellow spot. Having made him as comfortable as possible, Stan, Andy and I sat there and chatted to him.

He told us about the whole catalogue of scrapes he'd been through on Piper, before he'd managed to get away. At one point, he'd scrambled out of the searing heat into a container on the pipe-deck, where there were already about twenty people sheltering. Then something crashed on to the container and crushed it to a height of about four feet. Only Alec and one other man got out of there alive. After that, he jumped some one hundred and fifty feet into the sea.

As we were waiting for the helicopter, a Z-boat arrived with two more survivors. I left the back deck to check the extent of their injuries and see they were made as comfortable as possible.

They were Jim Russell and Andy Mochan, who worked for Wood Group. Both of them had burnt hands and feet. They'd had an horrific experience, being trapped for some time inside the modules. As the *Silver Pit*'s cabins were filled, we put them down below in the supposed rescue hold, which was the most uncomfortable place in the ship. With half a dozen people down there, it seemed crowded. Yet it was supposed to accommodate the entire crew of a rig. It would have been possible to squeeze them in only if none was injured. Even then, it would have been like the Black Hole of Calcutta.

I went off and asked George to go down to check them over. Then I saw they had a cup of tea and cigarettes.

When I went back on deck, I realised we'd been waiting an incredible time for the helicopter. Yet there were several of them flying about.

By this time, Stan was looking very green. He'd already said to me, 'Ed. I'm afraid my secret's out. I suffer from chronic seasickness! I'll do everything I can, but I'm going to have to stay out in the fresh air.' Despite this, he'd consistently done a magnificent job, keeping his eye on the skipper and what was happening on deck.

I decided to go onto the bridge and call Tharos. But then I spotted a helicopter close by, combing the sea for survivors. I picked up the radio and said, 'Helicopter, helicopter, helicopter, 300 metres off the starboard bow of *Silver Pit*. We've got several seriously injured people who need medivaccing urgently. Can you handle it? Do you copy?'

There was a brief pause, a click, and then the clear middle-class tones of an RAF pilot said, '*Silver Pit*, *Silver Pit*. This is Rescue 131. Please give details of your injured.'

I gave him the details.

'Message understood,' he said. 'Will come to the stern of your vessel and put the winchman on board. 'Fraid we're very short of space. Will take what we can.'

I rushed to the back deck to prepare for the helicopter's arrival. As it approached, the winchman was at the end of the cable. He pointed to something. Actually, he was showing us where he was going to land, but I thought he was pointing to what seemed to be a long dangling rope. Assuming it was meant to help hold him in the right position, I grabbed hold of what turned out to be the earthing strap and received a massive belt of static electricity.

This winchman was far less amenable than the earlier one. The first thing he said to me was, 'We're already topped up with dead bodies and so I hope you haven't got too many.'

I thought, 'Oh, well. I'll give him the benefit of the doubt. He looks as though he's had a hell of a time.' So I said, 'Look, there are some men who've really got to go. We'll get them here as soon as possible.'

The RAF helicopter took off the seven men we regarded as being in need of urgent medical attention.

Once that had been done, I began to feel more relaxed. I walked off the back deck, beside the bridge, intending to go to the galley for a cup of tea. But then, looking around the rescue deck, I realised there was nobody there keeping watch.

So I went into the galley and said, 'We ought to arrange a rota, fellers, so there's always somebody on deck looking for survivors. I'm happy to start. Is there anybody who'd like to come outside with me for twenty minutes?'

Everybody got the message and from then on there were at least half a dozen men on deck, keeping watch all the time.

When I'd organised that, I went down to spend some time with the injured men. I couldn't bear to be doing nothing. It just seemed ludicrous for me, being fit and able, to sit chatting in the galley.

By the time I went back on deck, we'd drifted quite a way from Piper, but the flames and the constant roar were an ever-present reminder of what had happened. As the *Silver Pit*'s engines were still shut down, were were no longer playing an active part in the rescue operation. But the sea was being constantly swept by the piercing searchlights of the helicopters and the other ships.

It was only then that I realised that the *Silver Pit*'s searchlights had never been switched on. So I went onto the bridge and said, 'Put on the searchlights.'

'We haven't got any,' the skipper replied.

Another astonishment! 'Well, what have you got?'

'There's a signal lamp.'

'I'll have it.'

When it was produced, I saw it had only a very short lead. So it had to be operated from close to the bridge. I switched it on and played it over the water to see if I could see any other survivors.

But we didn't pick up anybody else. Occasionally, we spotted things in the water at a distance and I'd call up a helicopter to say what we'd seen.

As we kept watch, Stan and I stood chatting – especially about our friends on Piper who might not have made it. What had happened to Barry Barber, Lens, Budweiser, Keith Cunningham?

'What a bloody industry this is!' Stan said.

As I nodded in agreement, I happened to catch sight of something shiny sticking out of his pocket. It was his patent lung-tester! 'You bastard! I don't believe it! You went back for that, didn't you?'

For the first time since we'd arrived on the *Silver Pit*, we laughed.

Later, Gareth joined us and talked quietly about what had happened to him that night. He'd been the diver in the water at the time of the first explosion.

At the start of his dive, he'd descended in the bell to a depth of fifty feet. There, he made his way to the flooded member, which he began to clean with the grit-gun. All the time, he was in constant communication over the intercom with John Barr, the diving supervisor. After he'd been working for about three quarters of an hour, Gareth heard a bang and saw a white flash to the west. Immediately, he thought the grit-gun had burst. When he checked, he found it hadn't. Then ten seconds later, there was another similar bang and flash.

Over the intercom, John Barr said, 'Leave everything and make your way back to the bell.'

Gareth knew that something was wrong, but didn't have a clue what it was. The diving procedure in an emergency is not to give any details to the diver in the water so he won't be unnecessarily alarmed.

He left everything and swam back as fast as he could to the bell. As he did so, he was aware that his heavy umbilical cord was not being retrieved. This was usually done by a manually operated hydraulic sheave. He passed on this information to John Barr.

Half-way back to the bell, the umbilical cord began to be jerkily retrieved. So it was obvious it was being done by hand. That was extremely disturbing. If the power to the hydraulics sheave had gone for any reason, there was always a back-up source of power that should have been used. But that appeared to have failed as well.

When Gareth had returned to the bell, he informed John Barr of his position and that he was ready to ascend. As the bell was being raised, John Barr told Gareth he was in 'free time', which meant he hadn't been underwater for long enough to need decompression on the surface.

The diving bell arrived on the dive-skid, and Gareth was helped out of all his diving gear, apart from his wet suit. He was then told by somebody he had to go into one of the decompression chambers. The surfaced diver has very little time in which to start decompression and so Gareth didn't argue. He knew he'd had an emergency ascent.

As he approached the two chambers, he saw that the entrance door of the one facing east appeared to have been blown off its mountings inwards. To do that must have taken a tremendous force – the door was made of inch thick solid steel and was on heavy hinges. Without really thinking what might have caused the accident, he entered the other chamber. Then he discovered its interior light wasn't working.

Gareth had been inside the decompression chamber for less than two minutes when he saw John Barr at the porthole, indicating that he was going to be taken out. After a short delay, the door opened and Gareth stepped out of the chamber. As he did so, a cloud of black smoke billowed towards him and through the grating above the dive module he could see flames. Streams of burning oil were running on to the dive skid. Although nobody was panicking, Gareth felt that the people around him were lost for words and appeared to be in a state of shock.

'Perhaps we were,' Stan said. 'And no wonder. I was most aware of the pools of blazing oil spreading towards us and the burning oil pouring on the oxygen bottles. As I was opening all the taps on the chamber trying to get you out, the depth gauge appeared to be static. I thought the chamber was never going to open. I just wondered if, when the whole thing went up, it'd hurt.'

After passing through an immense amount of smoke, Stan, John and Gareth eventually made their way to the north-east corner. Gareth, still wearing his hot water suit, and Stan followed me down the rope on to the spider deck. They were both with me in the first group to be taken off by the Z-boat and transferred to the *Silver Pit*.

It'd been a nightmare for all of us and there had been many miraculous escapes – but none more so than Gareth's, who pointed out that he owed his survival in great measure to the professionalism of his colleagues, the divers who had stayed to winch him up and especially John Barr and Stan MacLeod.

Just after half-past three, as Stan, Gareth and I stood beside the bridge of the *Silver Pit*, the sun came up over the horizon. It was somehow astonishing to see a brighter light than Piper appearing in the sky. As dawn broke, I became aware that a whole fleet of ships had come to the scene. As far as I could see, there were vessels of all shapes and sizes patiently combing the sea. It seemed oddly peaceful.

It was then that I was suddenly struck by a feeling that my father had been with me, keeping an eye on me, throughout the whole experience. It may seem to be a most fanciful idea – he'd been dead for almost ten years – but it was very real to me at that moment.

Then, for the umpteenth time that night, I wondered if there was any way Vicky might have heard there'd been a disaster on Piper that night. It was obviously unlikely – it had happened too late for all the major television news programmes. So I began to hope we'd arrive back in Aberdeen before she got up and heard the news. I felt convinced, however, that instinctively she'd know that I was all right.

But my mother was a different matter altogether. She had a

nervous disposition and a heart condition. If she found out about the accident, it would be seriously not OK. It was really important she received the message that I was fine before she was told what had happened to Piper. Yet it was impossible to do anything about it. There was no way I could get to a telephone. The only thing I could do was to hope the list of survivors on the *Silver Pit* we'd sent to Tharos had been passed on.

Suddenly, about four o'clock in the morning, George managed to repair the engines. We immediately contacted Tharos, who suggested we sailed straight into Aberdeen. There was no way any of us wanted to do that. Even if the engines held out, it would take many tedious hours to sail all that way, so I said, 'Isn't it possible to have a basket-transfer to Tharos?'

The idea didn't excite the skipper. 'It's really hard to manoeuvre the boat,' he said. 'Basket-transfers are a great problem. And what about the injured men? They canne be gi'en a basket-transfer.'

'Well, let's think again,' I said.

I spoke to Tharos and they said they were sending a Z-boat over with a doctor to see the seriously injured men. It was then suggested it might be possible to transfer us all by Z-boats to a supply boat. As that could be manoeuvred more easily, we could then be transferred on by basket to Tharos.

As we steamed closer to Tharos and the wreck of Piper, we began passing through the pathetic flotsam of hard hats, charred pieces of furniture, dozens of plastic storage bins, the occasional lifebelt, books and pieces of paper – all the things you might expect to see after the destruction of an oil rig.

A Z-boat arrived with two doctors who were taken down to have a look at the injured. They decided a couple of the men would have to be taken off by helicopter and set about arranging that with Tharos.

Shortly afterwards, a Z-boat arrived with the three men who'd been the crew of the *Silver Pit*'s Z-boat that had rescued me and the others. After their boat had been damaged, they in their turn had been rescued. Now, seeing us, they had looks of quiet satisfaction on their faces. And so they should. They'd done some tremendous work and certainly saved many lives, including my own. I thanked them as warmly as I could.

Piper was a terrible sight. Although there was still an immense amount of flame and smoke, virtually nothing was left apart from A Module. Off the east side, sticking out of the sea, was a substantial, unidentifiable piece of wreckage. I took some binoculars from the bridge down on to the deck so that anybody who wanted to could have a closer look.

All around were dozens of boats, following regular search patterns. We kept on recognising ones from our past – supply boats we'd known, diving-support vessels, the massive *Iolair* which was BP's emergency support vessel, and the *British Enterprise III* on which Mike Toy, a close friend of mine, was the photo technician. I knew he'd be somewhere on deck looking out for me – worried sick. I tried to find him with the binoculars. There was a whole group of people standing on the bridge and I just knew he'd be amongst them, but I couldn't pick him out.

As we approached Tharos, the Z-boat that had brought out the doctors reappeared. Being aware of Stan's sea-sickness, I said to him, 'You take the forward end of the party and I'll take up the rear. You can then be sure you hand over the list of survivors. Otherwise, we're going to have many unnecessarily worried wives, come breakfast-time.'

I went down to George's cabin and tied my wet clothes in a blanket. Then carrying this ethnic bundle, I went back on deck.

We organised life-jackets for everybody and it took four or five runs in the Z-boat to transfer us all to the supply boat. I made sure I was the last of the survivors due to leave the *Silver Pit*. Just before I transferred into the Z-boat, I took off the boots I'd borrowed and handed them back to their owner. I then put on a pair of flip-flops somebody gave me.

When I reached the supply boat, clambering out of the Z-boat was one of the most dangerous things I'd done all night. In the heavy swell, it was bashing against the ship's side and the ladder we had to use was shooting up and down. It was a nightmare.

When I at last got up the ladder, still carrying my bundle, the supply boat's crew was waiting with blankets. There were cups of tea and sticky buns everywhere.

I waited to make sure everybody from the *Silver Pit* had been transferred by basket on to Tharos and then I went up on the last run. On every other basket-transfer I'd done, I'd stood on the outside of the ring, holding on to the netting. But, on this occasion, we were gently escorted into the middle – which was normally absolutely taboo – and four men on the outside linked round to keep us protected.

On Tharos, another group of people was standing there with blankets, waiting to receive us. Every survivor was led away by an escort. As I stepped out, the first person I saw was Martin Richmond, an old friend of mine.

When he saw me, his jaw dropped and he said, 'Ed. Where the hell have you been?'

'Just on a quick excursion from Piper. What are you doing here?'

'Working. I came to pilot the flying bell. We should have been under Piper two hours before it all happened, but – thank Christ! – we were held back.'

It was great at last to be on something approaching terra firma. Even though the sea hadn't been rough, the *Silver Pit* had done a mighty lot of bobbing about.

Martin walked with me up a flight of stairs into the hospital. An orderly asked my name and he ticked it off on his list.

'Any injuries?'

'No.'

I was then waved through the hospital to the cinema. All the seats had been cleared and people were handing out mugs of tea. We were told that we'd soon be taken off but, if we wanted a meal, we should go down to the galley.

Stan and I wandered down there and to our astonishment met Keith Cunningham. Unlike the rest of us, he was clean and wearing crisp new overalls. Although his face showed signs of shock, his clothes were immaculate.

'What happened to you?' we asked.

'Well, I was with Tony Payne, Barry, Chris and the other guys. When there was that big explosion, we all jumped into the sea. It was just so hot I couldn't believe it. I was sure the sea was on fire. So I just swam under water. I swam and swam and swam, until I couldn't swim any longer. Then I came up, took a breath and did the same thing again and again. The third time I came up for breath, I realised the sea couldn't be on fire – otherwise I wouldn't be taking in any air. So I looked around. Piper was like a fireball and the air about me was still incredibly hot. So I swam to Tharos.'

'What!'

'Yes. I just swam here.'

'And what about your boots'

'I kicked those off half-way across.'

'So what happened when you arrived?'

'I saw some ladders going up the legs. I climbed up one of them and appeared on deck. A group of blokes was standing there looking at me. They said, ''Where have you come from?''

"I've just swum from Piper." "Bloody hell!" they said. And that was it. I must have been the first one to arrive on Tharos.'

'But it was over five hundred metres.'

'That's not so far,' he said.

'And what about the others?' I asked. 'Is there any news of Barry Barber?'

'No. Nothing as yet.'

As I didn't feel like eating, I went up to the radio room. There they had computer listings of all our names and addresses with asterisks marking those who'd been picked up. I was extremely impressed to see something so superior to the handwritten scraps of paper I'd been dealing with all night.

'Is Barry Barber on your list?' I asked.

They checked through and said, 'No. Sorry.'

I asked if I could look through the list and they handed it over. There were surprisingly few asterisks. Against many of the names I knew, there was nothing but an ominous blank space: Barry Barber, Brian 'Lens' Lithgow, David Wiser, and four of our riggers – Carl Mearns, Michael Short, Kenneth Stephenson and Bryan Ward. Another, Michael Bradley, was listed as rescued but injured. I later learned he was badly burned.

Only sixty-three men had been rescued from Piper Alpha. Of these, thirty-seven had been on the *Silver Pit*.

As I handed back the list, the radio operator said, 'The chopper will be here in five minutes.'

'Fine,' I said. 'I'll make sure I don't miss it.'

It was almost half-past six.

On the mainland, people would soon be waking up to the accounts and photographs of the Piper Alpha tragedy that dominated the television news and front pages of the daily newspapers. In Aberdeen especially, people would be stunned and horrified by what had happened. Many had sons, relatives, friends or neighbours working on the rig. In Aberdeen, everybody knew or knew of someone who was lost.

CHAPTER FIFTEEN

GOING HOME

After leaving the radio room on Tharos, I again bumped into Martin Richmond and asked him what things had been like on Tharos, after the explosion.

'Pretty grim', he said. 'As soon as possible, they evacuated almost everybody from here, apart from the divers. We were the only people deemed fit to deal with the dead bodies. They've been bringing them in all night. About a dozen of them are still in the hangar.'

'And Piper?'

'That really was horrific – watching all those men, running out on the pipe-deck and climbing up the drilling derrick to get away from the flames. One man even edged his way along a gas-flare boom. And there was nothing we could do for him, apart from scream, "Jump!" After the big explosion, there was no sign of him. Many of the others had also disappeared. The fireball started coming towards us and so Tharos had to be rapidly moved back.' Others later told me that the heat was so intense that the fire monitors had to be sprayed on to the deck, because the gases stored there were in danger of exploding. Another vessel apparently just winched all its gas cylinders over the side and dumped them into the sea.

We were interrupted by an announcement coming over the Tannoy to say that the helicopter had arrived. Martin and I said goodbye and I went to the helideck to join the party of survivors.

There wasn't enough room for all of us. Stan said I should go with the first group and he would travel with the next one. As I climbed into the Sikorski helicopter, I was again surprised to see a television crew there. It was, in fact, the same one I'd seen earlier, but at the time I began to have the feeling there were cameras everywhere.

As we took off, I suddenly realised something was missing. I'd left behind on Tharos the bundle of my clothes I'd so carefully carried with me from the *Silver Pit*.

On the flight, everybody else seemed dazed and subdued. But after hours of constant activity, I couldn't bear suddenly having to sit and do nothing. I kept on nudging people and pointing at things through the window, including a five-legged rig, just like the Alexander Kielland. Then we passed over what seemed to be a whole fleet of warships, heading towards Piper.

After about an hour, we saw land for the first time. It was so beautiful – fresh, green and lush. I knew then that life would never be the same again. Whatever happened, I'd just been through a born-again experience.

Within a minute or so of our landfall, we flew right over Occidental's headquarters. Irrationally perhaps, it seemed as if there should have been something different about it, that in some hardly perceptible way it would have changed. But it was exactly the same as it'd always been.

Instead of landing at the heliport, we were taken straight to Aberdeen Royal Infirmary. As we came down, I saw a row of five brand new ambulances waiting, looking extremely impressive with their built-in emergency lights.

When the door of the helicopter was opened, nurses and ambulancemen rushed forward with blankets and stretchers. But they weren't needed. Although some of the group had burns and other injuries, we were all able to walk.

Stepping on to the ground, I was struck with how wonderful the earth smelt. I beamed with pleasure. Then there was a blinding flash and I turned round to see the battery of film-cameras and photographers.

We were taken by ambulance to the hospital. 'Have you had many survivors in?' I asked the driver.

'A few,' he replied. 'But not dozens by any means.'

After a very short journey, we arrived at the front of the hospital. We walked in past a crowd of silent relatives, standing there, hoping their loved one would be amongst us.

Inside, the staff was all geared up to process us. First, a young woman had a seemingly endless list of names and addresses. She asked each of us who we were and handed us an identity bracelet to put round our wrist. It was then that I discovered I'd given the wrong address when I first went to work on Piper.

We were then directed further on into the hospital.

'Can I have a telephone?' I asked.

'Not till we know you're all right.'

'Please!'

'No. After.'

I went where I'd been directed. An extremely attractive doctor whisked me into a room and said, 'And what's the matter with you?'

'Nothing.'

'Nothing?'

'Oh, I had a bloody sock. I had a look at my foot, but couldn't find a cut or anything.'

'Let me have a look.'

I pulled off my flip-flop and sock. She wasn't very impressed by my foot. There was obviously nothing wrong with it.

She asked me if I'd breathed in any water or smoke. When I told her I hadn't, she said, 'You appear to be all right. Go and get a cup of tea.'

'Can I use a telephone first?'

The doctor called a staff nurse, who took me into a small office where there was a telephone on the desk.

I phoned Vicky who was terribly distressed. I told her she wasn't to worry. I was fine. Then I briefly explained what had happened.

Vicky said she'd heard the news that Piper had blown up on the radio at seven o'clock. She'd immediately called Occidental on the ordinary line, not the emergency number given out on the news. When the girl on the switchboard answered, Vicky said, 'My husband's on Piper. I want to know if he's OK.'

Vicky was connected to the emergency office and said, 'I'm Mrs Punchard. My husband's Ed Punchard and he's on Piper.'

There was a pause and then a voice said, 'Your husband is on our list of survivors.'

Vicky said she'd been fine up to that point, but that comment made her realise that, if there were survivors, there were also people who hadn't survived. She then began to cry, because she had no way of knowing whether or not I was badly injured.

A few minutes later, she received a call from David Jenkins, the safety manager of Stena. He told her that Piper had blown up and, unfortunately, he didn't know what had happened to me.

'It's all right,' Vicky said. 'He's on the list of survivors. Occidental told me.'

'Fantastic. We didn't know. Occidental are refusing to give information to anyone other than relatives.'

'But surely you should know! You're his employer.'

'You would have thought so, but Occidental must have their reasons.'

Before I rang off, I asked Vicky to phone my mother and break the the news to her gently.

As I'd been due to go on leave that day, I'd already arranged as usual to spend the night in Aberdeen with my friend Chip Scott and his girlfriend, Jean Lornie, who'd worked in the Comex office for years. I'd have normally phoned them up the night before, just to confirm the arrangements. But, of course, I hadn't been able to make that call.

So after speaking to Vicky, I called Comex and was put through to Jean Lornie.

'Jean,' I said, 'it's Ed.'

'Where the hell have you been?' she exclaimed. 'I was expecting to hear from you last night. I didn't know whether you were coming in or not.'

'Jean, haven't you heard?'

'Heard what?'

'Piper blew up last night. There're a hundred and eighty men missing.'

'Jesus Christ!' she gasped, obviously deeply shocked. 'Where are you?'

'At the hospital.'

'I'll be there.'

'No, no. Wait. They're probably going to take us up to the Skean Dhu in a short while. So why don't you go up there? Maybe, you could bring me some clothes, 'cause I'm wearing somebody else's wrecked boiler suit and it's full of holes.'

'Are you all right?'

'Don't worry about me. I'm fine.'

It transpired that she was the only person working at Comex who didn't know about the accident. She'd heard nothing about it before she'd left home. When she arrived at work, her boss, knowing that she and I were friends, asked her how she felt.

'There's nothing wrong with me,' Jean replied and walked on into her office.

As she obviously didn't know about the tragedy, her boss and the rest of the employees decided to say nothing to her about it, in the hope they'd first receive news that I was among the survivors.

Meanwhile, her boyfriend and my close friend, Chip Scott, had switched on breakfast-time television and heard the news. He'd spent the next half-hour getting the engaged tone from the emergency telephone number. It was only when Jean phoned him that he found out I'd survived.

After I'd finished making my calls in the office, I went for a cup of tea. By that time, Stan MacLeod had arrived. I sat next to him and had a chat, mainly about the vast number of men who were missing.

I also told him about my conversation with Vicky. As I was speaking about the call from David Jenkins, we realised that Stena probably still didn't know the fate of their employees.

'We'd better phone them now,' Stan said and we walked back to the office with the telephone.

Stan had been around a long time. He'd been diving for twenty-three years and so he'd started in the business long before there was a North Sea oil industry. In his time, he'd witnessed his fair share of tragedies.

He phoned Stena and asked to speak to Dave Reid, the projects manager. After he'd been put through, he said, 'Hello, Dave. This is Stan. We're back in the hospital. Most of the team got off safely, but not all. I'll give you a list of the known survivors: Edward Amaira, John Barr, Michael Bradley, Andrew Carroll, Keith Cunningham, David Elliott, Brian Jackson, Alastair Mackay, Stephen Middleton, Dusty Miller, Christopher Niven, Gareth Parry-Davies, Tony Payne, Edwin Punchard, Noel Ralph, Joseph Wells, John Wood and myself. That means five men from the team are still missing.'

Listening to his calm, clear voice, slowly reading out that roll-call, was one of the most moving experiences in my life.

After Stan had finished, I phoned my mother. Vicky had already spoken to her and so she'd adjusted to what had happened. 'That's all right, Ed,' she said. 'I know you're fine. Don't worry about me. I've just switched on the radio and I can hear they're talking about it, but I haven't had time to take it in. You just look after yourself now.'

When we arrived back in the waiting room, we discovered that most of the men had been put into taxis and taken to the Skean Dhu. They said there'd be another taxi for us and so we made our way towards the front entrance.

As we were walking along the corridor, a man came up to me and asked if I had any news of a man he named. It was his brother.

I'd never even heard the name. So I asked, 'Who does he work for?'

'Bawden International,' he replied.

'I'm terribly sorry, but I've heard nothing about him. But there are more helicopters on the way. Perhaps he'll be on one of those.'

The man was very calm, though subdued. 'Thanks,' he said, 'and good luck.'

By the time we'd reached the front door, a minibus had arrived, driven by a uniformed chauffeur. Stan, Noel Ralph, Brian Jackson and I got in with a couple of other men and, as we drove along, we just sat there and talked. Barry Barber, Lens and the lost riggers came into our conversation many times.

'I just can't understand it,' I said. 'Of all people, I thought that Barry would get off. He was just that kind of man. He'd been around for so long and had so many great stories. I keep on expecting to bump into him and for him to come out with some elaborate yarn about how he escaped.'

'He smoked too many of those menthol cigarettes,' Stan said quietly. 'He just wasn't as fit as he looked.'

Eventually, we arrived at the Skean Dhu. In the car park, a man was dithering around trying to back out his Rolls-Royce. For some reason, this unnecessary delay infuriated us and we all started bellowing at him to get out of the way.

When he'd completed his eighteen-point turn, we drove up to the hotel entrance and clambered out of the minibus. There were a few photographers waiting by the front door. They snapped away busily as we walked past them into the hotel.

We were directed to the bar area, which was also the place where the hotel guests ate their breakfast. So we arrived, scruffy and bedraggled, amongst a group of people in their best clothes eating bacon and eggs. On the floor, in a corner of the room, was a large heap of blue holdalls, all covered in dust. Beside them was a pile of brand new rig-boots, packed in cardboard boxes.

'Take one of these each,' we were told.

On the holdalls was a label. It said, 'Survivors' Clothing – 1 set'. The penny dropped. Somewhere, there was a warehouse-full of the kit needed after an oil-rig emergency. When something untoward happened, an order was placed, a lorry was laden and the stuff was dumped on to the floor of an hotel bar.

Inside each of the bags was a Javelin jacket, thermal trousers, a set of orange overalls and a pair of thermal socks. Trying to find the right sizes, we scrabbled over the contents, like a good-natured crowd at a charity bazaar – much to the bemusement of the people still trying to eat their breakfasts.

'I don't like the colour of these boots,' I heard one man say. 'Has anybody seen some dark-red ones?'

We'd each sorted out a set of clothes, when an assistant manager from the hotel came along and said, 'We've reserved three rooms for you so you can use the showers and telephones. If you'll follow me, I'll take you to them.'

We went with him to the rooms, where we took it in turns to clean ourselves up. After everybody had finished with the telephones, we wandered back to the bar area in our bright-orange overalls.

Then we sat about waiting for the debriefings that had been arranged. As nothing seemed to be happening, I collared a passing waiter and said, 'I want a trolley with two pots of coffee on it, two jugs of orange juice with ice and a crate of Coca-Cola.'

When the trolley arrived, we sat there luxuriating in the pleasure of an ice-cold drink. Just as when I'd seen the land for the first time while flying back from Tharos, it was a most wonderful experience. I'd never ever tasted Coke like it.

Shortly afterwards, Dave Jenkins, the safety manager from Stena, arrived with Andrea, who was Dave Reid's extremely attractive secretary. Seeing her again was yet another new experience. I was just overwhelmed by her beauty.

'Andrea,' I said, 'you look bloody gorgeous!'

Everybody knew exactly what I meant. It wasn't a crass, sexist comment. It was the heartfelt reaction of a man who was glad to be alive.

One of the hotel's receptionists came over to us and said, 'There's somebody here for a Mr Ed Punchard.' So I went along with her and saw Chip and Jean. They rushed up to me and gave me a big hug. Both of them were in tears.

'Good God,' I said to them. 'You look as though you need a drink!'

It was wonderful to see them. We hung on to each other for a while and then I took them back into the bar and introduced them to the others. After they'd had a coffee, Chip said, 'I've got the clothes for you outside in the car. We'll go out and fetch them.'

'That's all right,' I said. 'I'll come with you.'

As soon as we walked out of the front door, a dozen television cameras were switched on and a herd of journalists jammed microphones up to my face. 'What was it like? What was it like? What's your name? How did you escape? What caused the accident? How many of your friends are dead?'

It was an incredible shock. Not expecting to see them there, I had nothing to say and so I mumbled inanely, 'I can't say anything until I've spoken to my company.' Then I retreated back inside. It was astonishing that, when we'd arrived, there'd been only a small handful of photographers. Now the world's news-hawks had swooped down on the Skean Dhu.

As I was hurrying past the reception desk, I was called to the telephone. It was Doug Renwick, calling from Occidental.

'Are you OK?' he asked. 'I've only just found out.'

I said I was, briefly reported what had happened and told him there was no news of either Lens or Barry. He was obviously very upset by the tragedy. At one point he said, 'Honestly, Ed, I'd have been devastated if you hadn't come through. I brought you along on the contract and so, if you'd been killed, it would have been my responsibility.'

When I'd finished the call, Chip and Jean had returned. Mike Toy had been staying with them before he went out on the *British Enterprise III*, and so they'd brought along a load of his clothes.

'Poor Mike,' I said, 'I saw his ship close to Piper. He must be desperate not knowing what's happened to me, and here I am about to put on his clothes.'

'Don't worry about Mike,' Jean said. 'You go and get changed and I'll arrange for him to be sent a telex with the good news.'

So off I went. It was blissful to put on clean, newly pressed clothes. I then returned to the bar and rejoined the others – all still wearing their orange overalls. In response to a few whistles and cat-calls, I gave a quick twirl and said, 'Come on fellers. This is what all the best-dressed survivors are wearing this year!'

I was soon called to give a statement to Grampian Police. I

sat down at one of the tables set out in a large hotel room and related to a delightful policewoman what I'd seen and done the previous night.

As I walked out, I was met by the man with the wad of money who, I'd been told, turned up after the '84 explosion.

'What do you need for immediate expenses?' he asked. 'We'll be providing you with an air ticket home.'

'Sixty quid will be fine,' I replied and he handed it over without question.

'What's your best route home?'

'Via London and Newquay.'

'Your tickets will be here soon,' he said and moved off to deal with the next man.

I then went to the hotel lobby, where I gave exactly the same statement to an Occidental representative.

While I was doing so, Chip was continually supplying me with very large whiskies.

'But I'd rather have a Coke,' I protested.

'Drink the Scotch!' he insisted.

As soon as I'd completed my second statement, I was handed my air ticket. Six of us were going on the same flight south. Steve Middleton, the diver, and I were flying on from London to the West Country, although Steve was going only as far as Plymouth.

There were a couple of hours to kill before departure. So a group of us, including Chip and Jean, repaired to the hotel bar and had a few more drinks.

Then the journalists filtered in with notebooks and pocket tape-recorders clasped in their hands.

By that time, Gareth had drunk quite a lot and in his gentle South African accent he called out to one of them, 'Come over here, man. Sit down. This diver-hero'll talk to you,' he said, pointing to Chris Niven. 'What paper are you from?'

'The *Daily Mail*,' the journalist replied, sitting down between me and Chris.

He asked his first question and Chris was about to answer when Gareth slapped a hand over his mouth. 'The kid doesn't say a thing,' he said, 'until you buy us a round of drinks!'

The man from the *Daily Mail* seemed quite reluctant, but we sat there in silence until he'd wandered off and brought back the drinks. Then we talked to him.

At various times, people from Stena and Occidental called in but, seeing the speed at which the alcohol was being consumed, didn't stay long.

Eventually, the time came for us to catch the one o'clock flight. I phoned up Vicky to let her know what time I'd be arriving at Newquay. She said she'd be there and that many friends had already phoned to enquire if I was safe.

After I'd said goodbye to Chip and Jean, a taxi took the six of us who were London-bound to the airport. Rather than going the usual way, we were taken up to the security gate, which was immediately opened, then behind the aeroplane and to a back door in the terminal building. A stewardess was there to meet us and escort us straight into the VIP lounge. We sat there for a while, chatting and drinking much-needed cups of coffee.

When the plane was loaded, we were taken to it, where we were given the front row of seats. The cabin staff was superb. As soon as we sat down, they began plying us with drinks and continued to do so throughout the entire flight. As we were getting off, they filled our pockets with miniature bottles of whisky and gin.

At Heathrow, we were greeted by British Airways 'meet-and-assist' personnel, who arranged for the collection of our baggage and took Steve Middleton and me to the next bay where the western flight had been specially held for us.

Once again, the cabin staff were incredibly kind to us. Half-way through the flight, a stewardess came along and said, 'We've had messages from the airports at both Plymouth and Newquay to say that there are some journalists there. If you'd rather not speak to them, we'll arrange for somebody to take you past them.'

We thanked her and said we were both prepared to have a word with the press.

At Plymouth, Steve left the plane. It then flew on to Newquay, which is actually RAF St Mawgan, a Nimrod base. At the time, the runway was being refurbished. That didn't really matter to the plane we were in. It was so small that, at a pinch, it could have landed and taken off across the runway. But it meant that, instead of taxiing up to the terminal building, the plane had to touch down some distance away. Buses then took the passengers to the arrival lounge.

When we landed, I was told to get off first. Waiting for me was a car and the terminal manager. He said to me, 'Your wife and family are here to meet you. There're also some photographers and a TV crew from TSW. I've told them that, if you're not prepared to speak to them, I'll just drive straight past. They're not to hassle you or chase after you.'

'I don't mind about the TV crew,' I said. 'As long as they let me have ten minutes alone with my wife.'

He then switched on his walkie-talkie and relayed what I'd said to the people from TSW.

'They've agreed to that,' he said. 'They'll leave you alone until you've had some time with your family.'

I was driven to the airport terminal. Vicky rushed out to greet me and we embraced. It was absolutely delightful to be with her again and to hold Suzie, my little daughter, in my arms.

As we were walking to the entrance, I saw a television camera on the ground. Assuming it'd been left there by the waiting TSW crew, I thought no more about it.

Inside, Vicky handed me a fluorescent-green badge, on which was stamped the words, 'ENJOY LIFE. THIS IS NOT A REHEARSAL'. It was just right! The two of us chatted and hugged each other for ten minutes or so. Then some journalists came up, took some photographs and asked a few questions. Both Vicky and I were also interviewed by the reporter from TSW.

Driving home, we chattered away. I described what had happened to me and then Vicky told me about the people who'd phoned.

'The differences in their approach were fascinating,' she said. 'The first call was from Linda whose opening words were, "Is he dead?" I really appreciated that directness. Faffing around wasn't appropriate.'

One of the people who'd called was John Brooke, who'd been due to arrive on Piper that day to be my relief, while I was on my fortnight's leave. He'd said that he and his wife would like to pop round that evening to see how I was.

It was six o'clock by the time we arrived home. It was wonderful, incredible even, to be back there with Vicky and Suzie.

An hour later, John Brooke arrived with his wife and four bottles of wine which they obviously intended to ensure we drank that night. So we sat down and had some supper together.

That morning, John had set off at the crack of dawn on the first London train so he'd be able to catch the early flight to Aberdeen. When the train arrived at Reading, he'd heard a Tannoy announcement: 'Will John Brooke report to the station master's office immediately.'

'That's funny,' John thought. 'There's somebody else in this station with my name.' I took a few seconds before it sank in that the message must be for him. So he collected his bags and hurried off the train to the station master's office.

He was told that his wife had rung to say there'd been a serious accident on Piper and that he'd better phone Stena before going any further. The news didn't alarm him greatly, but he rang Stena just in case.

'Don't bother coming up,' they told him.'

'But it's no bother. I'm on my way.'

'Look, John. There isn't a Piper Alpha any more. Nobody is going to be working there. So don't bother coming up.'

Deeply shocked, he went to the booking office, bought a ticket and caught the next train back to Cornwall.

He and his wife were clearly still very upset – possibly much more so than Vicky and I.

As we were chatting, friends, relatives and journalists phoned constantly. It was lovely to receive calls from friends, some of whom I hadn't seen for years. I noticed their calls seemed to fall into categories. One group said, 'We knew Ed was on Piper,' even though most had no possible way of knowing any such thing. Then there were others who called out of curiosity, chatted for a time and then said, 'You must be glad you weren't on Piper.'

All three of my brothers called. Like everybody else involved in the North Sea oil industry that hadn't actually seen Piper ablaze, Bernie and Dave were devastated by the television pictures – initially far more than the people who were there.

My eldest brother, Bill, phoned later from the United States, where he'd lived for years.

'How did you hear about it?' I asked.

'You'd never guess,' he replied and then told me how he'd received the news. There was something wrong with his telephone earlier in the day. My mother tried to call him repeatedly. She'd decided it wasn't good enough not being able to get through and so she'd rung the international operator who connected her to the police department in Sudbury, Massachusetts, where my brother lived. She told the policeman who answered precisely what he was to do and what message he was to take.

Bill heard a knock on his door. When he opened it, he saw a police car outside and a policeman was standing at the door.

'Don't worry, sir,' the cop said. 'But there's a message from your mother in England. I'll read it to you. ''Your younger brother, Ed, has been in the worst ever offshore oil-field disaster. He survived a burning inferno, being dragged through the sea and a major rescue operation. He is uninjured and all is well. Love, Mum." '

That sounded just like my mother!

During the evening, the four of us also watched the television coverage of Piper on both BBC and ITV. It was peculiar to see myself, loading people onto stretchers that were being winched into a helicopter.

When the announcer explained that the footage had been taken by a television crew compiling a documentary on the rescue service, I realised why I'd seen the camera aboard the helicopter taking the injured off the *Silver Pit*.

Most unexpected of all was the coverage on the regional television programme. It showed Vicky and I embracing each other on my arrival at Newquay airport – the one thing the TWS crew had promised not to film. The camera I'd seen on the floor outside the terminal building had obviously been positioned and left switched on. Fortunately, after the event I didn't mind.

Very late that evening, after John and his wife had left, I suddenly felt exhausted. I realised it'd been over thirty-six hours since I'd last had any sleep.

Vicky and I threw all the cushions on to the sitting-room floor, turned the lights out and snuggled up together under a duvet.

Then I began to weep. It was for Barry and Lens and the others who hadn't survived – but I didn't have enough energy left to shed all the tears that were welling up inside.

CHAPTER SIXTEEN

STARTING ANEW

That night, I was unable to relax. I couldn't throw off the physical tenseness I felt. Though I was still charged with adrenalin, my body and mind seemed less able to cope with it.

Vicky was wonderful. Her words and actions were kind and loving and supportive.

Early the next morning, local reporters and photographers came round to do pieces on me that subsequently appeared in *The Times* and the *Daily Telegraph*.

Afterwards, I walked down to the small multi-purpose shop and post office called the 'Dock's Café', at the entrance to Falmouth Docks, and bought a copy of every national newspaper. I took them home and read their accounts of Piper with great interest. Unexpectedly, I was much impressed by the quality of all the initial reporting.

That evening, Vicky and I went out for a meal with her brother. We ended up drinking numerous bottles of champagne to celebrate my return home. It was a happy, relaxed, sociable occasion.

The following day, there were many follow-up stories in the press and on television. Many of them were concerned with the visits made by dignitaries to Aberdeen. Prince Charles and Princess Di were at the harbour to welcome back the *Silver Pit*. The crew were congratulated for their bravery in rescuing thirty-seven men from Piper Alpha. Not unexpectedly, no mention was made of the fact that much of the rescue work had been organised by survivors.

I was very shocked at the interpretation being put on a statement made by Armand Hammer, the Chairman of Occidental. It was widely reported that he'd be paying £100,000 to all the families of the bereaved. Typically, one tabloid reported on its front page: 'Dr Hammer, who flew from Los Angeles to Aberdeen for a briefing on the tragedy, said the grieving families will get £100,000 each and pensions for life.' That wasn't true and it never happened. What Armand Hammer meant was that only the families of men who'd been directly employed by Occidental would receive the money. That was thirty-one out of the one hundred and sixty-six who'd then died. This was because of the insurance scheme that provided for the Occidental workers. Once again, it proved to me that the majority of the North Sea workers, who were employed by contractors, were in every way – even in death – treated as second-class people. Since the accident some of the Occidental survivors tell me they have been treated no better.

My nights continued to be as sleepless and as tense as the first I'd spent back at home. It went on like that, night after night. For the next ten days or so, I only slept fleetingly and then I'd suddenly awake in a state of high anxiety. After lying awake for an hour or two I'd get up. There was no point in being in bed with my eyes shut pretending to sleep.

During most of the day, I was still as hyperactive as I'd been from the moment of the first explosion. I felt immensely enthusiastic, my thinking was more incisive, and I seemed to be far more articulate than before.

For much of the time I was awake, whether at night or during the day, I busied myself making notes about the work I had to do. All my previous records had been stored on floppy discs which together with my computer had been destroyed in the flames of Piper.

I knew it was most important for me to set myself goals – and I've been following those goals ever since. Paramount was the mission to inform as many people as possible that financial cutbacks and the resulting system of lump-sum contracts had led to inadequate and unsafe working practices in the North Sea oil industry. Despite all the warnings there had been, the disaster had finally happened.

In pursuit of my primary goal, I spent a lot of time chatting to Members of Parliament, journalists, trade unionists and anybody else who would listen. This book is a continuation of my determination to prevent another Piper tragedy in the North Sea.

I continued to live with the effects of the original explosion, every day and every night.

About a week after my return home, I was in bed when there was a sudden loud bang. Within a split second, I'd leapt into the air, with the duvet wrapped around me and Vicky grabbing on to my ankle.

'It's all right,' she was saying. 'It's all right. It's just the lifeboat maroon. Ed, the lifeboat's been called out. That's all. Don't worry. Come back to bed.'

Even when I was asleep, it seemed, there would still be the nightmares.

Everything concerned with Piper preoccupied me. If anything happened that I regarded as a miscarriage of justice, I responded instantly and with all my energy.

Immediately after the tragedy, a trust fund was established in Aberdeen to which Occidental and the government each immediately donated a million pounds. Shortly afterwards, I heard on the news that the Lord Provost of Aberdeen had stated that the trust fund would help out the bereaved and the injured, but it would also finance research into means of ensuring that a similar accident didn't happen again. I went berserk. One of the things that we'd been saying for years was that the oil industry was putting insufficient money into safety measures and ways of speedily evacuating the crews on oil rigs. But I felt that such research was the responsibility of the government and the oil companies. It wasn't the ordinary people of Britain and Aberdeen who should be financing it through the fivers they'd donated after the tragedy.

Over the phone, I voiced my concern to the PDA, the EEPTU, the AUEW and each of the journalists who'd spoken to me. Within twenty-four hours, the Lord Provost had backtracked from his original announcement. All the money would be used to help the families of the bereaved and survivors. It was the right and sensible thing to do. To have done otherwise would have been deeply distressing to the people of Aberdeen, who'd already been devastatingly affected by the tragedy.

A few days later, I heard that the Inter-Union Offshore Committee had formed a sub-committee to look specifically at the Piper issue. Membership consisted of the committee members of the parent body, plus the representatives of interested parties, including British Telecom who'd lost three of their employees on Piper. But the officers of both the PDA and the EEPTU (who'd lost eleven fully paid-up members) were excluded, because the two unions, which had just agreed to work closely together, were not members of the TUC. I thought it was despicable. At such a time, it seemed essential that such pettiness was forgotten. So I phoned the Inter-Union Offshore Committee and gave them hell. I then contacted my MP and phoned all the contacts I'd made in both the national and provincial press.

A short while later, I heard from Alan Miller of the PDA that the Department of Energy intended to invite representatives of the two excluded organisations to a separate meeting that would take place on the same day as one with the people from the Inter-Union Offshore Committee. I was pleased by that, but still sad that even such a tragedy couldn't establish unity among trade unions.

Subsequently, I was invited as a representative of the PDA to the separate meeting with Cecil Parkinson. The first was to take place at six o'clock in the evening of 18 July, eleven days after the explosion and two days before the memorial service for Piper's dead that was going to be held in Aberdeen.

Stena had already phoned me to ask if I wanted to attend the memorial service.

'I'll walk if I have to,' I replied. 'You just couldn't keep me away.'

Stena arranged and paid for all the survivors they'd employed on Piper to be flown with their wives to Aberdeen and accommodated for a couple of nights at the Moat House at Bucksburn, just outside Aberdeen.

So I could attend the meeting with Cecil Parkinson, I flew up to London with Vicky and Suzie on the 18 July. When we arrived at Heathrow, Vicky went dashing off to the Tie Rack to buy me a decent tie – an item of clothing for which I'd previously had little use.

We were met at the airport by a representative of the EEPTU who was to drive me to the union's headquarters at Hayes Court in Bromley. Alan Miller had requested me to attend a preliminary meeting there, before we went to the Department of Energy.

Before leaving Heathrow, I saw Vicky and Suzie to a taxi. They were going to Liverpool Street to catch a train to Colchester where they'd be met by my friend, Paddy Handscombe, with whom we were going to spend the night. I'd join them after seeing Cecil Parkinson and the next morning we'd fly to Aberdeen.

At the Hayes Court meeting, I discovered that a list of recommendations had already been compiled. However, the people who'd drawn them up had limited experience of the offshore diving industry, and so some of the things on the list needed to be revised.

For example, the first recommendation was that priority should be given to the immediate recovery by the Royal Navy of the bodies and the accommodation module.

'This is wrong,' I said. 'The naval divers may be very good in their way, but they don't know what an oil rig is. Then they'd have to rent a North Sea diving vessel to undertake the work. So why involve the Royal Navy when there's a wealth of talent and expertise already available? Within hours, you could assemble a group of North Sea divers who'd already worked on Piper and would know exactly what the rig looked like under water and how to find their way round an accommodation module in which they'd actually lived. Furthermore, under no circumstances can divers go straight into the submerged accommodation module. It has to be treated like any other diving job. You start at the top and clear off the debris, because you can't work beneath something that's likely to come crashing down on you. Once the area's been cleared, the bodies and the module can be recovered. You cannot do it before. It would be insane to risk unnecessarily the lives of divers while recovering Piper's dead. But I can guarantee that the North Sea divers will do everything they can to complete the task.'

It was agreed that the recommendation would be, 'The recovery of bodies will be undertaken as a major priority as soon as the structure is made safe.'

We spent three hours revising the document and then rushed off to town to see Cecil Parkinson at the Department of Energy. Before we went in, I decided that for the meeting I'd wear the badge that Vicky had given to me at Newquay airport.

We were taken upstairs and the group of us, including Eric Hammond and Roy Sanderson from the EEPTU and Alan Miller from the PDA, were led into a vast room with an antique and slightly wobbly conference table and walls bestrewn with paintings. Then, like a scene from *Yes, Minister*, in walked rosy-cheeked Cecil Parkinson and his junior minister, Peter Morrison, flanked by half a dozen starched civil servants.

As coffee was being handed round, we were all introduced to each other. When Cecil Parkinson heard I was a survivor from Piper, he was extremely surprised and genuinely solicitous as he asked how I was. 'You're the first person I've met,' he said, 'who was actually there.'

Cecil Parkinson then explained he'd had a meeting earlier in the day with the Piper offshoot of the Inter-Union Offshore Committee. He was unhappy about the situation of there having to be two separate groups, but he assured us he would never have a meeting with that group without also having one with ours.

We then started on the prepared agenda. Within five minutes, I could see that I was in another of those ineffective, dull meetings that I'd witnessed dozens of times in oil companies and liaison groups. For a time, I tried to restrain myself from speaking out, but then it suddenly occurred to me: 'If you can climb down that rope on a blazing oil rig and not be scared, Ed Punchard, what the hell are you worried about here?'

It was obvious to me that meetings such as this with the Minister were far removed from the sheer frustration and annoyance and stupidity of the things that actually happened offshore. It was no wonder that the matters they discussed were either diluted or not dealt with at all.

So I started talking. As each point was considered, I found that I was saying more than most in the meeting.

When Cecil Parkinson was told that North Sea workers were scared to come forward to talk about unsafe practices he said, in his quiet, calm, professional ministerial way, 'But we have a system that allows workers to speak to the department quite confidentially. There is a number they can phone at any time, twenty-four hours a day. And everybody is assured that their anonymity will be respected.'

So I said, 'I've no doubt that you believe there's a system. I've no doubt that when your civil servants made this provision, their intention was to stop victimisation taking place. But we cannot talk about it in this manner. We have to accept that the system doesn't work. Believe me, people are too scared to come forward. So the question that must be addressed is, "What would it take to make people come forward?" If the answer is "a new system", then you have to scrap the existing system.'

One of the civil servants then rather stroppily enquired if I could produce any proof of victimisation.

'No problem!' I said and described my experiences of having to resign from the executive of the association so I could find work.

I found it amazingly easy to get their attention and, at least for me, it became an extremely interesting meeting.

A whole range of issues was discussed. We asked if the provisions of the Health and Safety Act could be extended to offshore structures and the people employed by sub-contractors. The inadequacies of the survival training offered to offshore workers were pointed out. The matter that concerned me most was endeavouring to ensure that the public inquiry into the Piper accident would be able to hear evidence concerning other structures. As part of my case, I explained to Cecil Parkinson some of the working practices that existed in the North Sea, particularly the hazards to safety resulting from the system of lump-sum contracts.

By the end, nothing much had been decided, but Cecil Parkinson gave us two vital assurances. Firstly, the Piper inquiry would have the widest possible terms of reference. Secondly, all the bodies would be recovered as soon as possible.

Before he left, Cecil Parkinson peered at my badge, read it aloud and said, 'Ah! I understand.' Then he swept out, his retinue in train.

In the lobby outside, a representative of the Press Association walked up to Eric Hammond, who immediately pulled me to his side. He gave a general statement about the meeting. I added that the PDA was most anxious that there should be unanimity between all the unions representing offshore workers and that it would be disgraceful if previously established inter-union demarcations prevented this from happening. This was not the time for there to be bickering between the interested parties.

At the time, I was quite happy about the meeting. Later, however, I saw Cecil Parkinson being interviewed on television and it was abundantly clear that both of his assurances were worthless. He wouldn't guarantee that all the bodies would be recovered and he stated that the subject of the inquiry was what had happened on Piper Alpha. I realised then that I couldn't trust anybody.

After I'd left the Department of Energy, I caught the train to Colchester to rejoin Vicky and Suzie. When he met me, Paddy said he'd had a telephone call earlier that day from a researcher for 'Panorama' wanting information about Piper Alpha. He'd suggested she ring back later when she'd be able to speak to me.

Early the next morning, we rang the BBC and both Paddy and I spent a long time chatting to people in the 'Panorama' team. I found that what they had in mind sounded very promising. I suggested several contacts to them and it was agreed they would see me in Aberdeen in a couple of days.

Vicky, Suzie and I then caught the train back to London. Almost immediately, I fell asleep. Because of my sleepless nights, I'd found I was prone to peg out in the middle of the day, no matter where I was. Suddenly, somebody slammed the compartment door. In an instant, I was awake, out of my seat and crouching on the floor. The people around stared at me as though I was mad.

All the comedy sketches I'd seen about a shell-shocked grandpa jumping out of his skin whenever a car backfired were no longer funny. That was exactly what was happening to me. I was having to face the fact that the explosion and its aftermath were having a very real effect on me. Fortunately, I was being greatly helped by Vicky, who was incredibly understanding.

From Liverpool Street, a taxi took us to Heathrow.

I'd already decided that while I was in Aberdeen I'd visit the survivors who were still in hospital. Thinking that the Frenchman, Eric Brianchon, might not have had too many visitors, I went to the airport shop and bought a large pile of French magazines.

While Vicky stayed to buy something for Suzie, I went to the desk to check us in. The staff must have been briefed that Piper survivors would be passing through on their way to the memorial service, because the woman behind the desk said to me, 'What a terrible experience you must had had, Mr Punchard.'

I nodded, being impressed that at an airport, where everything is generally so impersonal, an effort was obviously made to look after those in more unusual circumstances.

Then the woman said, 'Wasn't it sad that the Frenchman died this morning?'

I was completely stunned. I stood, with the bundle of French magazines under my arm, unable to speak.

Realising that she'd said something I hadn't been expecting, the check-in clerk said, 'Oh, I'm very sorry. I didn't mean to upset you.'

'No, no, no,' I said. 'It's not your fault. I knew nothing about it. I'd just bought all these magazines for him.'

'I am sorry. Was he a friend of yours?'

'No, not a friend. I was just one of the people who rescued him.'

It was a bitter blow that upset me deeply. I wandered

disconsolately over to Vicky, who was still in the shop. But I couldn't say anything to her. I was completely choked.

She looked at me and said, 'What on earth has happened?'

'The Frenchman's died.'

'But you can't be sure. You can't be sure it was him. Let's ring up and find out.'

'No. It was apparently on the midday news. He was the worst injured. If anybody's died, it must be him.'

Seeing I was so upset, she held me tight in the middle of the shop. As thoughts ricocheted through my mind, I fleetingly felt amidst the grief an unreasonable sense of injustice that, after all his suffering and the trouble we and others had gone to, the man had still died.

Later, as we were queuing in the extension corridor waiting to get on to the plane, the whole structure began to shake – it must have been settling down on its hydraulics. It felt horrific and I was overcome with blind panic, convinced that we were all about to the thrown to the tarmac. As soon as I saw a small gap, I pushed Vicky and Suzie into the plane and clear of the door.

Vicky turned round and for a moment must have wondered what the hell was going on, but she quickly saw the state I was in and said nothing. I followed her and Suzie to our seats.

On the flight to Aberdeen, Vicky and I spent a lot of our time trying to hang on to Suzie, who was determined to wriggle like a fish up and down the aisle.

At Aberdeen, we went by taxi to the Moat House. Then for the first time in a fortnight I met some of the other survivors, including Stan MacLeod and John Wood who were both with their wives. One of the helicopter pilots who'd been on duty that night was also there.

There was much news and many reactions to share. Stan told me that Eddie Amaira, the diver, had apparently gone out to work offshore the day after Piper.

'He must be out of his mind!' I said. 'Isn't he feeling bad or anything? I'm sure I wouldn't even be able to make the beds offshore now!'

'Ah, you know Eddie,' Stan said. 'He's a man of iron.'

We spent a pleasant evening. It was great to see my friends again and meet their wives. But it was interesting to note, as we talked, how often there surfaced a thought that began, 'If only . . .'

If only I'd told Lens he couldn't go up to the accommodation' block to telephone his girlfriend; if only I'd invited Budweiser to do some work in my office; if only I'd managed to get a helicopter earlier to take the Frenchman off the *Silver Pit*; if only I'd made sure that Barry Barber was following me . . . would they still be alive?

At lunchtime the following day, Chip and Jean arrived to baby-sit with Suzie. About half-past one, taxis arrived to take the survivors to the memorial service. Dressed completely in black, including a natty trilby, Vicky looked incredibly elegant.

As Union Street was overflowing with people and closed to traffic, the taxi had to drive round the back to the Kirk of St Nicholas. It was clear that the whole of Aberdeen had closed down to honour the 167 men who'd died on Piper Alpha.

After getting out of the taxi, Vicky and I walked hand-in-hand through the avenue of photographers into the ancient granite church where we were shown to our pew among the mourners.

While we waited, I looked at the printed order of service. On the second page was a long, long list in alphabetical order of the men who'd died. I read slowly through the names, noting particularly the men I'd known. The eighth name was Barry C. Barber. Eric Brianchon was not on the list – it'd been printed before he'd died. Six of the dead shared the same surname – Alexander Duncan, Charles Edward Duncan, Eric Duncan, John Duncan, Thomas Irvine Duncan and William D. Duncan. Yet I didn't know any of them by name. They were just among the faces and places going through my mind. Then, like all the other survivors, I paused at the place in the list where my name might have been – in the third column between Raymond L. Price and Neil Pyman.

Among the last people to arrive were the four sombre government ministers – George Younger, Peter Morrison, Malcolm Rifkind and Cecil Parkinson.

When every seat in the kirk was occupied, the memorial service started with the words: 'We are here to remember those who died on the Piper Alpha.'

It was impossible to be there and not be moved. It was the hymns I found most difficult. After trying to sing a couple of lines, I had to bite the inside of my mouth to stop breaking out into uncontrollable tears. I barely had sufficient strength to support myself. I just had to stand there, rocking gently backwards and forwards, crushing Vicky's hand.

As the Rev. Andrew Wylie, the offshore chaplain to the oil industry, began his address, I saw that the woman sitting next to me on the other side from Vicky had broken down with grief. I didn't know who she was, but I put my arm round her and held on tight.

'God appears at such a time of bewilderment,' Mr Wylie was saying, 'in the sheer kindness of unspoken sympathy, the handshake, the arm around the shoulder, the hug, the understanding glance, the thoughtful gesture, the listening ear.'

He went on, 'In recent years, because Britain's offshore oil industry is over the horizon, it has been all too easy for those who work in it, through being out of sight, to become out of mind. This should not be. No matter the extraordinary level of technical achievement which makes complex exploration and difficult extraction possible, it is very much a people industry. And it is the people who are its most precious investment and give it its special character . . . This part of the offshore family is no more – but the family remains and proudly goes on.'

His words were extremely moving, striking exactly the right note for the inordinately sad occasion. As he spoke, the stillness in the crowded kirk was broken only by the distant crying of a child.

Then, after the final hymn, the service was over and the two thousand people who'd been present slowly made their way outside.

As we filed out, Vicky and I introduced ourselves to the young woman I'd sat next to and tried to comfort. She was the widow of Ian Piper, who'd worked for Bawden International. As far as I know, I'd never met him. But we expressed our heartfelt regrets and best wishes, all too aware at such a time of the total inadequacy of words.

When we walked outside, the sun was shining. There were hundreds of people standing there, many of them in tears. Among the drawn faces, I recognised a few who at one time or another had worked on Piper.

A tea had been arranged in a large pavilion for those attending the service, but for some absurd reason it had been arranged that the survivors would be taken back to the hotel so they could have a grief-therapy meeting with a psychiatrist. I was furious. I wanted to be with the other mourners. I felt that taking part in everything that day might help, in some way or other, to exorcise the ghost of Piper and expiate the grief.

I paced up and down in the hotel until Vicky and I eventually agreed to call a taxi to take us to the pavilion. But by the time we arrived, most people who'd been there had left.

In the evening, Occidental laid on a reception which was attended by several senior executives. It was a pleasant enough if somewhat subdued occasion, with plenty of wine. We all drank and talked a great deal – but to no great purpose.

In the morning, Vicky and I had a chat about when we should go home. I wanted to stay on in Aberdeen to talk to the people from 'Panorama', but Vicky was keen to get back to Falmouth as soon as possible.

'Don't worry,' she said. 'I'll go on with Suzie. We're flying all the way and so it'll be no problem. You stay here.'

I went with Vicky and Suzie to the airport. I waved goodbye and then stayed the next three days with friends in Aberdeen. That afternoon, I was invited to go along to Occidental, where all the information coming back from the wreck of Piper was being processed. I saw the drawings that had been made of what was found. It was astonishing. They were just like the ones I'd been used to working with, except these showed that most of the platform was missing. Vast steel members were bent and shattered. Vast piles of debris lay everywhere. On the bottom was the accommodation block where my cabin had been. Close by, at the north-east corner, lay the wreck of the tiny Z-boat. It was a terrible shock to see that so much damage had been done.

During the next couple of days, I spent some time briefing the researcher from 'Panorama'. In the evenings, I went out on the town with old diving mates and tried to get drunk.

I began to notice that creeping into conversations with friends who hadn't been on Piper there were comments like, 'You need to forget all about it now,' or 'You must get on and live your life.' I could see the beginnings of impatience. Two weeks after a disaster for those who hadn't been involved was a long time. But for me, that first fortnight was all part of the event.

In that time, people had thought me good company – even sparkling at times. I was a man who'd been given a new lease of life. Everything tasted extra good, jokes seemed funnier, the ordinary appeared special, and I enjoyed even the simplest of things.

But already I could feel that things were changing. I was beginning to suffer physical and mental strain from being unable to sleep. The adrenalin was still there with identical intensity, but it was somehow different. Faced with the routine of everyday life, I found myself becoming too easily annoyed by petty things. It was difficult for me to have a perspective on ordinary, humdrum, daily problems.

The tragedy of Piper and what should be done about it were becoming the only realities and my only real concern. I just couldn't shake off the intense arousal I felt about the whole business. There were still so many points to be made, so much information to be unearthed, so many journalists to be contacted and so many changes to be made.

These were the thoughts in my mind, as I flew back alone to Falmouth.

CHAPTER SEVENTEEN

NOWHERE TO GO BUT UP

On the 29 July, a few days after my return home from the memorial service, I was idly watching television. Suddenly, with a vivid jolt, I was back on Piper, experiencing the intensity of those first moments after the initial explosion.

The television programme I was watching dealt with the Korean War and a cameraman had captured the moments immediately after the explosion of a terrorist bomb. Debris was still falling from the surrounding buildings. People were rushing around, preoccupied and intense. Many were injured. Blood streamed down their shocked, bemused faces. Three men scrabbled to retrieve something precious from the wreckage.

There was no terror. People moved around me on the 64-foot level, actively if anxiously. An injured man was being carried down the metal stairs. I rushed to the compressor and tried to find a way of switching it off. Davey Elliott came to help me, blood still oozing down his face.

Yet around me, sitting there at home, were the noises of everyday life – Suzie playing happily with her toys on the carpet, cars speeding past the window, cups rattling in the kitchen, the cat purring on my lap.

The events on Piper were sliding away under the layer of domesticity and I realised that I neither wanted to nor could cope with this change. I was bickering with my wife and impatient with my friends. Memories of what had happened and thoughts of what should be done dominated my mind, making it impossible for me to indulge in the niceties of social chit-chat. I felt I desperately needed to hang on to the intense motivation that had driven me to take such positive actions after I'd been pulled from the water back on to the *Silver Pit*.

Watching those Korean scenes tore away the veneer of domestic life. I was forced to accept that my preoccupation with the essential reality of Piper was going to be with me for a very long time.

As a result, I made two important decisions. The first was that I'd start work on this book and the other was that I needed to seek the help of a psychiatrist.

If I was going to write, I felt I must do so away from home. My father-in-law, Mike, Laloë had an office by the docks. He and I had been getting on extremely well since Piper. As he'd been a Japanese prisoner of war and had been on a torpedoed prison ship, there was a feeling that we'd shared a similar experience. He readily agreed that I could use a part of his office. I borrowed a computer and bought myself a desk. Every day I was in Falmouth, I went down there and set to work.

I was also conducting a dialogue with several Members of Parliament. I was frequently on the phone to them, as I was to journalists and the people from 'Panorama'.

There was much to discuss. More and more stories about malpractices in the North Sea continued to surface. I was told about another diving bell that had been sent down empty to pretend an inspection was taking place. In this case, the divers weren't even in decompression. They were told to go to their cabins and keep out of the way. In another case, a flexible pipeline that had been damaged while being laid underwater was just left. The diving company was working on a fixed-priced contract. Replacing the section of damaged pipe would have meant operating at a loss. Then there was the case of divers being told to tighten the bolts on some riser-clamps with spanners, instead of using the time-consuming and, therefore, far more expensive but essential process of Hydratighting. One of the workers was so concerned about what he'd been asked to do that he informed the oil company, despite his not-unreasonable fear that by doing so he'd have trouble getting another job with a diving company.

As rumours of these and other such stories began to circulate and be picked up by various newspapers, I was contacted several times by the representatives of diving companies who wanted me to state publicly that their company hadn't been the one involved in a particular piece of malpractice. Of course, I couldn't do so. None of the stories had originated from me and I was unable to prove whether or not they'd actually happened.

The events that had taken place on Piper were a different matter altogether. When Occidental at first claimed that there'd been no smell of gas on the platform in the days before the explosion, I was outraged. Like dozens of others, I'd smelt and been affected by gas a couple of days before Piper blew up. Two days later, Occidental retracted their original statement and admitted that gas smells had been reported.

Initially, I found that going daily to the office reintroduced a feeling of normality into my domestic life. I'd become like other husbands and fathers who left home for work at half-past eight and came back again at five. So things seemed much better, although I was still inclined to be intolerant and irritable.

After a week or so, my appointment with the psychiatrist came through. I strongly believe in seeking professional advice. If you want to learn how to drive, you go along to a driving instructor. If you're being sued, you visit a solicitor.

Believing that the psychiatrist would be able to help me with my general nervousness and unacceptably extreme responses, I went hopefully along for my first session.

Things didn't get off to a good start. The psychiatrist's first question was, 'Well, what's wrong with you then?'

I found his approach somewhat aggressive and so I replied, 'I've just been blown up on a bloody oil rig, haven't I? What do you think's wrong with me?'

After that, the sessions did get slightly better. I found some of his comments useful. For example, he said, 'People who've been in an explosion always suffer from physical effects. Their whole body and internal organs have been shaken and their inner ears have popped in and out. These effects combine with the mental reactions to what has happened. And the mental effects can be shattering. People normally try to construct for themselves a life that is predictable. So they feather their nest and have around them their partner and family. But it is an illusion of predictability they have created. Life is full of sudden and unpredictable things. People die, have accidents, become disabled, suffer from financial problems. Those who have a major traumatic shock, no matter how well they cope with it at the time, experience a massive turn-around in their life. Previously, life was thought to be predictable: suddenly, it's known to be unpredictable. This understanding, this turn-around, has a significant and lasting effect. The premise of life and existence has been changed.'

I found much of what he had to say was interesting, but after a couple of sessions I didn't feel they were really helping me. Indeed, over the next month or so my symptoms got worse. My left eye developed a slight nervous tick, which was there something like three quarters of the time.

I'd also suddenly, for no reason, remember something that had happened to me on Piper, something that up to then I'd forgotten. At lunch once, I suddenly had the sensation of falling. I dropped my fork and grabbed on to my chair. At first I didn't know what was happening, but a second or two later I pieced all the feelings together and realised I was for the first time recalling the rope suddenly dropping as I climbed down the rig.

At times, an awful feeling of dread would suddenly sweep over me. I'd be expecting a bang or an impact. Then my forearms would go numb. Some nights, I'd wake up a dozen or more times with my hands clenched and my forearms in the air. Each time, I had to switch the bedside light on and rub my arms for a few minutes to restore the circulation. For a time, I just couldn't work out what was happening until I realised my arms felt just as they'd done after I'd been dragged through the water by the *Silver Pit*.

At five o'clock one evening, I was half gazing out of the window and half watching television. Suzie was on the floor playing with some bricks. All of a sudden, the house shook. There'd unmistakably been an explosion. With no sense of panic, in an instant, I'd picked up Suzie under my arm and was out of the room, through the hall and the front door, down the steps and on to the pavement. I was running up the street with Suzie still tucked under my arm, when suddenly I screeched to a halt like a demented cartoon Road-Runner. I realised I wasn't on an oil rig. The place wasn't on fire. I wasn't beneath a billowing cloud of black smoke. We weren't in mortal danger.

Suzie was giggling away. She clearly thought it was great fun to be carried by her father at high speed along the middle of the road.

I composed myself, put Suzie down, and looked around. I knew I'd been right. It wasn't a car backfiring or the lifeboat's maroon. There had been an explosion, but looking around I could see no sign of it.

I walked back towards home and knocked on the door of my next-door neighbour who's an ex-coastguard.

'Did you feel that?' I asked him.

'I bloody well did. Come in. We'll find out what's going on.'

He had a shortwave radio on which he could listen to the shipping traffic. He switched it on and we discovered that a mile offshore the Navy had blown up a 1100-lb wartime mine that had been brought up in the nets of a trawler.

I was still shaking a couple of hours later.

I began to feel that things were slowly falling apart. Instead of being driven by what seemed to be an inexhaustable supply of adrenalin, I began to feel drained and listless. Because of the pressures I'd begun to impose on her, my relationship with Vicky also began to deteriorate. Suddenly, her husband had become a single-minded obsessive, who was too preoccupied to help with domestic and family chores. Regularly, I'd become deeply upset because I'd discovered or heard something new about some aspect of the Piper affair. Then I'd be on the phone for another three hours or flying off again to Aberdeen to attend some meeting or other.

It seemed that, because I'd been through a trauma that my wife hadn't and couldn't share, there was an imbalance in our lives. Slowly and inevitably, we seemed to be drifting apart. Even though I knew it was happening, I was incapable of doing anything about it. All my time and energies were spent dealing with the aftermath of Piper.

One of the matters that came up arose from the sudden realisation that there was a strong possibility that survivors would be paid financial compensation for the trauma and loss of earnings. Occidental had strongly advised us all to get in touch with a solicitor. Mine in Aberdeen had already received reports about the state of my health.

One afternoon in late August, I was sitting in my office beside Falmouth docks when he phoned me. 'The maximum permissible in a Scottish court is fifteen years' loss of earnings,' he said in his flat, matter-of-fact voice.

'Yes,' I said, scribbling down what he'd said.

'As I say, that's the most they will allow. Even if it can be shown a person is unable to work again, fifteen years may not be allowed, because there's always the possibility that he might have decided at some stage in his career to have become a tramp rather than continue to work offshore.'

'I see. A tramp,' I said, scribbling it down.

'Then there's the question of the trans-Atlantic multiplier to take into account.'

'Yes,' I said, not having a clue what he was talking about.

As he went on, sounding ever more like an international financier, my mind began to cloud over and I could barely take in what he was saying: 'That leaves us with the trauma. Add that, multiply . . . in excess of . . . But we'll have to wait and see. I don't want a disappointment on my hands. Thank you, Mr Punchard.'

Click went the phone and I stopped scribbling.

Any compensation payment lay in the future. Meanwhile, most of the survivors who were unable to work were being helped financially. Within a fortnight, the trust fund had sent £3,500 to each survivor and Occidental had agreed that until the end of the year they would all be given stand-by pay, which was half the normal working wage. This was efficient and caring, but nobody was sure what would happen after that.

In mid-September, I unexpectedly received from the EEC a most pleasant letter and a gift-cheque for £600, that had similarly been sent to all the survivors 'to ease the pain and suffering'.

A few days later, on 23 September, the newspapers contained photographs and reports of another explosion and fire in the North Sea. The semi-submersible drilling rig *Ocean Odyssey* was working 130 miles east of Aberdeen when a gas bubble shot up the well and exploded in a sheet of flames. Sixty-six men were rescued – several of them after jumping over a hundred feet into the sea. After Piper, many said they weren't prepared to wait there to be rescued. The radio operator, who'd returned to his post, was killed.

It was the same day, 23 September, that the trustees of the Piper Alpha Disaster Fund chose to announce that no further payments from the £4.5 million collected would be paid to survivors. All the remaining fund would be distributed among the bereaved. I found this astonishing decision quite unacceptable, knowing as I did that several badly injured men were already experiencing financial hardship.

Determined to do what I could to have the decision reversed, I flew a couple of days later to Aberdeen for a meeting of survivors organised at the Athol Hotel by Piper Outreach, the support group established by Grampian's extremely efficient and caring Social Services Department. The team, led by Anne Bone, provided immeasurable help to both survivors and the bereaved. Links were also established with other similar groups, such as those formed after the Zeebrugge and Bradford disasters.

At the meeting, the fourteen survivors present discussed the decision of the trust fund. I then wrote down the points they'd made and used them to draw up a press release, which we all signed. Naturally, we were concerned that we might be misunderstood. We certainly didn't want to convey the totally unjustifiable impression that we didn't care about the bereaved and wanted to take money away from them. So the words were chosen very carefully.

The press release started: 'It is with very great regret that we must express our belief that the trustees have abdicated their responsibility to the survivors and their families.' It then listed a number of specific points, including: 'We have received no contact from the fund's trustees concerning our physical and mental condition or that of our families. Nor have we received any contact concerning our financial needs.'

We decided that we'd delay sending out the press release to give the trustees a chance to change their minds in response to the public outcry there had already been. If nothing had happened in a week, I'd send our statement to all the national newspapers on a fax machine I had available. With luck, it would then hit the headlines immediately after the publication of the report by the Department of Energy on the initial technical investigation of the Piper disaster.

The survivors' meeting was the first time since the accident that I'd seen Dusty Miller. He was covered in bandages which, afterwards at the bar, he had to rearrange so he could drink his beer. Where he'd been having lots of skin grafts, his bandaged face was badly swollen on one side. To some people, his appearance might have seemed hideous, but I gave him a great hug and said, most truthfully, 'Dusty, you look bloody marvellous.'

After we'd chatted for a while, he suddenly said, 'I don't know how I'm going to pay my mortgage next month, Ed.'

'Why's that?'

'The stand-by pay's going to be stopped at the end of September.'

'But Occidental promised it'd be paid until the end of the year.'

'Yes. But Stena say we wouldn't have been working after the end of September in any case and so that's when the stand-by pay stops.'

'It doesn't make any sense. Stena isn't paying it – Occidental is.'

It was insane that this man who'd been shattered by an explosion, had thirty-per-cent burns, spent every day in hospital and couldn't drink his beer properly without moving his bandages, had to be worrying about his mortgage.

As soon as I'd returned to Falmouth, I went to my office, sat down at the computer and wrote a personal letter to Armand Hammer, pointing out what was happening to the divers' stand-by pay. A few weeks later, I received a personal reply, in which he stated: 'The matter relating to pay has now been resolved and you will receive your stand-by payments until the end of 1988.'

On 19 September, the Department of Energy published its inspectors' interim report on the Piper disaster. (At the same time, after a four-year delay, the report into the 1984 fire on Piper was also published.)

The Department's interim report was clear and succinct. It suggested that the first explosion was most likely caused by gas escaping from a pressure-release valve which had been removed for maintenance work. This initial explosion triggered off a series of later blasts and started fires which were to engulf the platform. The major explosion, twenty minutes after the first, arose when the pipeline bringing gas from the Tartan field ruptured.

The report also pointed out a series of safety failures that had taken place. Because the fire pumps had been switched to manual for the safety of the divers, they could not start automatically and so there was no water in the fire-fighting equipment on the rig. Two of the inflatable life-rafts had failed to inflate when they'd been launched. There were also criticisms of the rig's design and safety procedures.

On the day the report was published, I was back in Aberdeen, taking part in a news conference called by a small group of survivors and Frank Doran, the MP for South Aberdeen. We affirmed our belief that independent inspectors should be appointed to oversee oil operations in the North Sea. I also stressed that there was a desperate need for a free movement of information if appropriate action was going to be taken. It was unacceptable that the government should have waited four years to publish its report on the 1984 Piper fire.

I then returned to Falmouth and faxed copies of the survivors' press release to the national press. It created quite a stir, especially in the Scottish newspapers. 'Piper fund handling under fire' was the lead headline in Aberdeen's *Press and Journal*. The trustees squirmed and said they'd review the decision and just before Christmas another £4,000 was sent to each survivor.

Because I was constantly commuting between Aberdeen and Falmouth, pleading the survivors' case on radio and television, working at my computer on Piper documents, and spending hours on the telephone, I was rarely at home. Yet, though Piper still obsessed me, I felt at times as though I was beginning to run out of steam. I'd have bouts when, for some unknown reason, it was as though curtains had been drawn across my mind. The only thing I could do was to crawl into bed and try to go to sleep. Sometimes, I'd wake up and the feeling would still be there and last for another couple of days. On other occasions, if I managed to have an hour's sleep, it'd be completely gone.

Deciding that I must be suffering from some form of depression, I went back to my doctor and asked if an appointment could be arranged for me with a different psychiatrist.

I got on better with my second psychiatrist. She was prepared to spend two or three hours with me at a time. Immensely practical, she reassured me that what I was experiencing was normal for someone who'd survived a disaster.

Vicky was so worried about me that she discussed my strange behaviour with a friend, who rang me to say that the Royal Naval hospital at Haslar had carried out considerable investigations into post-traumatic stress syndrome after the Falklands War and disasters like the Bradford fire. He suggested I should go to the hospital for therapy. It sounded a good idea, but when I rang them up I found out it was a three-week course. As my psychiatrist advised me not to attend until we had done some work together, and I felt I was far too busy to sacrifice so much time, I didn't enrol.

The irrationality of my behaviour came out in many ways. My driving was appalling. If I had to travel anywhere, I'd just put my foot down and drive like a bat out of hell. There was only one speed at which I drove – too fast. Several times, I nearly wrote off my car. On one occasion, I was on a sharp corner before I knew it and as I swung the wheel round the car started to understeer. I slammed on the brakes, skidded and just avoided a car coming the other way.

I compared notes with other survivors and they all said the same thing. They often found themselves behaving in an unpredictable, even aggressive fashion. One of them told me that, when he was driving round Aberdeen, he'd take on anything – buses, lorries, sports cars. Everything had to get out of his way – even though he was only driving a 2CV!

Most were also having real problems with their relationships. It was common, since Piper, to feel a sense of detachment about family affairs. At times, though sitting in a room, it felt as though one wasn't there. Everything was looked at as though through a television screen. Yet the feeling was not alarming – it actually gave great strength. If you weren't there, you couldn't be hurt.

It was such conversations that led me to conclude that the only people I was still able to relate to were other survivors. They alone knew what had gone on out there, and they alone could understand what I was talking about, without being bored out of their minds.

At home, I felt I had a growing lack of contact with my family life. I also became aware that, however irrational it may have been, I was scared of my wife. When Vicky said something like, 'We've got to talk about this,' I'd begin to shake. I couldn't even cope with talking. I was seriously frightened of any upset. If there was a row, I'd have to walk away from it. Yet at other times, I'd be irritable and unreasonable. My mental state rightly made Vicky increasingly worried about me. She didn't want me to drive the car with Suzie in it or do all manner of things.

Yet I felt no sense of not being in control when it came to dealing with an issue concerned with Piper. Then my determination and energy seemed to return immediately. And so many issues were arising that my mind and time were almost fully occupied.

On 13 October, just after work had started on recovering the bodies and raising the two accommodation modules, Basil Butler, BP's managing director, made a speech in which he revealed much about the prevailing attitudes of the oil companies to offshore safety. Addressing the Institute of Petroleum in Glasgow, he said, 'Everything has an economic cost. And if safety measures were to rule out entirely the risks which are inherent in extracting oil from a province like the North Sea – which is in any case impossible – then operations would of necessity have to cease. We have to draw a balance between our expenditure and the levels of safety we achieve. It is as simple, and yet as complex, as that.'

These comments created an angry furore, especially from the unions. It was an astonishingly insensitive statement to make at such a time, but it could also be interpreted as being a warning given by the oil companies to the government – if you introduce safety regulations that lessen our profits, we'll stop work in the North Sea.

It was not surprising that the oil companies were somewhat apprehensive, because tougher safety measures would inevitably be introduced – although it was by no means certain they would be adequate. The government had announced that the preliminary hearing of the Piper Alpha Public Inquiry, chaired by Lord Cullen, would take place on 11 November, when a date would be fixed to start the main inquiry, which was expected to last anything up to a year.

Two days before the preliminary hearing, the oil companies were obliquely attacked from an unexpected quarter. At a conference in Aberdeen, Jim Morrison, the chairman of the Association of Offshore Diving Contractors, delivered a hard-hitting key-note speech. First of all, he conceded that there was truth in the allegations of malpractice – such as the empty diving bell being sent down as part of an inspection programme. 'It shows,' he said, 'that our clients have work to do to improve the quality of their offshore supervision of the whole industry.'

He stated that, 'Top management strategy seems aimed at reducing cost, without regard to medium-term implications, or even to short-term cost-effectiveness.' He placed the blame for the cost cutting on the practice of fixed-price or lump-sum contracts. 'I believe that this trend towards lump-sum inspection is fundamentally flawed and should be outlawed, if necessary, by the Department of Energy, if the industry will not put its own house in order. After all, which of you would consider paying for a medical cancer diagnosis on a lump-sum basis?'

At last, the debate about safety in the North Sea oil industry was taking place in public. If this openness continues, there is a possibility that it will lead to safer working practices and reforms in the structure of the industry. If that happens, some good will has come out of the Piper Alpha disaster.

On 12 December, I flew up to Aberdeen for a meeting that had been arranged, months earlier, for survivors. Funding had been provided. We were all flown to Aberdeen and put up at the Altens Skean Dhu.

Just after I'd arrived, I was walking down Union Street when a tall skinhead, wearing a black coat, suddenly started walking straight towards me. I felt sure he was going to attack me. Then I realised it was Gareth Parry-Davies.

'Are you all right, Gareth?' I asked, staring at his newly shaven head and assuming he'd gone completely insane. I'd heard he'd had many unpleasant experiences since the explosion and it was certain he'd never dive again.

'Yes, fine,' he said breezily. 'Do you like the haircut?'

'Well . . . '

'I was in this pub and I was reading an article appealing for money to help feed starving kids in Africa. So I thought, ''That's bad, eh! I must do something about this.'' So I went round the pub, pointed to the article and said, ''How much will you cough up if I shave my head?'' So I collected fifty quid and shaved my head.'

It was brilliant.

We went for a coffee and then made our way to the Skean Dhu. After a shower, I went down to the meeting. It was good to see everybody again and catch up with all the news. I was relieved to learn that Barry Barber's body had at last been found, some distance north of the platform and beyond the area searched by divers.

There were several people there I hadn't seen since the night, including many who'd been on the *Silver Pit*. One of them shook my hand and said, 'Thanks! If ever I'm in a disaster, I want to be with you.'

I thanked him, but curiously I didn't know his name. I couldn't even remember his face.

Vince Swales told us about the trip he'd made back to Tharos. Occidental had flown him out so he could see what Piper looked like.

He was just getting ready to leave, when one of the crew came up to him and said, 'Did you get your boots back, Vince?'

'What boots?' Vince asked.

'The ones you left on Piper. They found them!'

'Is that right? You're joking, aren't you?'

'No, I'm not. They found your rubber boots and there's nothing wrong with them – not even a wrinkle!'

How amazing it was that Vince Swales's discarded rubber boots were among the few things left undamaged after the Piper inferno!

Dusty Miller was also at the meeting. Although he was allowed out occasionally, he'd been in hospital ever since the day after the explosion.

We chatted for a while and Dusty suddenly said softly, 'I've got something to tell you, Ed. When the explosion happened, I was able to make my way up towards the lifeboat, but then I got trapped by the smoke. When you guys were on the north-west corner, I was on the level higher up. There were literally only a few inches where I could stand. Above me were the big telephone dishes and two telephone engineers were calling down for me to throw them a rope so they could climb down. I couldn't see any rope and I was wondering what the hell to do when I heard the bang and saw the fireball coming towards me. I just curled up into a ball and fell over the side. The fireball hit me before I touched the water. I could feel all my back was burnt. My overalls had just gone. But it was cooler in the water. I managed to keep afloat and I could see a bit of wreckage with some guys on. You won't believe it when I tell you, but it was my dad that got me there. I could feel him with me, telling me I'd be all right and pushing me through the water. It was my dad, Ed, that got me away from there.'

Dusty was an extremely brave man and I found his story very moving.

We were all called to have something to eat. At the meal, we toasted absent friends.

Afterwards, we sat together and talked in the bar. But I must have been at a low ebb. It seemed as if I was there in body, but not in mind. Even though I enjoyed being with my friends, I found just sitting there drinking was a little bit of a strain.

Though the bonds forged between the survivors were retained, the camaraderie could no longer mask the inner tensions, even desperation, that people were enduring, especially in their domestic life. At least a couple of marriages had totally broken down and others only survived because of regular periods of mutually agreed separation. The aftermath of Piper continued to embroil many people other than the lucky ones who'd survived. They were able to provide each other with some support. But their wives and girlfriends were often left alone, the unacknowledged victims of a tragedy beyond their ken.

I was not sorry to return to Falmouth.

A few days later, I went out for a drink with my brother-in-law and ended up in a seedy nightclub. There I met a diver called Jim Norman, who'd been part of the team sent to recover bodies from Piper Alpha. In that bizarre environment, he told me about making the first bell-run to find the accommodation module.

While he remained in the bell, his dive partner went first.

'I could tell,' Jim said, 'just by the way the guy was breathing, how anxious he was. Then suddenly, I heard him say, "Oh, my God, it's here. It's right below me." '

When the bodies were found, most of them were piled in groups in the stairwells and the galley. Using remotely controlled vehicles, the divers brought many of them up. Those that the RCVs couldn't reach had to be left until the accommodation module was brought up from the sea-bed.

After Jim Norman and the other divers had finished their work, they were each given a special medical because there was much concern about the enormous amount of toxic waste deposited in the sea after the explosion.

The insulating fluid in the transformers on Piper was pcb (polychlorinated biphenyls), a toxic persistent compound. It is believed that 4.8 tons of pcbs were present on Piper. Although much may have been incinerated or evaporated during the blaze, quantities of pcbs must still be present in the sea around the wreckage.

Just before Christmas, the search for bodies was called off. Thirty bodies are still missing, lying somewhere in the bowels of the North Sea. One of them is Lens.

It was also announced that Occidental had been given permission by the government to cut the remains of Piper in half with explosives, leaving a 250-foot-high stump, assorted debris and the toxic waste on the sea-bed. This was despite the fact that an original condition of establishing the rig was that when it ceased to be operational it would be totally demolished, leaving the site exactly as it had originally been.

Christmas, 1988, was the worst I'd ever spent. Vicky and I were barely communicating and no longer under the same roof. I felt absolutely drained and, to cap it all, I caught flu on Christmas Eve.

By New Year's Eve, I'd just about recovered. Piper still dominated my life, but I toasted the arrival of 1989 with relish. With luck, it was going to be a much better year than the last – it could hardly be worse.

EPILOGUE

NO MORE PIPERS

The public inquiry, chaired by Lord Cullen, was given the responsibility of hearing evidence to discover the cause of the Piper Alpha tragedy. It is clearly important that this should be ascertained, but it is only part of the story. What also needs to be examined is the system operating in the North Sea to find out whether defects in it contributed to or permitted the disaster.

To do this, all the parties involved – oil companies, the Department of Energy, the contractors, certifying authorities, the trade unions and the government – must stop blaming each other and at least accept the possibility that changes can be made that will be beneficial to all. If these groups are to work together, there must be greater openness, with channels of communication established to allow information to be disseminated to and discussed by all involved in the industry.

Time and time again, in my meetings with various representatives – whether of the government, trade unions or oil companies – I've found no absence of ability or of plans to solve a problem. What they lack is information. People in positions of power too often believe they understand the essence of a problem when clearly, because they've been inadequately briefed, they're totally unaware of the full facts. It isn't then surprising that the North Sea oil industry just bumbles along, instead of being, as it could and ought to be, a paradigm of efficient, profitable and safe working practices.

It is a myth – and an unacceptable excuse – to believe that the North Sea is the romantic last frontier with waves one hundred feet high and a supporting cavalry of helicopters. It's an ordinary industry, employing clerks and cooks as well as roughnecks and divers. Are the duties of a cook working in a kitchen offshore very different from those of a cook in an Aberdeen hotel? Of course not. Then why do offshore cooks annually have more accidents? The absurd answer sometimes given is, 'That's why they get more pay.' That isn't often true and neither explains nor excuses unsafe working practices.

Of course, there are far more potential hazards and fewer means of escape on an oil rig than there are in a factory on land. That doesn't mean we should be prepared to accept more accidents. It does demand that the safety precautions and the means available to preserve life should be as effective and as comprehensive as possible. Not just the Piper Alpha tragedy but many other incidents referred to in this book show that this is not the case.

Why not? The answer is simple – money wrongly spent and supervision inappropriately applied.

Despite the vast sums originally spent on exploration and platform-building during the pioneering phase in the North Sea, the desire to get the oil out of the ground as quickly as possible led to such absurdities as Piper Alpha being installed with a damaged jacket that had no corrosion protection. Crammed on to the early platforms were buildings that, if spread out on land, would occupy ten acres. Yet, in the design, no use was made of risk analysis – nor, unlike the Norwegian sector, has it been much used since, although later designs have at least abandoned the insane practice of siting the accommodation block immediately above what is potentially the most dangerous part of the rig – the gas-compression module and the place where the risers bring in or export the oil and gas.

It has already been stated that the dramatic drop in oil prices that occurred at the beginning of 1986 led to cuts being made in the industry and the widespread adoption of fixed-price contracts, even for essential and unpredictable work, such as the underwater inspection of the platforms. This system has led to shoddy and deceitful practices, which even in the medium term will lead to further accidents and to losses of production and, therefore, profits.

There are numerous examples of how more money spent on safety would have actually saved money. It is absurd to have a system, as exists on many rigs, that requires fire-water pumps to be switched off because a diver is in the water. With proper cages round the water intakes, not even the pumps in the vicinity of the diver need to be switched off. The rest can remain on automatic. Where cages are not fitted, those pumps remote from diving activity can still be in use. If either system is in operation, water will always be available for fire-fighting, providing the pumps themselves have not been destroyed.

There are also many examples of how additional money spent on more appropriate safety equipment would have saved more lives. The main example of this dealt with in this book is the unsuitability of the stand-by boats, which are there to provide emergency evacuation. There should have been on the boat:

a. wider doors without a step so that people could be carried through more easily;
b. more ropes to help rescue people in the water;
c. a better system than the rope scramble-net to transfer people from Z-boats to the boat;
d. someone trained and able to take responsibility for co-ordinating rescue work;
e. adequate medical equipment;
f. more Z-boats;
g. more stretchers and blankets;
h. searchlights;
i. some form of heat-shielding; and
j. a fully trained crew.

Such additions demand adequately paid crews manning purpose-built stand-by boats, a few of which are already in service.

On the rigs, life-saving equipment is also inadequate. On Piper, there were not enough life-jackets and the inflatable lifeboats failed to function. It would be advisable for every offshore worker to carry with him a small case, containing his personal life-saving equipment, such as a survival suit, smoke hood, inflatable life-jacket, anti-flash gear and a torch.

The survival courses at present provided for all offshore workers are totally inadequate. They do little more than train people to act only when instructed and to do nothing on their own initiative.

Incredibly, many contract workers are expected to pay for their own survival training.

The oil industry relies heavily on contract workers. Unlike the employees of the oil companies, they have no security of employment and few opportunities for advancement. Despite being in the majority offshore, they are often treated as second-class citizens, sometimes even being given inferior accommodation or food. Needing, as they do, the approval of the oil company as well as the sub-contractor before they can be employed, they are naturally reluctant to complain about anything – not even the most glaring breaches of safety regulations. The hotline which allows workers to contact the Department of the Environment about safety concerns neither removes the workers' fears of losing their jobs nor ensures their anonymity.

By conniving at cost cutting on desirable safety measures, the government is as guilty as the rest of the oil industry of putting profits before people. Cecil Parkinson has already stated that it is unlikely that redundant oil rigs will ever be completely removed – thus cutting oil-company expenditure, while at the same time possibly creating a hazard to fisheries and marine life. It has also been established that the oil companies have persuaded the government not to demand that emergency shutdown valves should be fitted to pipelines on the sea-bed just before they enter a rig. If such safety devices had been fitted around Piper, it is likely the major conflagration would have been prevented.

The government also has the major responsibility for supervising safety in the North Sea. It would be ridiculous in a home-match between Liverpool and Manchester United for the Football Association to appoint as referee a Liverpool FC employee. Yet that's precisely what happens in the oil industry. The routine safety checks are carried out by employees of the oil-production company.

The government body that is responsible for the extraction of oil and therefore, ensures the profit for the national resource is the Department of Energy. It is also the body responsible for the application of safe working practices. Despite the best of intentions, this conflict of responsibility can only lead to confusion and inequity.

There should, therefore, be a separate offshore installations inspectorate with statutory powers, similar to the inspectorate for nuclear installations, which are likewise complex and hazardous. Failing this, the responsibility for health and safety should be transferred from the Department of Energy to the appropriate body – the Health and Safety Executive. Until one or other of these changes is made, there can never be any confidence in the present system of regulation.

In addition, the myriad of regulations should be reviewed and those that are kept must be made binding. At present, there exist far too many opportunities for rules to be bent and avoided, because many are issued only as 'guidelines' that can be dispensed with.

Similar problems exist in the fields of safety and inspection at even the lower levels of activity in the North Sea industry. Given the obvious proliferation of recent equipment and installation failures, it is essential that new and effective measures are taken to guarantee that work is undertaken correctly.

The conflicting interests of the Department of Energy that lead to the everyday abuse of people and the system can best be brought to an end by the creation of a new independent, monitoring body, responsible for health and safety. This body would appoint safety representatives that are trained, protected and with status – similar to those which already exist in the Norwegian sector. Because of their power to initiate the closure of an offshore installation, the very presence of such representatives would make it far less likely that such power ever needed to be exercised. Unfortunately, the current proposals of the British government fall well short of this.

Independent checks throughout the industry would transform both the working atmosphere and the effectiveness of safety and inspection control. To accomplish it requires only the will and a reordering of existing priorities. Those applying at present in the British sector are far different than those in Norway. Magne Ognedal of the Norwegian Petroleum Directorate states, 'In the Norwegian oil industry, the first priority is people. The second is the environment around the installations. The third priority is the investment made in installations and equipment. The fourth priority is the production regularity or the profits supplied to the society.'

The present inappropriate supervision in the British sector does not have this order of priority. The certifying authorities that are the oil industry's 'auditors' for much of the inspection work have proved incapable of weeding out unsafe practices. At times, it seems they're doing little more than review paperwork. One year's inspection findings may look pretty much the same as another – both have the same glossy cover and are produced by the same word processor on similar paper. Yet, how can they be the same, if in one year the inspection took six months and in the next was rushed through in less than six weeks?

There are perhaps lessons to be drawn from the aviation industry. As its stock and trade daily involves the safety of hundreds of thousands of people, it has been unable to avoid detailed public scrutiny. It is no wonder then that the aviation industry is regulated by an independent body and the everyday activities of maintenance and inspection are rigidly covered with detailed procedures. Every item of equipment has a log, a history, a maintenance schedule and a permitted life. Such procedures are unfortunately rare offshore.

In case there is any doubt about the severity of the problem, consider that in the six months since the Piper Alpha tragedy there has been a spate of accidents and problems in the North Sea:

a. On 28 July a gas leak on *Brent Bravo* caused a shut-down of production.

b. On 22 September there was a major fire on the *Ocean Odyssey*, as a result of which one man died and the exploration rig was virtually destroyed.

c. Ninian Central was shut down after a gas leak on 4 October. Corrosion was then found in the pipework of the gas compression equipment.

d. Brent Delta suffered a gas leak and shut down on 11 November.

e. The flooding of the accommodation on Brent Charlie resulted in 70 being evacuated.

f. The Department of Energy ordered checks to be made on seven jack-up rings because of suspected cracks.

g. Christmas Eve saw the converted supertanker storage vessel *Petrogarl 1* break free with its massive mooring tower and drift uncontrolled towards the Clyde platform. Eyewitnesses said it came within a few hundred metres. Being a quarter mile long with 100,000 tonnes of oil aboard the potential loss of life and scale of disaster was terrifying. It also caused the shut-down of Clyde, Fulmer and Auk and brought the total loss of UK production at that time to 25% of total.

h. The New Year's Day explosion on Brent Delta shut it down

and brought controversy as to why the coastguard were not informed of the potential evacuation and also allegations of drinking amongst senior management, leading to their suspension pending enquiries.

And so it goes on.

Throughout the industrial revolution, it was considered vital to Britain's economic development that as much coal as possible was brought up out of the ground. So men, women and children were sent down mines to labour for long, back-breaking hours in appalling and unsafe conditions. It didn't seem to matter to the rest of the population that miners were frequently injured, contracted hideous lung diseases or were inadequately paid. Even the occasional disaster that killed hundreds of miners barely moved the nation, the colliery owners or their friends in government. The product and the profit were all that mattered. Beneath the ground, the miners were out of sight and out of mind.

Now, we consider that the working conditions endured in the nineteenth-century collieries were unacceptable.

Today, it is considered vital to Britain's economic development that as much oil as possible is brought up out of the ground. So, workers labour on oil rigs for weeks at a time in appalling and unsafe conditions. It doesn't seem to matter to the rest of the population that the accident rates are far higher than for other workers, that divers may be irreparably damaging their health or that the oil workers are inadequately paid, considering the unacceptable risks they have to take. The product and the profit are all that matter. Out on the rigs and in the sea beneath, the workers in the North Sea oil industry are out of sight and out of mind.

The Piper Alpha disaster and the resulting deaths of 167 men must change the attitude of the nation, the oil producers and their friends in government. We cannot wait until the next century before it is accepted that the working conditions endured in the North Sea are *un*acceptable.

POSTSCRIPT

This book is dedicated to the men who died in the Piper Alpha tragedy. It concludes with these, the names of my fellow survivors:

Edward Amaira
Robert Ballantyne
John Barr
William Barron
Geoffrey Bollands
Michael Bradley
Fred Busby
Harry Calder
Robert (Roy) Carey
Andrew Carroll
Neil Cassidy
Alexander Clark
William Clayton
Richard Common
James Craig
Keith Cunningham
Iain Duguid
Derek Ellington
David Elliott
Ian Ferguson
Ian Fowler

Barry Goodwin
Erland Grieve
John Gutteridge
Derek Hill
Brian Jackson
Michael Jennings
Mahmood Khan
David Kinrade
Charles Lamb
David Lambert
Ian Letham
William Lobban
Alastair Mackay
Stanley MacLeod
James McDonald
Robert McGregor
Ian McKenzie
Joseph Meanen
Steve Middleton
John Menzies
Harold Miller

Andrew Mochan
Dean Naylor
Christopher Niven
Gareth Parry-Davies
Robert Paterson
Adrian Powell
Anthony Payne
Steven Rae
Noel Ralph
Alex Rankin
Mark Reid
James Russell
Anthony Sinnet
Vincent Swales
Donald Thompson
Roy Thomson
Joseph Wells
Alexander Wood
John Wood
William Young

GLOSSARY

ACPD	Alternating Current Potential Drop. A technique for assessing the depth of a crack in steel, usually in a weld.
AIR-DIVING	Diving conducted in the comparatively shallower depths of less than fifty metres, where the divers breathe air not a mixed gas.
AQUAPRINT	A technique for obtaining a highly-detailed reproduction of a weld or other feature underwater.
BASKET	This is used as a lift in, out and through the water by air divers to their required working depth.
BEACON PLATFORM	Small area below the corners of the cellar deck on many rigs. The place where many Piper survivors made their escape.
BELL RUN	A bell dive. This usually starts at the time that the bell is 'locked off' the saturation system and lowered. It ends when it is 'locked back on' after the dive, which usually lasts about eight hours.
BIX	British Industrial X-rays. A diving company.
BOAT BUFFER	The large steel tube attached to the rig legs around water level to prevent damage should a vessel nudge the rig.
CATHODIC PROTECTION	The system used to prevent the corrosion of oil rigs or other items below water.
CELLAR DECK	The lowest working deck on a rig.
CERTIFICATE OF FITNESS	The equivalent of an MOT for an oil rig.
COFLEXIP	A type of flexible umbilical or pipeline.
CONTROL ROOM	The nerve centre of the rig where the oil and gas production process is controlled.
DECOMPRESSION CHAMBER	This is where a diver is put back under pressure as he was under water either to complete his required decompression or to treat an ailment such as decompression sickness.

DECOMPRESSION SICKNESS	'The Bends'. This is caused by gas coming out of solution in the diver's body following a dive and forming a bubble. The pain causes some to bend over hence the name.
DIVE CONTROL	This is where the diving supervisor sits and runs the dive. He monitors and adjusts the air supply and other life support functions. He is in contact by voice with the diver and often has a video picture coming from a camera on the diver's helmet.
DIVE MODULE	On Piper, the area above dive control where the superintendent, inspection controller and diving representative had their offices.
DIVE SKID	On Piper, the small deck below the cellar deck from which the divers operated. Here the wet bell was brought up and down with the diver in it. The wendy hut was also here.
DIVING BELL	The pressurised sphere that takes divers from the decompression chamber complex to their working depth. It contains a great deal of support and control equipment.
DIVING REPRESENTATIVE	Contracted as an independent supervisor to the oil operator to monitor the diving work underway. Relays information and instructions to the diving contractor.
DIVING SUPERINTENDENT	The offshore manager for the diving contractor, in overall charge of the diving operation.
DIVING SUPERVISOR	The person who runs the dives and is legally responsible for the diver's well-being whilst the diver is in the water.
DP	Dynamic Positioning. Computer controlled positioning for dive ships etc.
DSV	Dive Support Vessel.
ESD	Emergency Shut Down.
ESV	Emergency Shut Down Valve. A valve provided to isolate a section of pipework or plant in the event of an emergency.
EXPLORATION RIGS	Mobile drilling rigs used to look for oil, may be supported by barges, ships, jack-ups or semi-submersibles.
FLARE	A means of burning off excess or unwanted gas.
FLARE STACK	The support column for the flare.
FLASH	A process where gas is released from a liquid due to a drop in pressure.

FLASH DRUM	A vessel for the collection of flashing liquids and separation of the associated gas.
HABITAT	A structure that is used to create a dry controlled environment suitable to undertake a high-quality weld, often on an underwater pipeline.
HOT WATER SUITS	Diving suits used offshore that release a steady and controlled stream of hot water all over your body.
H_2S	Hydrogen disulphide. A highly toxic gas that is sometimes found with oil and gad as a result of bacterial action.
INSPECTION CO-ORDINATOR/ INSPECTION CONTROLLER	Usually someone with diving experience who organises and plans the diving activity.
JACKET	The supporting structure of a platform installation. In the case of Piper, the jacket is fixed to the sea-bed by twenty-eight piles and the topside modules are mounted to it by the deck support frame.
JACK-UPS	Exploration rigs with legs that extend down to the sea-bed and allow the rig to be jacked-up clear of the water. These are used in shallower water, say up to sixty metres.
KELLYS	The large gas storage vessels for divers' air or helium.
KIRBY 17's	Modern diving helmets made of yellow fibre glass.
MCP-01	Total Oil Marine's manifold compression platform on the Frigg to St Fergus gas pipeline.
MEDICAL LOCK	The smaller transfer lock on decompression chambers that allows food and other items to be transferred to the divers inside.
MEMBER	Steel tubes that form the basis of the steel jacket structure of a rig.
MODULE	A subsection of the topside structure.
MOL	Main Oil Line. It carried a large portion of the oil recovered from the North Sea.
MOON-POOL	Opening in the bottom of dive ships and rigs to allow the bell to enter the water.
MPI	Magnetic Partial Inspection. An inspection technique to allow cracks to be seen in metals, usually welds. It involves the magnetisation of welds and the use of coloured magnetic inks

that will gather in any crack present.

MUD | Mud is a liquid that is made up of a variety of different chemicals. By circulation in the well during the drilling, it cools the drilling bit, removes cuttings from the bottom of the hole and prevents the hole behind the bit from caving in. It also prevents water, gas or oil from intruding in the well until it is completed and lined with steel piping, and prevents oil and other hydrocarbon fluids from kicking back out of the hole.

OIL FIELDS | A reservoir or group or reservoirs related to a single geological structure.

OIL RESERVOIR | A formation of porous rock containing fluid or gas sealed by an impermeable rock cap. The oil is contained in microscopic spaces between rock particles.

OIM | Oil or Offshore Installation Manager.

PIG | A device inserted into a pipeline to displace or separate products, clean or inspect the pipeline.

PILES | Driven through pile guides into the sea-bed to anchor the rig firmly to the sea-bed.

PILE GUIDES | Large metal rings clustered around the rig's legs that hold the piles in place.

PRODUCTION PLATFORM | Usually fixed platforms, not floating, of steel or concrete jacket construction. They provide a drilling base, production and processing facilities, personnel accommodation, communications, storage and transport facilities.

PSV | Pressure Safety Valves. A pressure relief valve.

QUADS | Frames containing a number of gas cylinders. Often divers' air or helium.

RISER | Section of an export or an import pipeline extending from the sea-bed to the ESV on the platform above.

RISER CLAMPS | Attachment between the riser and the steel members of the rig.

ROV/RCV | Remotely Operated/Controlled Vehicle. An unmanned submarine. Their design and function varies from the simplest swimming TV camera to large equipment carrying machines with manipulators used for inspection and other sub-sea work.

SACRIFICIAL ANODES	Alloy blocks attached electrically to the rig. They corrodae faster and in preference to the structural steelwork of the rig thus protecting it from corrosion.
SAT-SYSTEM	Complex of decompression chambers where the divers live during periods of deep diving.
SATURATION DIVING	Deep diving where divers' bodies become saturated with the breathing gas. Owing to the long decompression they then require, they are stored under pressure for long periods making regular bell dives to their working depths.
SEMI-SUBMERSIBLE RIGS	Normally for oil exploration but also used as emergency support for diving vessels such as Tharos, Iolair and Stadive. They float on two submerged hulls. For oil exploration they are used in deeper water than jack-ups.
SINGLE BUOY OR POINT MOORING	Large buoy or column attached to the sea-bed. Used as an oil collection point by tankers.
SPIDER DECK	The area of the rig just above the water. It is not decked over and is a series of companion ways welded to the members to allow workers access.
STAND-BY VESSEL	The vessel that is continuously stationed in the vicinity of an offshore production or exploration rig to provide support in the event of an emergency.
SURFACE DECOMPRESSION	A controversial technique of decompressing a diver after his dive. This involves a quick transfer from the sea to the chamber where the diver is then decompressed. This then enables the next diver to carry on working and is therefore economical, allowing a quick turnaround. However, it has been indicated by research that it results in brain damage.
SWINDELL	A free flow diving helmet usually seen in use on inshore diving jobs.
TUGGER	Air or hydraulically driven winch.
WENDY HUT	A shelter for the divers on the dive skid when they are working on deck and awaiting instructions.
WET BELL	An open non-pressurised bell used to get the diver in and out of the water.
WOOLLEY-BEAR	A diver's thermal undersuit, which resembles a large babygro.